North Carolina Headrights:

A List of Names, 1663-1744

This is to certify that these per[sons] [...]
proved their Rights at a Court held for the Precinct of
Carteret July [...] 1680

[...] proved there [...] freedom Rights [...]

[...]

Thomas [...]

[...] German his own Right being a freedom Right
[...] transportation Rights
John [...]
[...] John [...] [...] transported [...]
[...] [...]

John [...] three freedom Rights [...]
John Clarm
Mary his [...]
Edward [...]

[...]dwick Williams three freedom Rights & two transportation
Rights viz

[...]dwick Williams { William Stinson
Hannah William { John [...]
Elinor Williams

Thomas Harris[...] [...] freedom Rights [...]
Thomas Harrison { Elizabeth Harrison
Elizabeth his wife

[...] Macdonnell [...] freedom Rights [...]
Michael Macdonnell [...] { Mac[...]
[...] his wife { Frances

William Morbury five freedom Rights [...]
[...] William Morbury
Hannah his wife

As attest Paul Latham Court Clerk

This document of 1680 from Carteret Precinct lists numbers of individuals claiming "freedom rights"—land grants to which servants were entitled after expiration of their term of service. CCR 187, State Archives.

The Colonial Records of North Carolina
Special Series
Jan Poff, series editor
Robert J. Cain, series editor emeritus

North Carolina Headrights
A List of Names, 1663-1744

Compiled by
Caroline B. Whitley

Office of Archives and History
North Carolina Department of Cultural Resources
Raleigh
2008

Printed by Edwards Brothers

Illustrations

FOREWORD

As general editor of this special series of *The Colonial Records of North Carolina,* I am pleased that two such competent people as Caroline Banks Whitley (a former member of the staff of the Colonial Records staff) and Susan M. Trimble (a current member) have brought this useful work to fruition. Thanks are also due to another present member of the staff, Dennis Isenbarger, for his assistance.

Robert J. Cain
January 2001

INTRODUCTION

The colony of North Carolina followed the method of making grants of land that was common throughout the mainland British American colonies—by *headright*, also known as *landright*. Although there were numerous refinements and variations, the system allotted each grantee a certain amount of land based on the number of persons he or she brought into the colony. Acquisition of land by purchase grant was generally an option also, but a much less common one than acquisition of land by headright.

Although details varied from time to time, the usual practice in North Carolina allowed persons imported for a claim of headright to be slave, bondservant, or free, male or female, and of any age. Until 1712, when the practice was abolished as an abuse of the proprietors' rights and an unfair evasion of payment of fees to local officials, persons who had no intention of remaining in the colony could not claim a headright. Thereafter, one had to reside at least six months in the colony before making a claim. Similarly, in the period before 1712 multiple importations of the same person was allowed. This meant that when someone left the colony and returned, he or she was entitled to a grant. A notable example of this is John Blany, who in 1697 successfully claimed a landright of 50 acres for each of the 33 times he had "transported" himself into the colony (page 30, below). A requirement dropped very early was the one for maintaining an armed servant on each tract granted. One of the claims of 1679 (page 128, below) included the assertion that the claimant and his servant possessed "guns Poder and Shott." The size of the grant became settled at 50 acres in the 1690s, having fluctuated between twenty and 100 until then.

Headrights could be "proved" by oath in precinct or county courts, higher courts, the governor's council, and until 1734 before a single magistrate. In that year the royal governor's council, noting that being able to prove a claim before a single magistrate "was sometimes of ill consequence," ordered that henceforth such proof could only be presented to the council, to the precinct court in which the claimant resided, or to the General Court, the colony's highest lawcourt. Servants were entitled to a "freedom" headright at the conclusion of their term of service. Headrights were commodities that could be assigned to persons other than the original claimant, and examples of this abound in the records printed in this volume.

Over time, as available land became increasingly scarce, fewer and fewer headrights were proved in courts and council. Also, the practice gradually ceased of naming the people for whom the headright was claimed. The latest such entries in the following list are a few from the early 1740s, but the great majority are from the 1690s.

The records printed here comprise all headright names, both manuscript and published, that the compiler was able to locate during a lengthy search. Undoubtedly many others will never be known because of missing records. Multiple versions of the same document are included, since significant differences sometimes occur between them. Variant spellings of personal names have been treated as main entries, and no attempt has been made to differentiate between and among different people bearing the same name. Geographical names have been rendered as given in the document. A limited number of subjects have been included in the index. Not included here are applications for grants that include only the applicant's name, the practice during the later colonial era.

A notable feature of named headrights is that very often familial relationships are indicated, as are the names of slaves and servants included in the household. In addition, the first reference to an individual in any document of the colonial era may well be in a headright claim. For many others, the same source constitutes the sole surviving record of their existence. It may be presumed that most of the individuals named in the lists below did in fact become permanent residents of the colony of North Carolina, although it should be noted again that doubtless some, at least, did not.

For a more detailed treatment of the topic of headrights, as well as of land grants generally, interested readers may wish to consult the introductions and documents in Mattie Erma Edwards Parker, William S. Price, Jr., and Robert J. Cain, eds., *The Colonial Records of North Carolina* [*Second Series*], 10 vols. to date (Raleigh: Division of Archives and History, Department of Cultural Resources, 1963—), I-IX.

Robert J. Cain
January 2001

North Carolina Headrights:
A List of Names, 1663-1744

Nell Marion Nugent, *Cavaliers and Pioneers, Abstracts of Virginia Land Patents and Grants, 1623-1666*, vol. 1 (Richmond, Va.: Dietz Print Company, 1934-; reprint, Richmond: Virginia State Library, 1979).

Patent Book No. 4 [No. 5 on mf.]
p. 425
Henry Palin, 450 a. at the mouth of New begin Creek, 25 Sept. 1663, p. 93 (584). Transportation of 9 persons: Wm. Gailer, Tho. Giles, Hen. Sterne, Roger Simons, Isaac Scott, John Atkins, John Sheffild, Nich. Wilson, Ralph Sharpe.
[Marginal note: "Carolina."]

Thomas Hodgkin, 1000 a., in a bay of Carolina River, beginning at a small Creek called Cannaughsaugh, running up same to a branch of Mattacomecke Creek etc. 25 Sept. 1663, p. 93 (584). Transportation of 20 persons: John Philpot, Jno. Tyler, Mary Lewis, Samll. Burton, Math. Hewes, Wm. Bateman, Mich. Wills, James Rogers, Alex. Mont, Marke Allister, Geo. Rayman, Roger Cleyton, Tho. Kintly, Robt. Herne, Wm. Strood, Simon Allen, Ger. Ward, Rich. Card, Cutt. Fletcher, Fard Downes.

William Munday, 300 a. in Carratucks Creek, falling into Kecougtancke River, which river falls into Carrolina; beginning at the mouth of a swamp where John Harveys land ends, running E.S.E. etc. 25 Sept. 1663, p. 94 (584). Transportation of 6 persons: Wm. Edmonds, Joseph Gibson, Robt. Read, Rich. Smith, Samll. Warren, James Bard.

p. 426
Thomas Sherwood, 880 a. on the North side of Carolina River, running N.W. by trees of Samll. Davis, then E. by N. etc. 25 Sept. 1663, p. 94 (585). Transportation of 18 persons: Tho. Davis, Edward Sneath, Wm. Tanner, Robt. Wheeler, Henry Weston, Wm. Lewis, Tho. Waad, Wm. Badger, Jno. Gafer, Eliz. Waad, Lidia How, Rich. Webb, Abell Jason, Sus. Alcocke, Sam. Francis, Wm. Glover, Fr. Glover.

Thomas Keely (Keele), 800 a. in a bay of Paspetanke River, 25 Sept. 1663, p. 94 (585). Transportation of 16 persons: Wm. Badger, Jno.

Gaffer, Danll. Merick, Tho. Joanes, Ed. Seare, Margt. Williams, Ann Robinson, Abell Jason, Rich. Bullock, Tho. Mann, Rich. Evans, Edward Evans, Robt. Evans, Jno. Sharpe, Ja. Fuller, John Carey. [Marginal note: "Carolina."]

John Battle, 640 a. on Westward side of Paspetanke River, beginning on a point which parts this and land of Mrs. Fortsen, running S.W. etc. 25 Sept. 1663, p. 94 (585). Transportation of 13 persons: John Garey, Ed. Maurice, Jno. Curtain, Tho. Cooly, Tho. Mory, Wm. Crow, Wm. Hutton, Samll. Cornix, Abra. Travers, Wm. Fowler, Jacob Carew, Wm. Hughes, Mary Stevens. [Marginal note: "Carolina."]

James Murdah, 420 a. on W. side of Chowanoke River, 25 Sept. 1663, p. 95 (586). Transportation of 9 persons: Josias Pew, Jno. Boyce, Tho. Crafford, Wm. Morry, Nath. Bridges, Wm. Clarke, Hen. Kent, Ral. Bowles. [Marginal note: "Carolina."]

Mr. John Laurence, 625 a. on W. side of Chawanoke River, running S.W. along land of Mr. Robert Lawrence etc. to land lately surveyed by James Murdah etc. 25 Sept. 1663, p. 95 (586). Transportation of 13 persons: Geo. Teague, Kath. Cornelius, Wm. Sharpe, Ann Bleach, Wm. Hare, Fen. Nackington, Tho. Hill, Giles Wake, Hugh Farthy, Sar. Helior, Wm. Brickenton, Jane Doughting. [Marginal note: "Carolina."]

Mr. Thomas Stampe and James Noakes, 300 a. on the N. side of Carolina River, beginning at marked trees deviding this and land of Henry White, running E. etc. 25 Sept. 1663, p. 95 (587). Transportation of 67 persons: Hen. Leanord, Robt. Flake, Rich. Baker, Eliz. Hancoke, Wm. Preston, Duncumb Pantwell.

Lt. (St.) Mount Wells, 600 a. on W. side of Chowanoake River, running by land lately surveyed for James Murdoh, running E. etc. 25 Sept. 1663, p. 95 (587). Transportation of 12 persons: Tho. Poore, Jos. Hill, Ed. Suckett, Wm. Clarke, Tho. High, James White, Jno. Giloe, Tho. Bayly, Tho. Wood, Wm. Wood, Jno. Marly (Marky), Mary Fain.

Mr. Robert Lawrence, Junior, 625 a., on W. side of Chowanoke River, 25 Sept. 1663, p. 96 (587). Transportation of 13 persons: Wm. Yelding, Wm. Hare, Jno. Shaply, Tho. Turner, Ed. Morgan, Jno.

Goffe, Ed. Stephens, Wm. Chester, Mary Cant, Tho. Stroud, Ja. Smith, Ed. Hawly.

Katharine Woodward and Philarete Woodward, her daughter, 750 a. on W. side of Paspetanke River, beginning at a point above the mouth of a large Creek falling into said river, etc. 25 Sept. 1663, p. 96 (588). Transportation of 15 persons: Fra. Ost, Jno. Garnell, Mary Well, Alice Jeffry, Jno. Newton, Christian Grene, Jno. Barnwell, Mary Taylor, Robt. Cox, Ja. Johnson, Ja. Corke, Rich. Harman, Tho. West, Jno. Smith, Tho. Turvell.

Robert Peele, 350 a. on S.W. side of Pasbetanke River, between land of Doctor Relfe and John Battle, running S.W. etc. 25 Sept. 1663, p. 96 (588). Transportation of 7 persons: Wm. Cornix, Jno. Shard, Mary Carter, Jno. Sarmar, Wm. Whiter, Mary Jones, Jno. Shalpe.

p. 427
Mr. William West, 2500 a. on the E. side of Pequimmin River, about 6 or 7 miles up the same, beginning on a point of land neere A great Marsh nigh an Indian feild, running N.E. etc. to the mouth of a small creeke called Curraticke and from thence up the said river of Pequemin. 25 Sept. 1663, p. 96 (589). Transportation of 50 persons: Jno. Mison, Tho. Cox, Wm. Camp, Wm. Jones, Mary Yong, Tho. Carew, Ed. Frith, Wm. Stephens, Jno. Shans, Marke Williams, Jno. Sarson, Tho. Cooly, Mary Karp, Jno. Sanders, Wm. Fewell, Marke Lun, Wm. Capp, Tho. Stone, "and thirty two More"

Samuell Davis, 950 a. on the N. side of Carolina River, beginning at the mouth of a swamp, running N. by W. etc. 25 Sept. 1663, p. 97 (589). Transportation of 19 persons: Robt. Suite, Jno. Blete, Oliv. Williams, Tho. Soare, Eliz. Jones, Eliz. Smith, Eliz. Willmson, Eliz. Kitchin, Wm. Turner, Jane Doughting, Geo. Oakely, Hen. Henre, Luke Lunn, Morg. Wms., Edw. Coll, Robt. Hughes, Tho. Holder, Ma. Carr.

Mr. Thomas Relfe, 750 a. on S.W. side of Paspetanke River, beginning at the mouth of a swamp and running by land of Thomas Keele etc. by Mr. Fortsons marked trees etc. 25 Sept. 1663, p. 97 (590). Transportation of 15 persons: Jno. Rouse twice, Tho. Rouse, Steph. Harris, Jno. Shorebury, Kath. Dolbin, Percy Whitty, Ann Maine,

Ann Joanes, Mary Bayly, Tho. Relfe, Wm. Blech, Mary Belson, Jos. Rogers and his wife.

Mr. John Harvey, 600 a. in a small creeke called Carrawtucks, falling into the river of Kecoughtanke, which river falls into Carolina River. 25 Sept. 1663, p. 97 (590). Transportation of 12 persons: James Harvy, Hump. Evans, Ann Wombwell, Jos. Poole, Seph. Farrell, Tho. Elmes, Tho. Poole, Wm. Basse, John Davis, Rich. Blunt, Sam. Jnkins, Art. Brown, Cha. Sawe[*torn*]

Roger Williams, 350 a. on N. side of Carolina River, 25 Sept. 1663, p. 97 (590). Transportation of 7 persons: Man. Rogers, Thos. Jones, Tho. Jeffries, John Rosse, Cha. Seward, Jno. Daniell, Jone Roper.

William Jennings (Jenings), 550 a. in New begin Creeke, beginning at the mouth of a great swamp, which parts this and land of Robert Lawry, running up the Creek etc. to the mouth of a swamp which parts this and land of Phillip Evans etc. 25 Sept. 1663, p. 98 (591). Transportation of 11 persons: Samll. Henricke, Steph. Peirson, Samll. Moses, Tho. Peram, Tho. Richmond, Mich. Parram, Peter Janson, Sarah Marshall, Eliz. Jenuer, Peter Dennis.

Mr. John Harvey, 250 a. on the River of Carolina, beginning by Roger Williams land, running down same to the miles end of said Williams etc. 25 Sept. 1663, p. 98 (591). Transportation of 5 persons: Vergis Smith, Steph. Johnsey, Geo. Moore, Jane Parnell, Tho. Poole.

Robert Lawry, 300 a. in a bay at the mouth of New begin Creek, beginning at the mouth of a small swamp which parts this and land of Henry Palin, running S.W. etc. up the said Creek to a marked gum in the midst of the mouth of a great swamp which parts this and land of Mr. Jennings etc. 25 Sept. 1663, p. 98 (591). Transportation of 6 persons: Robt. Lawry, Jno. Maior, Rich. Woodart, Jude Wilson, Geo. Preston, Jno. Turfe.

Thomas Woodward, Senior, and Tho. Woodward, Junior, his sonne, 2500 a. on the N. side of Paspetanke River, beginning at the head of the eastermost branch of Aranews Creek etc. towards the head of the North River. 25 Sept. 1663, p. 98 (592). Transportation of 50 persons: Eliz. Elaerton, Xpher. Davis, Richard Marr, Edw. Rycroft, Hen. Greene, Tho. Patman, Jno. Brathwite, Tho. Robinson, [*torn*] Morris, [*torn*] Hiliard, Thos. Oliver, Nich. Woford, Ja. Charlton, An.

Bring, Wm. Lovet, Mary Spencer, Jno. Hollum, Rich. Wyatt, Mohan Hogan, Kat. Kadlin, Jno. Rich., Robt. Chambers, Tho. Hamton, Ma. Lenox, Row. Denson, Rob. Shepard, Sil. Ward, Jno. Barker, Hum. Chapman, Tho. Beffin, Ja. Murdah, Geo. Petit, Tho. Gilnett, Leo. Hathorne, Wm. Thomas, Rob. Walters, Jno. Simpson, Jno. Partridge, Tho. Carver, Jeff Mumford, Mary Cross, Jno. Olton, Rich. Hamond, Rich. James, Mary Simons, Alex. Frizell, Wm. Hazlewood, Wm. Famill, Tho. Clement, Arspell Forstive, Dan. Fenny.

p. 428

Phillip Evans, 300 a. in New begin Creeke, beginning at the mouth of a swamp which parts this and land of Mr. Jenings etc. 25 Sept. 1663, p. 99 (593). Transportation of 6 persons: Richard Whitty, Henry Catchmaid, Dina Farnes, Tony Negro, Jno. Scott, Mary English.

Mrs. Mary Fortson, 2000 a. on W. side of Paspetanke River, beginning at the mouth of a swamp etc., N.E. by land of Thomas Keele etc. 25 Sept. 1663, p. 100 (594). Transportation of 40 persons: Wm. Welldon, Hen. Benns, Wm. Carne, Jno. Robinson, Ed. Hawley, Geo. Warter, Tho. Roberts, Amosse Damsy, Jno. Wright, Tho. Steward, Tho. Mountfort, Ben. Perey, Susan Johnson, Roger Stroake, Mary Adams, Robt. Melclaugh, Stephen Brewer, Edward Barrett, Mary Young, John Peeterb, Tho. Starpe, Wm. Frizell, Tho. Marmaid, Thomas Hawley, Edward Moulson, Sarah Samwayes, Wm. Howard, Fra. Chalke, Tho. Baxton twice, and his two Wives, Tho. Harper, Jane Allen, No Brer., James Percy, Eliz. Steel, Abiather Flarrell, Margt. Thurloe, and Eliz. Newcomb.

Thomas Woodward, Senior and Thomas Woodward, Junior, 2000 a. on W. side of Chawanoke River, beginning 50 poles below the small Creeke which is at the lower part of the old Indian Towne, running W.S.W. etc. 25 Sept. 1663, p. 100 (594). Transportation of 40 persons: Humph. Pawle, Tho. Pryer, Ann Sutten, Robt. Black, Arth. Holder, Jacob Browne, Symon Prichard, Ezekell Williams, Wm. Miller, Wm. Holden, Robt. Corner, John Stevenson, Anth. Wyn, John Hamlin, Xpher. Woodward, twice, Tho. Marshall, John Bird, Robt. Hancoke, Peter Dennis twice, Eliz. Jemer(?), Sarah Marshall, Peter Janson, Ester Ruke, Mich. Talin, Tho. Richmond, Tho. Parin, Samll. Moses, Steph. Persian, and Samll. Henry.

Henry White, Senior, 250 a., on N. side of Carolina River, bounded on W. with John Harvies line, E. with Thomas Stamp and James Noakes, on N. with the woods and S. with the river. 25 Sept. 1663, p. 100 (595). Transportation of 5 persons: Ann Donkaster, Geo. Jenkin, Edward Barrett, Danll. Walker, Ann Jeakin.

Henry White, Junior, 750 a. in a small creek called Corawtucks that falls into Kecoughtanke River, beginning toward the head of the same, running W.N.W. etc. 25 Sept. 1663, p. 101 (595). Transportation of 14 persons: Perry Greene, Eliz. Howson, John Bruck, Richard Roods, Dan. Walker, Edward Morgan, Rich. Staples, Ann Dasor, Hestor Morgan, Eliz. Emnes, Edw. Parrett, Sarah Wadman, Danll. Walker, John Pine, James Rudder.

Mr. Richard Buller, 1200 a. lieing in New begin Creeke, beginning at the mouth of Doctors Creeke, running up the first mentioned Creek etc., together with a small Island against the mouth of Doctors Creek. 25 Sept. 1663, p. 101 (595). Transportation of 24 persons: Math. Smither, Artick Slatter, Joane Risding, Richard Ward, John Carey, Hester Sarkett, Robt. Mason, James Cranedge, Thomas Horne, Robt. Marson, Henry Warner, Thomas Turvor, John Mathews, John Pargetor, Sence Johnson, And. Armestrong, Dorothy Bankes, Tho. Rich, Edward Mosby, Tho. Read, Mary Memorish, Sarah Read, John Tapt, Wm. Sacum.

Nell Marion Nugent, *Cavaliers and Pioneers, Abstracts of Virginia Land Patents and Grants, 1695-1732,* **vol. 3 (Richmond, Va.: Dietz Print Company, 1934-; reprint, Richmond: Virginia State Library, 1979).**

Patent Book No. 13 p. 353
Aaron Blanchard, of North Carolina; 152 a. (New Land), Upper Parish of Nansemond Co., adj. George Spivey, in the Back Branch; 28 Sept. 1728, p. 362. Importation of 3 persons: Mary Lackey, Effra Nearne, and William White.

William L. Saunders, ed., *The Colonial Records of North Carolina,* **vol. 1 (Raleigh: State of North Carolina, 1886).**

p. 393: Perquimans Precinct Court, Feb. 1693/4
Mr. Tho. Lepper has proved Ten rights whose names are as followeth Tho. Kent Ann Kent Sarah Kent Rebecca Kent Ann Kent John

Thomas Wm. Brown Wm. Brickstone Tho. Lepper Nicholas Robeson

Caleb Calloway enters Foure Rights: Danll. Pembrooke Tho. Merrett and Indian Boy in all Foure. Arthur Long

p. 394

Thomas Lepper has proved ten Rights in the County Court Tho. Kent Ann his wife Sarah Kent Rebeccah Kent Ann Kent Junior John Thomas Wm. Brown Wm. Brickstone Tho. Lepper Nicholas Robeson

John Barrow proves three rights by importation Robert Tester Simon Smith and a negroe Jean

Thomas Pierce has proved his rights being Thomas Pierce John Pierce Susanna Ruth Pierce Dorothy Pierce Mary Pierce Mary Bridges John Wilkeson and John Pierce in all nine Rights

Hannah Gosby has entered nine Rights Jno. Gosby Jno. Anderson John Kinsey Richard Waterlow Kathrine Kinsey Jean Anderson and 3 hands from Jno. Northcoate Joseph Hepworth Jeremiah White and Henry Clay senior in all nine Rights

Peter Gray Proves two Rights for himselfe transporting twice into the Governmente and one given him by John Twegar

John Bently enter for importation Richard Bently Jean Bently Mary Bently Sarah Bently a negroe Boy a Negroe Woman an Indian Boy in all Seven Rights

Roger Snell enters for importation Roger Snell Rebecca Snell John Snell Walter Castle in all five

Jenken Williams enter one right for himselfe

Timo. Clare has proved foure Rights Timo. Clare Francis Belchamp Edmond Rodman Richd. Fox Junior in all foure.

Samll. Niccols has proved his rights being Chrissor. Niccolson Hannah his wife Deliverance Sutton Samll. Niccolson Frances Simons Hannah Niccolson in all Six Rights.

p. 395

Thomas Harloe has proved his Rights Thomas Harloe Mary Harloe Mary Harloe Jno. Harloe in all Foure.

Christor. Butler has proved his Rights Christor. Butler his wife and two children and a negroe girl in all five.

John Durant has proved his rights. John Durant Sarah Durant one Servantt named Judith in all three

William Godfrey has proved his rights being Prudem Hallum John Hallum Elizabeth Hallum Wm. Godfrey Sarah Godfrey in all five rights

James Fewox has proved James Fewox Ann Fewox Robert Fewox Edith Batchelor James Wilson Ann Wilson Alice Wilson John Wilson in all eight Rights.

Edward Mayo has proved his rights being Edward Mayo Senior Edward Mayo Junior Sarah Mayo Ann Mayo Elizabeth Mayo three negroes John Nixon Em. Nixon Ann Nixon Affrica Pike Samuel Pike in all thirteene

Turlo Fee has proved his rights namely Turlo Fee Daniel Fee being two

John Mason has proved his rights being Morgan Thomas and his wife and two children and a highred man named John Haws: in all five Rights.

William Butler proves his rights being William Butler Diana Butler in Number two.

Richard Nowell has proved his rights being Richard Nowell Joan Nowell John Smith Ellinor Nowell Charles Taylor George Taylor Mary Taylor Olliver Nowell Alice Nowell in all nine.

George Deere has proved his rights being Jeane Gritchell and John Dear and by Hannah Harrison Edward Harrison Hannah Harrison Joseph Williams Wm. Fyan Hannah Fyan Mercy Fyan Elizabeth Fyan Lydia Harrison in all tenn persons.

George Young has proved his rights namely Edward Foster Perthesia Foster and George Young in all three.

Tabitha Haskett has proved her rights being John Gray and Tabitha his wife John Gray Thomas Gray John Gray in all five Rights

Charles Mackdaniel has proved his Rights being Charles Mackdaniel Elizabeth Mackdaniel Thomas Wallingforde Samuel Powel in all Foure.

William Lacy has Proved his Rights being Martha Rouse John Rouse Mary Rouse Martha Rouse Wm. Lacey Senior Grace Lacey John Davis Jean Davis Wm. Lacey Junior in all nine Rights

James Loadman has proved his Rights being Hubbart Lambert Jeane Buyard his Mother and James Loadman in all three Rights

p. 396
Stephen Manwering has proved his rights being Edward Berry Andrew Kinsley John Deadman Robert Brightwell Senior Alice Brightwell Robert Brightwell Junior Richard Parker John Caselton Stephen Manwering being in all nine Rights

Thomas Hossold has proved his Rights being himself twice transported Mary Hossold Thomas Hossold Junior Thomas Snowden in all five Rights

John Northcoate has proved his Rights being Henry Clay Senior Mary Clay Henry Clay Junior Precilla Clay two Servants Joshua Hepworth Jeremiah White John Northcoate. Three of these rights are sold to Hannah Gosby being in the whole Seven Rights

Anthony Dawson has proved his Rights being himselfe and John Chapman in all two Rights

Mr. Patrick Baly has proved his Rights being himself Lucy Harvy a Negroe Woman Margrett Hamelton two Rights John Hudson Simon Daxter in all Seven Rights

Richard Fox has proved his Rights being Richard Fox George Fox William Fox Mary Fox in all Foure Rights

William Bartlett has proved his rights being Wm. Bartlett Senior Elizabeth Batlett William Bartlett Junior Thomas Bartlett Michael Bartlett in all five Rights

Robert Beasley has proved his rights being himselfe Sarah Beasley his wife James Beasley Johanna Beasley Richard Chestone Sarah Chestone in all Six Rights

p. 405: Albemarle County General Court, 25 Sept. 1694
Georg Ferdice upon his oath proveth that he hath right to two hundred and fifty acres of land by the importation of George Ferdice George ferdice his wife Mary his wife Sarah and Hanah Ferdice his daughter

Wm. Plater upon his oath proveth that he hath right to two hundred acres of land by the importation of Wm. Plater Martha Grace and Thomas Plater.

p. 413: Albemarle County General Court, 26 Sept. 1694
James Fewox proveth his rights to land by the importation of Rich Bachelor and John Haswell

p. 415: Albemarle County General Court, 27 Sept. 1694
Anne Stuart Senior proveth 6 rights viz. four negroes one English servant and Virgill Simons.

p. 418: Albemarle County General Court, 27 Sept. 1694
James Fewox proveth his right to one hundred acres of land by importation of Richard Bachelor and Jno. Haswell

Jno. Symons proveth his right to fifty acres of land by the importation of himself.

p. 420: Albemarle County General Court, 28 Sept. 1694
Leonard Loften proveth rights for himself and Eliz. his wife.

Jno. Previt proves his right three hundred acres of land by the importation of Jno. Previt twice transported An his wife Philip Warde Jno. Previt Junior Mary Previt

Major Saml. Swann proveth his right to six hundred and fifty acres of land by the importation of Saml. Swann, Sarah Swann, Wm., Sam,

Samson, Henry and Thomas Swann, Eliz. Hunt, Tom, Mary, Hanah Eliz. and Jane Servants

p. 432: Albemarle County General Court, 28 Nov. 1694
Henry Brooks proves his right to fifty acres of land by the Importation of himselfe

p. 435: Albemarle County General Court, 29 Nov. 1694
Danl. Halsey proveth his right to one hundred acres of land by the importation of John Aires and Rich. Wakefield

p. 436: Court of Chancery, 29 Nov. 1694
James Mills proves his right to eight hundred and fifty acres of land by the Importation of James Mills, Edw. Conquest, Geo. Sutton and his wife Nathanl. Sutton, Joseph Sutton, Mary Gosby, Eliz. Sutton, Wm. Hague, Nathaniell Marker, one Negro servant, James Hunds Jno. Pinck and his wife Jane Garrett, Jno. Overton Joseph Pitts.

p. 443: Albemarle County General Court, 25 Feb. 1694/5
Jacob Overman proves his right to four hundred acres of land by the importation of Jacob Overman Dorathy Overman Jacob Overman junior Tho. Overman Ephrim Overman Margery Overman Charles Overman and Anne Overman and Warrant Given

p. 479: Perquimans Precinct Court, Jan. 1696/7
Francis Segrave proved five Rits for five persons transported into this county Whoes Names are under wretten viz. himselfe, Lucretia his Wife Thomas his Sonn Francis his Soon William Powel.

John Dunston proved three Rits whose names are under Wreten viz. himselfe Francis his Wife Sarah Moore.

Thomas Speight proved tenn Rits Whoes Names ar under Wretten viz. himselfe Richard Mallone Nich. Perru John Morres Elizabeth Morres John Morres Junior William Morres Mare Morres Nathaniel Rave Fone a Negro

Charles Scot Proved fower Writs for fower persons transported into this County Whoes Names are under Wretton viz. himselfe Mary Scoot Elizabeth Scot Charles Scot on for his Servetue

Denis Meclenden proved aleven Rits Whoes Names are under Wretten viz. himselfe Charles Cafen Mary his Wife Margaret Dun Dennes Dun Rebecka Carpender Elisabeth Mackclenden Brient Mackclenden Dennes Mackclenden Francis Mackclenden Thomas Mackclenden

John Oden proved Six Rits for Six persons Whos Names are under Wretten vis. Himselfe Ann his wife Ann his Daughter Jan his Daughter Mary his daughter Rachel his Daughter

Abraham Williams proved fower Rits whoes Names are under Wretten vis. himselfe Anne his Wife Edward Williams John Williams.

p. 480: Perquimans Precinct Court, Jan. 1696/7
Francis Foster proved Six Rits Whose names are under Wretten William Foster John Foster Elisabeth Foster Francis Foster Jeane Swetman a Negro Hanna.

p. 487: Perquimans Precinct Court, July 1697
Edward Homes proved Writs for fifteen persons transported Into this County Whoese name are under Wretten vis. him Selfe Elizabeth his Wife Tho. Homes Edward Homes Junior Edward Homes Senior Elizabeth his Wife Tho. Homes Edward Homes Junior Sarah Homes Elizabeth Homes Edward Homes Senior Elizabeth his Wife Thomas Homes Edward Homes Junior John Homes.

p. 488: Perquimans Precinct Court, 18 Oct. 1697
John Spence proved three Rits for three persons transported Into this County Whoes names are under Wretten vis. him Selfe Cattern his Wife Robart Spence.

Alexander Spence proved Rits for five persons transported Into this County hoes names are under Wretten vis. himselfe Dorety Spence John Spence Daved Spence James Spence.

John Shaw proved on Rite for his transportation.

p. 493: Perquimans Precinct Court, Apr. 1698
Daniel Hall proved two Rits one for his transportation And one for his freedum

Robart Smith proved on Rite for his transportation into this County
And Asigne It to John Dawson

John Dawson proved on Rite for his transportation into this County

Rose Ingan proved one Rite for hir transportation Into this County
And Asigned It to John Dawson

p. 494: Perquimans Precinct Court, July 1698
Samuel Hearst proved Rits for fower persons transported Into this
County Whos Names are under Written vis. himselfe Jane
Chaddock John Doughatre Jane Jane Daughatre

Hennery Norman proved Rites for eight persons transported Into
this County Whoes Names are under Wreten vis. him Selfe Mary
his Wife Andrew Ross Mary Ross Thomas Ross John Simmons
Georg Waide James Ross

p. 523: Perquimans Precinct Court, Apr. 1699
John Watts Proved Writs for three persons transported Into this
County Whoeses Names ar under Wretten John Watts Senior John
Watts Junior Catterin Watts

p. 533: Perquimans Precinct Court, Apr. 1700
William More Proved two Writs for two persons Transported
Into this County Whoes Names Are under Written vis. Himselfe
Elisabeth His Wife

Thomas Hancock Proved five Writs for five persons transported Into
this County Whoes Names Are under Written vis. Him Selfe Mary
His Wife May his daughter Elisabeth his daughter John His Sonn

John Hare proved three Writs for three persons transported Into this
County Whoes Names Are under Wretten vis. Him Selfe Sarah his
Wife Sarah Shadock

William Fryle proved on Rite for His transportation and Asigned It to
Robart Murre

Robert Murre proved on Rite for His transportation

p. 534: Perquimans Precinct Court, July 1700

John Benet Proved Rits for Six persons transported Into this County Whoes Names Are under Written vis. Him Selfe Rose His Wife John Benet Junior Elener Benet Jean Benet Thomas Benet

p. 565: Perquimans Precinct Court, Nov. 1702
Timothy Clare Proved too Rites for too persons transported into this County Whose Names Are under Wretten John Dixson Elisabeth Jackson.

p. 566
Thomas Winslo Proved on Write for His Freedom An Asignd It to Timethy Clar.

p. 568: Albemarle County General Court, 28 Oct. 1702
Wm. Hutchison Provd Rights to 700 Acres of Land by the Importation Viz. Moses Whitaker twice Imported Frans. [*blank*] twice Imported Wm. Thomas twice Imported Jno. [*blank*] Tho. Cowlisle Jno. Gray Jno. Oliver Wm. Hutchison [*blank*] times Imported: And Assigned to Nathanl. Chevin

Simon Knight provd his Right to 100 acres of Land by Importation of Himself and Eliz. Knight

Mr. Jos. Reading Provd his Rights to 270 Acres of Land by Importation of Edw. Dickason

p. 576: Perquimans Precinct Court, 9 Feb. 1703
Upon a Petition of Mary Coffen Widdow
The said Mary proves three rights being for the transportation of Francis and Mary Coffen and Jno. Thursten and Assignes them to her Sonne in Law Richd. Rose.

p. 577: Perquimans Precinct Court, 9 Feb. 1703
Richd. Rose Proves one Right to 50 acres of Land by transportation of himselfe

p. 580: Perquimans Precinct Court, 13 July 1703
James Foster by a Petition requests leave to prove five rights (videlicet) two for himselfe Hannah Forster Samll. Wright and Mary White and is granted

p. 582: Perquimans Precinct Court, 12 Oct. 1703

Thomas Speight proves Rights for 350 acres of Land by the Importation of Mary Speight Senior Ditto Junior John Hetterter Mary Fitt Garratt Elizabeth Do. Negro Hannah and himselfe.

Thomas Dorton proves his Rights to 150 acres of Land by the Importation of himselfe Thomas Davis and Anne Davis.

p. 589: Albemarle County General Court, 29 July 1703
Wm. Rayfield proves his Rights to 200 acres of Land by Importation of Wm. Rayfield Ann Patience and Wm. Rafield.

p. 612: Perquimans Precinct Court, 11 July 1704
Wm. Williams proves his Right to 50 acres of Land by the Importation of himselfe.

p. 613: Perquimans Precinct Court, 10 Oct. 1704
Upon Petition of Captain James Coles praying to prove Rights to two hundred and Fifty acres of Land by the Importation of himselfe John Brock, John Falconar Edward Daniel Pison and Charles an Indyan and is admitted.

p. 618: Perquimans Precinct Court, 9 Jan. 1704/5
Upon Petition of Danl. Snooke praying to prove Rights for Four Hundred and Fifty acres of Land by and Importation of John Williford and Jane Williford Wm. Williford Sarah Williford Mary Watts Mary Avengton Phillis Love Saml. Boatman and 1 Child and is admitted.

Upon Petition of Dennis Macclendon praying to prove Rights to a Hundred Acres of Land by the Importation of two persons videlicet Michael Downing and Habella a Negro and is Admitted.

Upon Petition of Henry Spring praying to prove Rights to a Hundred acres of Land by the Importation of two persons videlicet himself twice and is admitted.

p. 619: Perquimans Precinct Court, 9 Jan. 1704/5
Upon Petition of Timothy Clare Esqr. praying to prove A right to A Fifty acres of Land by the Importation of Jenny A Negro is Admitted and Assignes the Same to Dennis Macclendon.

p. 650: Perquimans Precinct Court, 6 Jan. 1705/6

Isaac Wilson by his Subscription proves Rights to Twelve Hundred acres of Land by the Importation of Mary Boasman Eliz. Boasman John Morris Richd. Ruckman Negroe Phebe Indian Mall Negroe Patt Negro Maria James White 2 Anne Barker George Baits 2 my wife Rebekah Ratcliffe George Rice Richd. Gove Simon Alderson Joseph Canerle Richd. Turner Wm. Barnstable John Hooks Isaac Ricks and Abraham Ricks.

Upon Petition of Ralph Boasman praying to prove Eight Rights is admitted and proves Rights to Four Hundred acres of Land by the Importation of himselfe 3 times for his wife for Eliz. Boasman and 3 times for Saml. Boasman.

Upon Petition of Saml. Bond praying to be admitted to prove Eight Rights is Admitted and proves Rights to Four Hundred acres of Land by the Importation of Saml. Bond Eliz. Bond Mercy Bond Susannah Bond Eliz. Bond Mathew Potter Sarah Johnson and Luke Grace.

p. 651: Perquimans Precinct Court, 6 Jan. 1705/6
Upon Petition of James Nuby praying to prove Six Rights is Admitted and proves Rights to Three Hundred acres of Land by the Importation of John Nuby Magdalen Nuby John Nuby Eliz. Nuby and James Nuby 2 and assignes the same in open Court to Isaac Wilson.

Upon Petition of Saml. Bond praying to prove Three Rights is admitted and proves Rights to one Hundred and Fifty acres of Land by the Importation of Henry Grace James Hurt and William Bruing, and assignes the Same in open Court to Isaac Wilson.

pp. 653-654: Perquimans Precinct Court, 8 Oct. 1706
Upon Petition of Mr. James Minge praying to be admitted to prove Rights is admitted and proves Rights to one Thousand Acres of Land by Importation of James Minge Six times Ruth Minge Thrice Robin A Negro Four times Bob. Sam Sue Jane and Doll Sam and Voll

p. 654: Perquimans Precinct Court, 8 Oct. 1706
Richd. Turner by his Subscription proves Rights to Four Hundred and Fifty acres of Land by the Importation of Richd. Turner Thrice

his wife Bridgett Turner William Barnstable 2 Elizabeth Turner John Turner and John Hooks.

Saml. Charles by his Subscription proves Rts. to Two Hundred acres of Land by the Importation of Charles Scott Mary Scott Eliz. Scott and Mary Scott

Mattie Erma Edwards Parker, editor, *North Carolina Higher-Court Records, 1670-1696*, vol. 2 of *The Colonial Records of North Carolina* [*Second Series*], (Raleigh: Division of Archives and History, 1968).

pp. 14-15: [CCR 189]
Upon a petition of Francis Penrice for to prove his rites wich accordingly, he has done viz. Tho. Penrice Puriana Penrice Temperans Penrice Mary Penrice Eliz. Penrice Mary Cooke Francis Cooke Francis Penrice. (4 Feb. 1690/91)

p. 19: [CCR 189]
Willm. Stuard Proved ten Rights by his oath in oppen Corte the names Jno. Williams, Mary his Wife, [Wm.] Williams, Jno. Williams, Wm. Steward, Eliz. Steward [*illegible*]. (Mar. 1693/94)

p. 30: [CCR 101]
Georg Ferdice upon his Oath proveth that he hath right to two hundred and fifty acres of land by the importation of George Ferdice, George Ferdice his Wife Mary his wife Sarah and Hanah Ferdice his daughter. Ordered that a certificate therof be made to the Secretarys Office. (Albemarle County General Court, 25 Sept. 1694)

[CCR 101]
William Plater upon his Oath proveth that he hath right to two hundred acres of land by the importation of William Plater Martha, Grace and Thomas Plater. Ordered that certificate thereof be made to the Secretarys Office. (Albemarle County General Court, 25 Sept. 1694)

p. 37: [CCR 101]
James Fewox proveth his rights to land by the impor[tation] of Rich. Bachelor and John Haswell. (Albemarle County General Court, 26 Sept. 1694)

p. 39: [CCR 101]
Anne Stuart Senior proveth 6 rights viz. four negroes one English servant and Argill Simons. (Albemarle County General Court, 27 Sept. 1694)

p. 42: [CCR 101]
James Fewox proveth his right to one hundred acres of land by Importation of Rich. Bachelor and Jno. Haswell. (Albemarle County General Court, 27 Sept. 1694)

[CCR 101]
Jno. Symons proveth right to fifty acres of Land by the importation of himselfe. (Albemarle County General Court, 27 Sept. 1694)

p. 44: [CCR 101]
Leonard Loften proveth rights for himself and Eliz. his Wife. (Albemarle County General Court, 28 Sept. 1694)

p. 45: [CCR 101]
Jno. Previt proves his right to three hundred acres of Land by the importation of Jno. Previt twice transported An his Wife Philip Warde Jno. Previt junior Mary Previt. (Albemarle County General Court, 28 Sept. 1694)

[CCR 101]
Major Saml. Swann proveth his right to six hundred and fifty acres of land by the Importation of Saml. Swann, Sarah Swann, William, Saml., Samson, Henry, and Thomas Swann Eliz. Hunt, Tom, Mary, Hanah Eliz. and Jane Servants. (Albemarle County General Court, 28 Sept. 1694)

p. 80: [CCR 187]
To the Honorable Thos. Harvey Esqr. Deputy Governor the honorable the Lords Proprietors Deputies and members of the grand Councell. The humble petition of George Ferdice Sheweth That your Petitioner Haveing Five rites whose names are under written transported into this County Humbly prays that they may be proved and a warrant grannted upon them An he shall pray.

Geo. Ferdice
George Ferdice
Geo. Ferdice
his wife Mary

his wife Sara
and Hannah Ferdice
his [daughter]

Petition of Rights
Proved by the oath of George Ferdice (Sept. 1694)

[CCR 187]
To the Honorable Court
 James Fewox sheweth That he hath right to 100 acres of land by the importation of Rich. Batchelor and John Haswell for which he craves certificate and he shall pray. Proved by the Oath of Fewox.

James Fewox.

(Sept. 1694)

p. 82: [CCR 140]
Albemarle To the Honorable Cort
 Wm. Plater humbly sheweth that he hath right to 200 acres of land by the importation of William Plater Martha Grace and Thomas Plater for which he Craves certeficat and he shall pray.

William Plater Signum

 [*Endorsed:*]
 Proved and assigned to William Turner (Nov. 1694)

[CCR 187]
 To the Honorable the Depity Governor and members of the generall Court
 The humble petition of Ann Stewert Sheweth That she hath transported 6 rights. Humbly prays they may be proved. And she shall pray.

Ann Stewart

Being 4 Negroes One English
servant and Argill Symons:
Proved by her (Nov. 1694)

[CCR 140]
To the Honorable the Generall Court
 Samuel Swann Sheweth that he hath Right to 640 acres of Land for the Importation of 13 persons Into this Countrey (viz.) Samuel

Swann and Sarah his wife, William, Samuel, Samson, Henry and Tho. Swann, Eliza. Hunt Tom Mary, Hannah, Elizabeth and Jane negroes.

Samuel Swann proved

Rights (Nov. 1694)

[CCR 187]
Albemarle To the Honorable Court
The Petition of John Symons sheweth that he hath right to 50 acres of land by importation of himself for which he crav and shall pray. Proved and assigned to Nicho. Symons by him to W. Glover (Nov. 1694)

p. 95: [CCR 101]
Henry Brooke proves his rights to fifty acres of land by Importation of himselfe. (28 Nov. 1694)

p. 98: [CCR 101]
Danl. Halsey proveth his Right to one hundred acres of land by the Importation of himselfe and Mary his wife. (29 Nov. 1694)

[CCR 101]
Danl. Halsey proveth his right to one hundred acres of land by the Importation of John Aires and Rich. Wakefeild. (29 Nov. 1694)

p. 99: [CCR 101]
James Mills proves his right to Eight hundred and fifty acres of land by the Importation of James Mills, Edw. Conquest, Geo. Sutton and his Wife, Nathanl. Sutton, Joseph Sutton, Mary Gosby, Eliz. Sutton, William Hague, Nathaniell Marker, One Negro servant, James Hunds, Jno. Pinck and his Wife, Jane Gunnell, Jno. Overton, Joseph Pitts. (Court of Chancery, 29 Nov. 1694)

p. 129:
Jacob Overman proves his right to four hundred acres of land by the Importation of Jacob Overman, Dorathy Overman, Jacob Overman junior, Tho. Overman, Ephrim Overman, Margery Overman, Charles Overman, and Anne Overman, and Warrant Given. (29 Nov. 1694)

pp. 237-238: [CCR 102]

Mr. Cuthbert Phelps Senior proves by his Oath his Right to One Thousand and Fifty Acres of Land by the importation of himself Frances Phelps Derby Phelps, Edward Phelps Bartholomew Phelps, Precilla Phelps, Cuthbert Phelps Junior Daniel Makee George Hadawell, William Ryder John Hawkiat, Robert Glascow Nicholas Wakefeild, Thomas Ross, [blank] Garrett, Robert Fowler Mary Fowler Richard Rooks, Mary Rookes, Edward Rooks, Elizabeth Rooks. (General Court, 26 Feb. 1695)

pp. 263-264: [CCR 102]
Eliz. Jones proves on behalfe of Tho. Holloway right to two hundred acres of land by the Importation of Tho. Holloway senior and Tho. Holloway junior each two times. (General. Court, 30 Sept. 1696)

p. 264: [CCR 102]
William Glover proves rights to three Hundred acres of land by the Importation of himselfe and Charlesworth Glover Joseph Glover Mary Glover Eliz. Davis William Davis. (30 Sept. 1696)

pp. 288-289: [CCR 189]
Evin Jones proves right to 400 acres of land by Importation himselfe and wife twice Evin Jones Junior James Jones Uphrasia Jones Eliz. Hallaway and assignes two to William Jackson Junior. (General Court, 2 Dec. 1696)

pp. 295-296: [CCR 102]
Evan Jones by his Oath Proveth Rights to four hundred acers of Land by the Importation of himself and his wife Each of them twise Evan Jones Junior James Jones Euphratia Jones and Elizabeth Holiway And Assigns two of them to William Jackson Junior. (2 Dec. 1696)

pp. 402-403: [CCR 101]
Mr. Tho. Lepper has Proved Tenn rights whose Names are as Followeth Tho. Kent Ann Kent Sarah Kent Rebecca Kent Ann Kent John Thomas Wm. Brown Wm. Brickstone Tho. Lepper Nicholas Robeson. (Feb. 1693/4)

Caleb Calloway enters Foure Rights: Danll. Pembrooke Tho. Merrett an Indian Boy in all Foure. Arthur Long. (Feb. 1693/4)

p. 404: [CCR 101]
   Thomas Lepper has Proved Ten Rights in the County Court Tho.
   Kent Ann his Wife Sarah Kent Rebecah Kent Ann Kent junior
   John Thomas Wm. Brown Wm. Brickstone Tho. Lepper Nicholas
   Robison. (Feb. 1693/4)

John Barrow Proves Three Rights by Importation Robert Tester
   Simon Smith and a Negroe Jean. (Feb. 1693/4)

Thomas Pierce has proved his Rights being Thomas Pierce John
   Pierce Susanna Ruth Pierce Dorothy Pierce Mary Pierce Mary
   Bridges John Wilkeson and John Pierce in all Nine Rights. (Feb.
   1693/4)

Hannah Gosby has entred Nine Rights John Gosby Jno. Anderson
   John Kinsey Richard Waterlow Katherine Kensey Jean Anderson
   and 3 hands from Jno. Northcoate Joseph Hepworth Jeremiah
   White and Henry Clay Senior in all Nine Rights. (Feb. 1693/4)

Peter Gray Proves Two Rights for himselfe transporting Twice into
   the Govornmente and one given him by Jno. Twegar. (Feb.
   1693/4)

John Bently enter for Importation Richard Bently Jean Bently Mary
   Bently Sarah Bently a Negroe boy A Negroe Woman an Indian
   Boy in all Seven Rights. (Feb. 1693/4)

Roger Snell enters for Importation Roger Snell Rebecca Snell John
   Snell Mary Snell Walter Castle in all five. (Feb. 1693/4)

Jenken Williams enters one Right for himselfe. (Feb. 1693/4)

Timo. Clare has proved foure Rights Timo. Clare Francis Belchamp
   Edmond Redman Richd. Fox Junior in all foure. (Feb. 1693/4)

p. 405: [CCR 101]
   Samll. Niccols has proved his rights being Christopher Niccolson
   Hannah his Wife Deliverance Sutton Samll. Niccolson Frances
   Simons Hannah Niccolson in all Six Rights. (Feb. 1693/4)

Thomas Harloe has Proved his Rights. Thomas Harloe Mary Harloe
   Mary Harloe Jno. Harloe in all Foure. (Feb. 1693/4)

Christopher Butler has proved his Rights Christopher Butler his Wife and Two Children and a negroe Girle in all five. (Feb. 1693/4)

John Durant has proved his Rights: John Durant being Prudence Hallum John Hallum Elizabeth Hallum Wm. Godfrey Sarah Godfrey in all five Rights. (Feb. 1693/4)

James Fewox has proved James Fewox Ann Fewox Robert Fewox Edith Batchelor James Wilson Ann Wilson Alice Wilson John Wilson in all Eight Rights. (Feb. 1693/4)

Edward Mayo has proved his Rights being Edward Mayo Senior Edward Mayo Junior Sarah Mayo Ann Mayo Elizabeth Mayo Three Negroes John Nixon Em Nixon Ann Nixon Affrica Pike Samuel Pike in all thirteene. (Feb. 1693/4)

Turloe Fee has Proved his Rights Namely Turlo Fee Daniel Fee being Two. (Feb. 1693/4)

John Mason has Proved his Rights being Morgan Thomas and his Wife and Two Children and a highred Man Named John Haros: in all five Rights. (Feb. 1693/4)

William Butler Proves his Rights being William Butler Diana Butler in Number Two. (Feb. 1693/4)

Richard Nowell has Proved his Rights being Richard Nowell Jean Nowell John Smith Ellinor Nowell Charles Taylor George Taylor Mary Taylor Olliver Nowell Alice Nowell in all Nine. (Feb. 1693/4)

George Deere has Proved his Rights being Jeane Critchell and John Dear and by Hannah Harrison Edward Harrison Hannah Harrison Joseph Williams Wm. Fyan Hannah Fyan Mercy Fyan Elizabeth Fyan Lydia Harrison in all Tenn Persons. (Feb. 1693/4)

George Young has proved his rights Namely Edward Foster Perthesia Foster and George Young in all Three. (Feb. 1693/4)

Tabitha Haskett has proved her Rights being John Gray and Tabitha his Wife John Gray Thomas Gray Jahn Gray in all five Rights. (Feb. 1693/4)

pp. 405-406
    Charles Mackdaniel has Proved his Rights being Charles
    Mackdaniel Elizabeth Mackdaniel Thomas Wallingforde Samuel
    Powel in all Foure. (Feb. 1693/4)

p. 406
    William Lacy has Proved his Rights being Martha Rouse John
    Rouse Mary Rouse Martha Rouse Wm. Lacey Senior Grace Lacey
    John Davis Jean Davis Wm. Lacey Junior in all Nine Rights. (Feb.
    1693/4)

James Loadman has proved his Rights being Hubbart Lambert Jeane
    Buyard his Mother and James Loadman in all three Rights. (Feb.
    1693/4)

Stephen Manwering has Proved his Rights being Edward Berry
    Andrew Kinsley John Deadman Robt. Brightwell Senior Alice
    Brightwell Robert Brightwell Junior Richard Parker John
    Caselton Stephen Manwering being in all Nine Rights. (Feb.
    1693/4)

Thomas Hossold has Proved his Rights being himselfe Twice
    Transported Mary Hossold Thomas Hossold Junior Thomas
    Snowden in all five Rights. (Feb. 1693 /4)

John Northcoate has Proved his Rights being Henry Clay Senior Mary
    Clay Henry Clay Junior Precilla Clay Two Servants Joshua
    Hepworth Jeremiah White John Northcoate Three of these
    Rights are sold to Hannah Gosby being in the whole Seven
    Rights. (Feb. 1693/4)

Anthony Dawson has Proved his Rights being himselfe and John
    Chapman in all Two Rights. (Feb. 1693/4)

Mr. Patrick Baly has Proved his Rights being himselfe Lucy Harvy: a
    Negroe Woman Margrett Hamelton Two Rights John Hudson
    Simon Daxter in all Seven Rights. (Feb. 1693/4)

Richard Fox has Proved his Rights being Richard Fox George Fox
    William Fox Mary Fox in all Foure Rights. (Feb. 1693/4)

William Bartlett has Proved his Rights being Wm. Bartlett Senior Elizabeth Bartlett William Bartlett Junior Thomas Bartlett Michael Bartlett in all five Rights. (Feb. 1693/4)

Robert Beasley has Proved his Rights being himselfe Sarah Beasley his Wife James Beasley Johana Beasley Richard Chestone Sarah Chestone in all Six Rights.
[*signed*:]

Alexander Lillington, Caleb Callaway, John Barrow, Tho. Lepper. (Feb. 1693/4)

pp. 406-407: [CCR 140]
To the Honorable Court
The Humble petition of James Fewox humbly shewing That your petitioner hath 5 Rights which he is Ready prove and Craves Certificate Viz. James Fewox Ann his Wife Robert Fewox Edward Batchellor [*illegible*] Bachelor and shall Pray etc.

James Fewox
(Feb. 1693/94)

Mattie Erma Edwards Parker, ed., *North Carolina Higher-Court Records*, 1697-1701, vol. 3 of *The Colonial Records of North Carolina* [*Second Series*] (Raleigh: Division of Archives and History, 1971).

p. 7: [CCR 102]
Mr. Thomas Lovett proveth Right To one hundred and fifty acres of land by the Importation of himselfe Eliz. Adams and William Herne. (General Court, 25 May 1697)

p. 8: [CCR 102]
Elizabeth Dean proves Right to two hundred and fifty acres of land by Importation of Peleg Dunston Elizabeth Dean, Mathew Scot Sarah Scot and Elizabeth Scott. (General Court, 25 May 1697)

p. 9: [CCR 102]
George Kingerley proves Right to two hundred acres of land by the Importation of himselfe Eliz. his wife Mary and Elizabeth his daughters. (General Court, 25 May 1697)

p. 14: [CCR 102]

Jno. Byrd proves Rights to three hundred acres of land by the Importation of himself Mathew Anderson Mary Byrd James Basford Rich. Wiggins. (General Court, 25 May 1697)

p. 15: [CCR 102]
　　Rich. Nowell proves right to two hundred acres of land by Importation of Mary West Saml. West Phebe West William West. (General Court, 25 May 1697)

[Robert Laton proves Rights to five hundred acres of land by Importation of An Laton Mary Laton himselfe Eliz. Laton James Laton Olive Offee and the four last transported a second time. (General Court, 25 May 1697)

p. 19: [CCR 102]
　　Mr. Jno. Durant proves Right to one hundred acres of land by Importation of two Negroes named Sampson and Ruth. (General Court, 28 May 1697)

p. 29: [CCR 102]
　　Jno. King proves Right to a hundred and fifty acres of land by Importation of Jno. King Sarah King Eliz. King. (General Court, 1 June 1697)

p. 70: [CCR 187]
To the Honorable Court
　　The humble Petition of Jno. Bird Humbly Sheweth That he hath six Rights viz. himseffe Mathew Anderson Mary his Wife Jno. Bird Junior James Bassford Richard Wiggins which he is Ready to Prove and Craves a Certificate and he shall Pray etc.

　　　　　　　　　　　　　　　　　　　Jno. Bird
　　　　　　　　　　　　　　　　　　　(April-June 1697)

p. 72: [CCR 187]
North Carolina SS. To the Honorable Generall Court
　　Mr. Jno. Durant humbly Sheweth that he hath right to one hundred acres of land by importation of Sampson [and] Ruth Negroes which he is ready to prove and craves certificate and shall etc. pray.

　　　　　　　　　　　　　　　　　　　John Durant
　　　　　　　　　　　　　　　　　　　(April-June 1697)

pp. 72-73: [Mf. Reel C.024.30024]
To the Honorable Court
    The humble Petition of George Kinserley humbly Sheweth that he
    hath 4 Rights: viz. himself Eliz. his wife Mary Kinserly Elizabeth
    Kinserly Junior which he is Ready to prove and crave certificate and
    shall pray.

George Kinserly
(April-June 1697)

p. 73: [CCR 187]
North Carolina SS. To the Generall Court
    Robert Laton sheweth that he hath right to 500 acres of Land by
    Importation of himselfe and Eliz. his wife James Laton Mary Laton
    Olive Fee An Laton and from Virginia a 2d Importation himselfe
    and wife and Mary Laton and Olive Fee which he is ready to prove
    and craves certificate and shall pray.

William Glover Clerk

[*Endorsed*:]
Robert Laton (April-June 1697)

p. 73: [Mf. Reel C.024.30024]
North Carolina SS
To the Honorable Governor and Lords proprietors Deputys
    The humble petition of Tho. Lovett Sheweth that your
    Petitioner hath Right to two hundred acres of land by the
    Importation of himselfe twice and of William Herne and
    Elizabeth Adams which he is ready to prove and Craves a
    certificate and shall etc. Pray.

W. Glover Clerk

May the 25th
Proved and granted and assigned to Major Lillington W. G.
(1697)

p. 74: [CCR 187]
North Carolina SS. To the Generall Court
    The humble petition of Rich. Nowell sheweth that he hath right to
    200 acres of Land by Importation of Mary West Saml. West Phebe
    West Will West which he is ready to prove and Craves certificate
    and shall etc. pray.

W. Glover Clerk

p. 79: [CCR 102]
  Samuel Parsons proves by his Oath his right to fifty acres of Land by the Importation of himselfe. (General Court, 5 Oct. 1697)

[Robert Munck proves his Right by his Oath to two hundred acres of land for the Importation of himselfe Elizabeth his wife John Munk and Jone Stephens. (General Court, 5 Oct. 1697)

p. 80: [CCR 102]
  Mr. James Damerell proves his Right to eight hundred acres of land by the Importation of William Stephens, William Neal, James Jones, William Jones, Eliz. Evins, William Rig, Frederick Jones, Jno. Kent, Adam Gamball, Jno. [Figgis], Michael Linch, Jno. Crummell, Jacob Stephens, Mary Stephens, An Hughes, Thomas Pinor. (General Court, 6 Oct. 1697)

pp. 91-92: [CCR 102]
  Capt. John Hunt Attorney of William Thirrell and Gidion Therrell sons and heires of William Thirrells deceased Proveth the said Thirrells Right to four hundred acres of land by the transportation of William Therrell Senior William Thirrell junior four Indians and two Negros. (General Court, 11 Oct. 1697)

p. 101: [CCR 189]
  Sam Person proves his right. (General Court, 5 Oct. 1697)

Robert Munk proves rights for him Eliz. his wife Jno. his son Jone Stephens his servant. (General Court, 5 Oct. 1697)

p. 102: [CCR 189]
  James Damerell Rights. W. Stephens William Neal James Jones Wm. Jones Eliz. Evins W. Rig Fred Jones Jno. Kent Adam Gamball Jno. Wiggons Mic. Linch Jno. Crummell Jacob Stephens Mary Stephens An Hughs Tho. Pinor. (General Court, 6 Oct. 1697)

p. 110: [CCR 189]

William Thirrells Rights by Capt. Hunts Oath viz. himselfe his son William 4 Indians and 2 Negroes. (General Court, 11 Oct. 1697)

p. 175: [CCR 148]
To the honoribil governur and Counsell now siteng the petision of Christopher Butler humbly sheweth that your petishnor has bin kept A Long time out of his Right which I hope your honors will Cosedor of that Stephen Manwaring shall apear before your honors the next asemble to Know what he has against your petisinor and duty he is bound to pray. Chris Butler October the 11th 1697

pp. 175-176: [CCR 187]
To the Generall Court
James Damerell prays to prove his right to 800 acres of land by Importation. <*Wm. Stevens, Wm. Keale, James Jones, Wm. Jones, Elez. Evens, Wm. Rigg, Frederick Jones, Jno. Kent, Adam Gamball, Jno. Wigings, Mich. Lynch, Joh. Crummell, Jacob Stevens, Mary Stevens, Ann Hughs, Thos. Pynor.*>

[*Endorsed:*]
Damerell (March 1697/98)

p. 176: [Mf. Reel C.O24.30024]
North Carolina SS. To the Generall Court
Capt. Jno. Hunt attorney of W. and Gidion Thirell humbly Sheweth that William Therrell deceased imported into this Government himselfe his son Wm. 4 Indians and two Negroes for which noe land hath been taken up which he is ready to prove and prays a certificate and Shall pray.

W. Glover Clerk
(Mar. 1697/98)

p. 185: [CCR 102]
Henry Hartley proves his Right to eight hundred and fifty acres of land by the Importation of himselfe and Eliz. his Wife William, Henry, An, Eliz., James, Archibald, Frances Hartley An Wharton Robert [Wharton] [*illegible*] Children Bartholomew Wood George Dawkins and William [Sanders]. (General Court, 1 Mar. 1697)

p. 186: [CCR 102]

Mr. Jno. Blany proves his Right to sixteen hundred and fifty acres of land by the transporting himselfe thirty three times. (General Court, 1 Mar. 1697)

pp. 221-222: [CCR 102]
Rich. Ashford and Johadan his wife in right of the said Johadan and of Ruth Lewis daughters of William Watkins deceased prove their right to three hundred and fifty acres of land by the Importation of Wm. Watkins Ruth Watkins Nathanl. Watkins Jno. Watkins Ruth Watkins William Watkins Johadan Watkins And the said Richard Ashforth proves his right to fifty acres by his owne Importation. (General Court, 26 July 1698)

p. 225: [CCR 102]
Anthony Alexander proves his right to two hundred acres of land by the Importation of himselfe An his Wife Anthony his son and Jno. Mason. (General Court, 28 July 1698)

p. 233: [CCR 187]
N. Carolina SS. To the Generall Court
Anthony Alexander humbly Sheweth That he hath right to 200 acres of land by the Importation of himselfe An his Wife Anthony his son and Jno. Mason his servant which he is ready to prove and prays a Certificate and shall pray.
W. Glover Clerk

[*Endorsed:*]
Antho. Alexander (Oct. 1698)

p. 234: [CCR 102]
John Burkhead proveth right to two hundred acres of land by the importation of himselfe two times and his wife and Child. Ordered that Certificate therof be made to the secretarys Office. (General Court, 25 Oct. 1698)

p. 244: [CCR 102]
James Mackdaniel proves his Right to One hundred Acres of Land by importation of Michaell Mackdaniel and Joan Mackdaniel. (General Court, 29 Oct. 1698)

pp. 269-270: [CCR 102]

Thomas Morgan proves his Right to 200 acres of Land by the Importation of himselfe Dorathy Gennit and her two Children. Ordered that Certificate therof be made to the secretarys office. (General Court 7 Mar. 1698)

p. 280: [CCR 102]
March 10th 1698 Court meet present Swann Semons Hawkins. Tho. Morgan Rites Dorathy Jenit and 2 Children and himselfe.

p. 308: [CCR 187]
March the 10th 1698/9. To the Honorable Court now sitting
The Humbell petition of Tho. Morgan shewing unto your Honorable bench that whereas I have transported unto this Country my self and three persons more which three is here under specified therefor youer pititieoner hath acording to the Costom of youer Country redy to prove and your petitioner shall pray.

The wife of John Jenet Dorothy
Jenet and two Children

Thomas Morgine

p. 371: [CCR 102]
James Fewox proved his Right to 250 Acers of Land by the Importation of five persons Viz. James Fewox and An his wife Robt. Fewox Eady Batchellor and Edward Bachellor. (General Court, 30 July 1700)

p. 402: [CCR 102]
A Letter of attorney from John Oadam of Virginia
To Thos. Spight was Proved by the oath of Henry Hill and Robt. Roundtree. (General Court, 29 Oct. 1700)

Henry Hill proved his Rights to 400 acres of Land by Importation of Henry Hill Mary Hill Abraham Hill John Hinton Wm. Hinton Eliz. Hinton Jno. Moaldy John Webb. (General Court, 29 Oct. 1700)

Mr. Jno. King proved his Rights to 450 acres of Land by the Importation of Jno. Morson: Jno. Howell: Michaell King: Henry Hill Wm. Stevens Tho. [Porter] George Okeham John King John Falkes. (General Court, 29 Oct. 1700)

p. 405: [CCR 102]
Dennis Mackelendon Proves his Rights to 650 Acers of Land by
the Importation of Charles Gastin: Mary Gastin: Eliz. Gastin:
Margarett Donn: Denniss Donn: Mathew Bryan: Mary Watts: Eliz.
Macklendon: Bryan Macklendon: Francis Macklendon: Tho.
Macklendon: Deniss Macklendon Junior: Dennis Macklendon
senior. (General Court, 31 Oct. 1700)

p. 421: [CCR 102]
Archibald Holms per his oath proved his Rights to 250 Acres of
Land by the Importation of himself Magdalen his wife Archibald
Holms Junior Edw. Phillips James Jimpson John Stewart. (General
Court, Perquimans, 25 Mar. 1701)

Richd. Davenport proved his Rights to 200 acres of Land by the
Importation of Richd. Davenport Johannah Davenport Richd.
Davenport Junior John Davenport. (General Court, Perquimans,
25 Mar. 1701)

Gabriell Nuby Proved his Rights to 200 acres of Land by the
Importation of Wm. Nuby Gilbert Smith Ralph Buffkin Gabriell
Nuby. (General Court, Perquimans, 25 Mar. 1701)

Alexander Gordaine proved his Rights to 350 Acres of Land by the
Importation of Allexander Gordaine senior Mary Gordaine
Alexander Gordain Junior Wm. Gordaine Charles Nyer Morriss
Cuningam Ann Gordaine. (General Court, Perquimans, 25 Mar.
1701)

p. 448: [CCR 102]
James Damerill proves Rights to 700 Acres of Land by
Importation of Tho. Newman: Alice Newman: Jane Newman:
Wm. Bush: Martha Bush: Martha Bush Junior: Wm. Bush Junior
Sarah Bush Elinor Bush William Collins Abraham Rattson: Eliz.
Battson: Rose Bush: John Hopkins. (General Court, 3 Aug. 1701)

pp. 474-475: [CR 2.002]
To the Honorable Deputy Governor and Councell Leon. Loften
sheweth That he hath imported Leo. Loften and Eliz. Loften which
he is ready to prove and craves with certification.
                                                    Leonard Loften

Proved by his Oath W. Glover (no date)

p. 523: [CCR 187]
To the honorable the Deputy Governor and Lords Deputies The
humble Petition of Henderson Walker Sheweth That whereas there
is 12 Rites due to your Petitioner for transportation of them into
the County. Wherefore your Petitioner humbly prays an Order that
it may be entered upon Record. And your Petitioner shall pray.

Henderson Walker

John Crene and his wife [*illegible*] Eliz. Crane his Child One Negroe
one servant woeman named Elizabeth Todd and one other
servant Woeman Henderson Walker one servant Robert Evans
Francis Middleton Richard Pryer one Negroe woeman One
servant Hanna Hayle in all 12 rites. (no date)

William S. Price, Jr., ed., ***North Carolina Higher-Court Records,***
1702-1708, **vol. 4 of** ***The Colonial Records of North Carolina***
[Second Series], **(Raleigh: Division of Archives and History,**
1974).

p. 42: [SS 310]
Wm. Hutchison Provd Rights to 700 Acers of Land by Importation
Viz. Moses Whitaker twice Importd Franc. [*torn*] twice Importd
Wm. Thomas twice Importd Jno. [*torn*] Tho. Cowlisle Jno. Gray
Jno. Oliver Wm. Hutchson [*torn*] times Imported And Asignd to
Nathanl. Chevin. (General Court, 27 Oct. 1702)

[SS 310] Simon Knight provd his Right to 100 Acers of Land by
importation of Himself and Eliz. Knight. (General Court, 27 Oct.
1702)

[SS 310] Mr. Jos. Reading Provd his Rights to 250 Acers [*torn*] Land by
Importation of Edw. Dickason [*torn*] Jno. Coverty Joseph [*torn*].
(General Court, 27 Oct. 1702)

[SS 310] Jos. Chowne provs [torn] to 150 Acers of Land [*torn*]
Importation of himself 3 times. (General Court, 27 Oct. 1702)

[SS 310] Mr. Tho. Babb provd his Right to one hundred [*torn*] of Land
by Importation of himself twice. (General Court, 27 Oct. 1702)

pp. 44-45: [CCR 140]
To the Honorable Court
    The Humble petition of Joseph Chowne shewing that he hath
    Rights Viz. Edw. Dickison Thos. Smith Joshua Evins Jno. Coverly
    Joseph Babb Jos. Chown 3 times transportation Jno. Ellis Ready to
    prove and Cravs Certificate and shall pray.
                                                        Joseph Chowne
    (General Court, Oct. 1702)

p. 45: [CCR 187]
To the Honorable Coart
    The Humble Petition of Wm. Hutchison Shewing that he hath 14
    Rights viz. Moses Whittaker twice Imported Fra. Elliss twice
    Imported Wan Thomas twice Imported: Jno. Lamlette Tho.
    Cowlisle Jno. Gray Jno. Oliver Wm. Hutchison 4 time Trasportd
    Read to pro and Cravs Cort and shall Pray etc.
                                                        Wm. Hutchison
    (General Court, Oct. 1702)

[CCR 140] To the Honorable Generall Court
    The Humble petition of Simon Knight praying to prove 2 Rights
    himself and Eliz. his Daughter and shall Pray.
    I Do Declare in the presence of god and under the penallty of
    perjury Declare that the said Rights Do properly belong to me and
    that no Land has been taken up for the same by me nor maner of
    person to the best of my Knowledge.
                                                        Simon Knight
    (Oct. 1702)

p. 57: [CCR 103]
    Wm. Rayfeild provs his Rights to 200 Acres of Land by
    Importation of Wm. Rafeild Ann Patience and Wm. Rafeild.
    (General Court, 28 July 1703)

p. 67: [CCR 102]
    Upon Petition of John Torkington praying to be admitted to
    prove five Rights is admitted and Proves five Rights to 250 acres

of Land by the Importation of himselfe Martha his wife Wm. Torkington Anne Starke and Francis Starke. (General Court, Oct. 1703)

p. 80: [CCR 187]
To the honorable Generall Court
 Jno. Tarkinton humbly Sheweth That your pettitioner humbly prays that he may be Admitted to prove five rights and your pettitioner as in duty bound Shall pray.
 <John Tarkington, Martha his wife, Wm. Tarkington, Anne Starke, Francis Starke.>

p. 148: [CCR [103]]
Upon Petition of Saml. Payne praying to prove Nyne Rights is Admitted and proves the Same by his Oath videlicet Saml. Payne John Day Paul Wakefield [*torn*] McBride Truman McBride Hugh Clarke John [*torn*] James Oughay and one Negroe. (General Court, 27 Mar. 1705)

p. 149: [CCR 103]
Upon Petition of John Pettiver praying to prove Eleven Rights is Admitted and proves these following Rights by his Oath videlicet John Pettiver Willm. Davis Edward Clarke Danl. Dyer Judith Clack Mary Downe Negroe Peter Indyan John Indyan Tom Negroe Naunce Indyan Jenney. (General Court, 29 Mar. 1705)

p. 473: [CCR 187]
To the Honarable the grand Court of north carolina:
The pition of william Maund Senior Sheweth that hee having Imported himsilf four times in this province and having brought in Sundry porsangers and Sirvants request rites for the Same whose names are under written

Wm. Maund Sinior	4
Emanuel Clienet	1
Philip Bayly	1
Joseph breiding	1
Samuel wilson	1
Henry Smith	1
Thomas [*illegible*]	1
Jno. Bryan	1
	11

Wm. Maund Junior 11
Thomas [*blank*]   1
Samfri a nigro   1
Thomas Youngblood 1
Onicald Francis   1
Thomas Lake   <u>1</u>
                     6
in all   17

Robt. Humble   1

[*Endorsed*:]
The within rights Sworn to by Wm. Maund

Robert J. Cain, ed., *Records of the Executive Council, 1664-1734*, vol. 7 of *The Colonial Records of North Carolina* [*Second Series*], (Raleigh: Division of Archives and History, 1984).

p. 33: [GO 111]
Madam Catha. Hyde Came before this Board and was admited to prove upon Oath the Importation of Eight persons into this Government (Videlicet) Edwd. Hyde Esqr. Mrs. Penelope Hyde Wm. Clayton Jno. Lovick Mary Tudo James Gregory Andrew Stephenson and her Selfe. (Chowan Precinct, 12 Jan. 1712/13)

[GO 111] Major Christo. Gale was admitted to prove upon Oath the Importation of Four rights for which he has not as Yett taken up any Land (Videlicet) himselfe twice his Daughter Eliza and Arthur Harris And Assigned the Same over to Colonell Wm. Reed. (Chowan Precinct, 12 Jan. 1712/13)

J. R. B. Hathaway, ed., The North Carolina Historical and Genealogical Register, vol. 1, (Edenton, North Carolina).

Vol. I, No. 1. The office of the Clerk of the Superior Court of Chowan County, Edenton, p. 139:

Wm. Symons proved 5 rights, Wm. Symson, Robert Smith, Emanuel Altooy, Maria a negro transport, Hannah Symson freedom right. Court of Grand Council, 29 Mar. 1680.

p. 140
John Nixon proved his rights as follows, for importation, Jno. Nixon, wife Elliner, Edward London, Robert Griffin, John Davis, Zachariah Nixon, John King, Lawrence Rasten, Griffen Lawrence, Joseph Jones, Richard Bishop, William Bodees; 1675-'6.

John Watts proved his rights, Jno. Watts, wife Jane, daughter Sarah; 1672.

Richard Tidmarsh, proves rights, himself, wife, sons Richard and John; 1672.

p. 141
Francis Penrice proved his rights, viz: Thomas Pennice, Puriana Penrice, Temperance Penrice, Mary Penrice, Elizabeth Penrice, Francis Penrice, Mary Cook, Francis Cook; February 4, 1690.

Robt. Break proves his rights, himself, Elee his wife, Son John, and John Stephens, his servant. (1697)

James Daniel, proves his rights, 25 October, 1697. Mr. Stickey, Wm. Keel, James Jones, Wm. Jones, Elizabeth Evans, W. Rig, Fred Jones, John Keat, Adam Gamball, John Wiggins, Nice Lynch, John Crumwell, Jacob Stephens, Mary Stephens, Mr. Hughs, Sr.

p. 142
George Kimberly, proves his rights. Self, wife Elizabeth, daughters Mary and Elizabeth.

John Bird, proves his rights, Mary, his wife, John Bird, Matthew Andrews, James Buesgin, Richard Wiggins.

Robert Laton proves his rights, himself, wife, James Laton, Mary Laton, Ann Laton, Olive Fee.

Richard Nowell proves his rights, for importation of Sam'l West, Mary West, Phebe West and Will West.

Mary Cotton proves her rights, Mary, and Francis Cotton, and John Thurston. Assigned to Richard Rose; February 9, 1702-'3.

Jonathan Tailor proved his rights, himself, wife Elizabeth, Thomas Tailor, Jonathan Tailor, Mary Tailor, Thomas Evalen; January, 1695-'6.

John Wilford proved 5 rights, himself, wife Jane, daughters Sarah and Mary and John Wilford.

p. 143

Capt. Blounts' own proper rights in one warrant, Thos. Blounts all in one warrant. These rights of Thomas Blount to be put into one warrant for his brother James, that is, James, his wife, and son; 1674.

p. 145: Court Records, Book B, No. 1—Register of Deeds Office John Waugh proves rights for importation of himself, Priscilla Jackson, Deborah and Cullen Flynn. (18 Jan. 1714)

January 19, 1714. The Court met. Saml. Merritt proves rights for the importation of himself, Mary Ann, Mary and Elizabeth Merritt, Wm. Yates, Phillip, and Temsela Brown.

p. 146

Wm. Mixon proves rights for importation of himself, wife and 3 children. (19 Apr. 1715)

Thos. Beale proves right of importation of himself, wife, and one child. (19 Apr. 1715)

Wm. Wade proves rights for importation, William and Elizabeth Wade, and Ann Perlain. (20 Apr. 1715)

p. 147

Patrick Laughly proves rights for importation of John Welch, Sr., John Welch, Jr., Elizabeth Welch, Edward Welch, John Gordon, Daniel Butler, Thomas Lamb, Henry Lamb, Richard Marshall, Na. Tucker, Matthew Dyer, Henry Clark, and Wm. Pratt. (20 July 1715)

John Williams proves rights of importation of himself and wife. (20 July 1715)

Tomazen Wykan proves rights for importation of himself and wife. (21 July 1715)

Lawrence Martin proves rights for importation of Lawrence, Patience and Ann Martin. (21 July 1715)

Matthew Capps proves rights for importation of Matthew, and Elizabeth Capps, Sr., Elizabeth, Jr., Mary and Ann Capps, Mary and Elizabeth Powell. (21 July 1715)

p. 148
Thomas Crank proves rights for the importation of Thomas Crank, Sr., Thomas Crank, Jr., Ann Crank, Sr., Ann Crank, Jr., Elizabeth Crank, and Daniel Storey. (19 Sept. 1715)

Lewis Bryan proves his rights for importation of Symon, William, Edward, Janette, Lewis, Elizabeth, Mary, Joanah, Sarah, and Ann Bryan, Lewis Bryan, Jr., and Elizabeth Bryan, Jr. (19 Sept. 1715)

p. 150
Epaphroditus Benton proves his rights, for importation of Elizabeth Jr., Lawrence, Job, Sarah and Epa Benton, and Wm. Hardy. (Chowan Precinct Court, 17 July 1716)

p. 152
Benj. Foreman proved rights for importation of Benj. Foreman, Sr., Venity, William, Mary, and Benjamin Foreman, Jr. (Chowan Precinct Court, 16 July 1717)

Thomas Rountree proves rights for the importation of Frances, Ann, William, Joan, Susannah, Moses, John, Sarah, Elizabeth, Jethro, and Christian Rountree. (Chowan Precinct Court, 16 July 1717)

James Griffin proved rights for James Griffin, Sr., James Griffin, Jr., Sarah Griffin, Sr., Sarah Griffin, Jr., John, Joseph, Susannah, and Moses Griffin. (Chowan Precinct Court, 16 July 1717)

Moses Hill proved rights for importation of Moses Hill, Sr., Moses, Jr., Dorothy, Elizabeth, Gray, and Susannah Hill, and Thos. Fullinton. (Chowan Precinct Court, 16 July 1717)

p. 290: Chowan County Register of Deeds, Book B, No. 1

Andrew Salsbury and wife Ann, to John Dopson. 100 acres west side Chowan River, binding upon land of Col. Thomas Pollock, known as Vixes Branch; December 11, 1714. On the back endorsed I assign over all my right and interest to John Howcott; September 18, 1715. Test, Robert Holbrook

p. 305: Miscellaneous Items Taken from Loose Papers Among the Records of Albemarle County at Edenton (7 Oct. 1701)
Christopher Buftin proved his rights, viz: Christopher Buftin, Wm. Winn, Rd. Bond, Doz. Winn, Elizabeth Winn, John Forman, Eliz. Forman, Grace Winn, Wm. Winn, Jr., Ed. Winn, Mary Winn, Lamuel Winn, John Brise, Simon Alderson, Henry Slade, Jr., Hester Dareby, John Wormington.

Jeremiah Goodridge proved his rights, viz: Jeremiah Goodridge, Walter Craddock, Jacob Littelwood, Jon Mosley, Obadiah Prenguellon, John Billousley, Henry Clark, Thos. Webb.

Benjamin Barrington proved his rights, viz: Benj. Barrington, Eliz. Barrington, Mary Barrington.

John Nelson, Sr., proved his rights, to-wit: Jon Nelson, Sr., his wife Jane, Eliz, Mary, Thomas and Aron Nelson.

Capt. Henry Smith proved his rights: Henry Smith, Wm. Brown, Richd. Stanley, Eliz. Davis, Ed. Davis, Alis Davis, Wm. Davis, Thos. Davis, Ed. Pitts, An Stephens, Eliz. Toogood.

Jo. Rodgers proved his rights: Joseph Rodgers, Charles Hoplin, Jos. Bowden, Mary Rodgers, Hannah Cockarum, Joseph Franks, Eliz. Dearham, Nathl. Cockarum, Joseph, Lydia and Mary Cockarum, Magdalin Napkin, Jon James, Henry, Mary, Henry, Jr., and Francis Fleatwood, William and Richard Holeman.

Lodovick Martin's Rights: Lodovick, Mary, Eliz, William and Lodovick Martin, Jr.

Hannah Cockrum proved her rights: Hannah, Nathl., Joseph, Lydia and Mary Cockrum, Magdalin Napkin.

George Mungummery's rights proved: George, Elizabeth and Jon Mungummery.

Geo. Birkenhead proved his rights: Goerge and Thomas Birkenhead.

James Hogg's rights proved, viz: Jacob, Mary, Jon and Mary Crulson, Jr., Jon Crocker.

Jacob Littelwood proved his rights, viz: Jacob Littelwood Walter Craddock Jno. Anesley, Obadiah Bengumellton.

Wm. Reed's rights proved, viz: John Read 3 passages.

Jno. Nelson's rights proved: Jno. Nelson, Jr., Jno. Nelson, Sr., Judith Woodis, Will Capps.

Thomas Dearham's rights proved, viz: Francis Sprye, Benj., Eliz. and Mary Barrington, Bobert [*sic*] and Margaret O'Neale, Oliver Smith, Thomas, Elizabeth, Mary, Richard, Ann, Joseph, Francis and Elizabeth Dearham, Jr., Stephen the niger, Jon. Kindred, Wm. Rowland, Thomas Dearham, Sr., Robert Brite, Susanna King, Eliz. Knight, William Cunningham.

p. 306
James Fewox proved his rights, viz: himself, wife Ann, Robert Fewox, Edward Bacheller and Edward Bacheller.

Vol. I, No. 4. Miscellaneous Items From loose papers among the Records of Albemarle County at Edenton, p. 609:

Simon Knight proved two rights, himself and his daughter Eliz. (1702)

William Hutchinson proves his right for importation of 14 persons, Moses Whitaker twice, Fra Elliott twice, War Thomas twice, John Gray, Thos. Carlisle, John Lamlelle, Jno. Oliver, Jno. Hutchinson 4 times. (1702)

Joseph Chewne proves his right, imported Edw'd Dickison, Thos. Smith, Joshua Eisup, Jno. Cowerly, and Joseph Babb. (1702)

John Hard, Jr., proves his rights, importation himself, wife Sarah and Sarah Shadock. (1700)

p. 611

Augt. 5th, 1702, Elias Alexander Garganus proved 6 rights, viz: Himself, Ann his wife, Robert Garganus, Catharine Garganus, Sarah Garganus, Mary Garganus, Levi Truewhitt, Cot. Clark.

p. 612

George Fordice proved his rights, himself, Geo. Fordyce, his wife Mary, his wife Sarah, Hannah Fordyce. (no date)

Ann Stewart proves her rights, viz: One English servant, 4 negroes, Argile Symons. James Fewox proves his rights for Rich'd Batchelder and John Haswell. (no date)

Samuel Swann proves his rights, viz: 13 persons, himself and wife Sarah, William, Samuel, Sampson, Henry and Thomas Swann, Elizabeth Hunt, and five negroes. (no date)

p. 613

John Porter proved his rights for importation of himself, wife and four children and 13 others from Pennsylvania here. (1699)

p. 614

William Plater proves his rights for 200 acres land for importation of self, Martha, Grace and Thomas Plater. (1698)

Pamtecoe the 4th, August, 1702. These are to certifie that John Bird assigned over unto Francis Garganus in open Court Held at Wm. Barrows the fourth day of August 5 Rites of Transportation into this Government, (viz.): John Bird 2 passages, Ann Bird, Elizabeth Smith, John Smith, Levi Truewhett, Court Clk.

J. R. B. Hathaway, ed., *The North Carolina Historical and Genealogical Register*, vol. 2 (Edenton, North Carolina).

Vol. II, No. 1. Miscellaneous Items. From the Records of Albemarle County at Edenton, N.C., p. 150:

John Hardy at a Court held Oct. 7, 1695, proved his rights for importation of himself, Charity Hardy, William Hardy, Mary Hardy, John Hardy, Jr., Thomas Hardy and Jacob Hardy, Nath'l Chevin Clk. Court.

April 1696. Timothy Clare proves rights for himself, wife Elizabeth.

Jane Byer proves her rights, Self, Richard Byers, Laurence Nogall, Jane Byer, Robert Boge, Wm. Boge, Margaret Boge, Wm. Moore, Jas. Loadman.

Chas. McDaniel proves his rights, himself, wife Elizabeth, Jon. Stepney Clk. Court.

p. 151
    Evan Jones proves his rights for importation, himself twice, wife twice, Evan Jones, Sr., James Jones, Uphrasia Jones, Eliz. Holloway.

James Thigpen proves his rights, self, wife, sons James and John.

Vol. II, No. 2. Miscellaneous Items. From Records of Albemarle County and Chowan County at Edenton, N.C., p. 299:

James Pettinger for himself, Elitia his wife and Mary Johnson, assigned to Isaac Guilford. (no date)

Oct. 1712, William Barefield for himself twice, John Shepherd, Sam'l Gayward, Thos. Matthews, John Robison, John Lahay and Joyce his wife, Ann their daughter assigned to Col. Wm. Reed.

Dec., 1702. James Fewox for importation, Sarah Wood, Eliz. Wood, Henry, Richard, Mary, John and Henry Smith, Jr., William and Francis Casswell Edith and Edward Batchelor, Mark, Elizabeth Deborah and Jane Wheeler, Daniel, Elizabeth, Sarah, John, Thomas and Abraham House, John, Rachel, John, Jr., Elizabeth, Mary and Sarah Smith, Cornelius and Elizabeth Dunevare, John and Thomas Word.

Robert Saunders for himself six times, George Saunders, George Beshar, Job Woolyard, John and William Tooke, Phillip Sexton, Sam'l Hopkins, John Duisdall, John Farrington. Thos. Abington, Clk.

July 5, 1697. Nicholas Tyler, 2 passages, Katharine his wife, Kellam, Mary, Rose, Ann, William and Katharine Tyler, Archibald McCarrell, Daniel Bathell, Farnifold Green, in all 12.

Michael O'Neill Sr., himself, wife Deborah, Michael O'Neill, Jr., Deborah O'Neill, Ann O'Neill, Sam'l Cowenton, Chas. Smith, Clk.

James Neville, himself 2 passages. Dorothy his wife, Rebecca, Richard, James, John and Thomas Neville.

Nicholas Tyler for importation of Francis Garganus, Leonard Jones, Jane McDaniell, himself twice and John Hogan.

John Buntin for Edward Keisland, an Indian named Frank.

pp. 299-300
Wm. Hancock for William, Susanna, William, Jr., Frances and Israel Johnson, James Therell, Richard Ashworth, Roger Monteigue, Susannah Monteigue.

p. 300
Joseph Leathworth for himself, wife Sarah, Tabitha Leathworth, Susanna Edwards, Charles a negro. Test, Chas. Smith, Clerk.

Aug. 19, 1701. Pasquotank Court, Peter Gregory and wife Letitia, Rich'd Belington assigned to Thos. Abington and by him to Thos. Boyd.

Cornelius Jones for Edward Blackburne, Mary Howden, Dyana a negro, Sarah and Sambo Indians, John Parker, Adam, Sythee and Wapping negroes.

Oct. 20, 1701. Sam'l Pike for himself twice, Jane his wife.

John Nash for himself.

James Forbes for himself, Alice his wife, John, James, Jr., Elizabeth, Thomas, Bayley and Edward Forbes, Lewis, Hester and Maria Knight, assigned to Isaac Guilford.

John Tooke for himself twice, Francis Britton, John Swann, William and James Tooke, Margaret Tooke assigned to Thomas Abington. Thos. Abington, Clk.

Augt. 19, 1701. Mrs. Ann Pope widow, Perisho a negro.

Samuel Pope, himself twice and Jane his wife.

Henry Creath, himself, Richard Creath, Richard Stanley, Wm. Clarke.

Joseph Peiry, himself, wife Ann, Elizabeth his second wife, Joseph, Susanna, Alice and Sarah Peiry, Obodiah Fair.

Henry Mandeville for Richard Burtonshall and wife Priscilla, Richard, Jr., Priscilla, Jr., Elizabeth and Dorcas Burtonshall, David, Mary, David, Jr., Mary, Jr., and Margaret Jones.

Aug. 1702. Richard Prince, for himself twice, Daniel Sullivant and wife Alice, Eliz Lucas and Jeremy Sullivant, Jno. Bernard, Henry Spring, Wm. Write, assigned to Thos. Agington.

Att a Court held for the precinct of Cartaret July the 15, 1680, the following persons proved their rights, viz: Richard Jones for freedom rights; Richard Jones, wife Mary and Wm. Jones, Edward German himself a freedom right, Jno. Sawyer two freedom and one transportation right, Mary his wife, Mary Sawyer transported Servant.

Jno. Dann, (freedom rights) John Dann, Mary his wife, Edward Golfe.

Luodovick Williams, (3 freedom and 2 transportation rights) Luodovick Williams, Hannah and Ellinor Williams, Trans' Wm. Wilson and John Jones.

p. 301
   Thomas Harrison (3 freedom) Thomas, wife Elizabeth and Elizabeth Harrison, Jr.

Michael Macdonnell, (4 freedom) Michael, Jane his wife and Mary Frances Macdonnell.

William Mowbray (2 freedom) William Mowbray and wife Hannah.

p. 305
Oct. 29. Henry Hill proved his rights for importation of Henry, Mary and Abraham Hill, John, William and Elizabeth Hinton, John Maulby and John Webb. (prior to 1710)

Vol. II, No. 3. Head Rights, p. 457
   Mr. Nixon proved his Rights; Isaac Page, Damerous his wife, Mary, Damerous and Elizabeth his daughters and Stephen Hanrork, new

Rights Zach Nixon, Elliner his wife and Eliz his wife, Robin an Indian.

Solomon Poole proved his rights, himself and 3 pruved.

Timo. Mead 2 wives or husbands, Elliner Brown, a young daughter. Will Travers proves his rights; Saray his wife, Francis Wilmot, Sam Morris, Jno. King.

[Editor's note following the above 3 headrights states that this record, undated, "is very old, probably about 1680."]

p. 465: Miscellaneous Items. Edenton Court House
Court held Feb'y. 12, 1694, for the Precinct of Chowan. George Branch proved his rights, for himself, wife, William, George, Elizabeth and Phyllis Branch and Margaret Thomas. Assigned to Nicholas Crisp.

Jon. Pettiver's rights, for himself, Wm. Davis, Edward Clarke, Daniel Dyer, Judeth Clark, Mandy Doune, Negro Peter, Indian John, Indian Tom, Negro Nan, Indian Jeanny. (no date)

Vol. II, No. 4. Miscellaneous Items. From Court Records of Bertie Co. at Windsor, N.C., p. 622:
John Jenkins proved ten white rights, viz: Jon. Jenkins, wife Anne, James, Elizabeth, Casia, Mary, John, Anna, Cader and Lewis, his children. (Bertie County Court, 14 Aug. 1744)

Benjamin Warren proved his rights, viz: himself, wife Esther, James, Benjamin, Margaret, Mary, Patience, William and Esther. J. W. to pay. (Bertie County Court, 14 Aug. 1744)

p. 624
Jos. Wynns proved his rights, viz.: himself, Judith, Geo. Pallaciah Wynns, Clara Anna Wynns, Jos. Perry Wynns and Anna Hubbard (whites), Phyllis (a black). (Bertie County Court, 13 Nov. 1744)

Wm. Outlaw proved his rights, viz.: himself, Mary Outlaw, Anna and James Outlaw. (Bertie County Court, 13 Nov. 1744)

Wm. Outlaw proved Thos. Finch's rights, viz.: Thomas and Mary Finch (whites), Mary and Toney (blacks). (Bertie County Court, 13 Nov. 1744)

Thos. Walker proved his rights, viz.: Sam'l., John, William and George Walker (whites). (Bertie County Court, 13 Nov. 1744)

Daniel Hysmith proved six of his rights, viz.: Daniel, Ann, John, Mary, Daniel and Sarah Hysmith. (Bertie County Court, 13 Nov. 1744)

James McDowall proved his rights, viz: Himself, wife Margaret and 13 blacks. (Bertie County Court, 14 Nov. 1744)

Thos. Odam proved his rights, viz.: Himself, wife Sarah, Susannah and Jacob Odam (whites). (Bertie County Court, 13 Nov. 1744)

John Williams proved 10 rights, viz.: Primus, Kinney, Grace, Guye, Phillis, Cezar, Betty, Sarah, Jack and Asha. (Bertie County Court, 12 Feb. 1744)

Wm. Bly proved his rights, viz.: John and James Bly (whites). (Bertie County Court, 12 Feb. 1744)

p. 625

Moses Horn proved his rights, viz.: Moses, Joel and Mary Horn (whites), and Edward Wever (black). (Bertie County Court, Feb. 1744-5)

John Jarnegan proves his rights, viz.: Jon. Jarnegan, Elizabeth, James Bolton, James Jarnegan and Dempsey Brasswell (whites), Jack (a black). (Bertie County Court, 14 Feb. 1714-5 [sic])

p. 626

George Hughes proved ten rights, viz.: Himself, wife Sarah, Mary, Ann, Elizabeth, Elisha, Jemima, William, George and Thomas (all whites). (Bertie County Court, 14 May 1745)

John Thomas proved four rights, to-wit: Himself, wife Martha, Phoebe and Elizabeth (whites). (Bertie County Court, 14 May 1745)

p. 627

Robt. Howell proved his rights, viz.: himself and Sarah Howell and 2 blacks. (Bertie County Court, 13 Nov. 1745)

Jacob Sharp proved his rights, viz.: Jacob Sharp and Elizabeth Sharp, John Glass, Sarah Bennett and Starkey Sharp whites and 3 blacks. (Bertie County Court, 13 Feb. 1745-6)

p. 628
John Holder proved one right himself. (Bertie County Court, 13 Aug. 1746)

John Barber proved his rights, himself, Wife Anna and Sarah Barber. (Bertie County Court, 13 Aug. 1746)

J. R. B. Hathaway, ed., *The North Carolina Historical and Genealogical Register*, vol. 3 (Edenton, North Carolina).

Vol. III, No. 1. Miscellaneous papers from Edenton Court House.
p. 67: Henderson Walker's Head-Rights
To the Honoble the Deputy Governor and Lords Deputies.
The humble Petition of Henderson Walker, Sheweth. That whereas there is 12 Rites due to your Petitioner for transportation of them into the Country, Wherefore yor Petitioner humbly prays an Order that it may be Entred upon Record. And yor Petitioner shall pray etc.

Henderson Walker.

John Crew and his wife, Eliz. Crew his child, one Negroe, one Servant Woman Named Elizabeth Todd and one other Servant Woman, Henderson Walker, one Servant, Robert Evans Francis Middleton, Richard Poyer, one Negroe Woman, One Servant Hannah Hayte, in all 12 rites. (no date)

p. 138
Mr. Snoden. You are required by Jabez Olford to Send him a warrant for these Rights underwritten, viz. Chowan precinct, Janr. Court 1703/4 Present the Justices, Jabez Olford proved 4 Rights viz. Jno. Olford Senior, Jno. Olford Junior Wm. Olford Jabez Olford and by assignment of N. Chevin Owen Daniell, it makes 250 acres. Test N. Chevin Clk. (no date)

p. 139: Miscellaneous Items. From Court Records of Albemarle County at Edenton, N.C.
To the Honorable Court—The Humble Petition of Jno. Bird Humbly Shewing—That he have six Rights viz.: himself Mathew Anderson Mary his wife Jno. Bird Junior James Bussfon Richard Wiggins which he is ready to Prove and Craves a Certificate and he shall Praye etc.

> Jno. Bird. (no date)

No. Carolina Ss.—To the Honorable Generall Court. Mr. John Durant humbly Sheweth that he hath right to one hundred acres of land by importation of Sempsones and Ruth negroes which he is ready to prove and craves Cert. etc.

> Jno. Durant (no date)

Thos. Lovett hath right to 200 acres of Land by the Impotation of himselfe twice Wm. Horn and Elizabeth Adams. Assigned to Major Lillington (no date)

Jno. Hunt attorney of W. and Gidion Therell Sheweth that Wm. Therrill dec'd imported into this Government himself his son Wm. 4 Indians and two negroes etc. W. Glover Cl'rk (no date)

George Kingsley hath 4 Rights, viz.: himiselfe Eliz. his wife Mary Kinserly Elizabeth Kinserly Junior, etc.

> George Kinserly
> (no date)

Rich Nowell hath right to 200 acres of land by Importation of Mary West Saml. West Phebe West etc.

> W. Glover Clk.
> (no date)

Robt. Laton hath right to 500 acres of Land for Importation of himselfe and Elizabeth his wife James Laton: Olive Fee An Laton and from Virginia a 2d Importation himself wife Mary Laton and Olive Fee. Etc. W. Glover Clk. (no date)

p. 140

John Tarkinton humbly prays he may be admitted to prove five Rights to Jno. Tarkinton Martha his wife—Wm. Tarkinton Annie Starke Francis Starke. (no date)

p. 141

To the Honorable Grand Court of North Carolina the Petition of William Maund Senier Sheweth that he haiving Imported himself four times into this Government and having brought in Sundry partyes and he warrants and signest rites for the same whose names are under written. Wm. Maund Senior 4 Emanual Cleaves 1. Philip Bayly 1 Joseph breeding 1 Samuel Wilson 1 Henry Smith 1 Jno. Bryan 1. [*blank*] 1. Wm. Maund Junier 1 Thomas Maund 1 Sampson a negro 1 Thomas (Youngblood) 1 one Ould Francies Thomas Later 1 Robt. Humble 1 in all 17. (no date)

pp. 141-142

To his Masties Jastices of North Carolina in Chowan presink—The humble petition of George Lasiter dweller in Nansy Mond county in Verjenia umbly Sueth That youre petishtioner of late transported into this countree five persons in the month of March last past 1702 and the names thereof is your petishtioner his Son Robert and Thomas Davis Peter Daugherte Joseph Ashlee and umply prays he may have the benefitt of five rights etc. prov'd and Entered

p. 144

To the Honorable the Deputy Governor and Members of the Generall Court. The humble petition of Ann Stewart Sheweth That she hath transported 6 rights being 4 Negroes, one English Servant and Argill Simons Humbly prays they may be proved etc. Ann Stewart.

[Editor's note: "No date, but prior to 1700 from land grant to Argill Symons."]

p. 146

Pamticoe the 5th day of August 1702. These are to Certifi whom it may Concerne; that Elias Elexander Garganus proved 6 Rites of Transportation into this Government at a Court Holden at the house of Mr. William Barrow July the 7th 1702 viz. Elias Elex Garganus, Ann his wife Robert Garganus, Catherine Garganus, Sarah Garganus and Mary Garganus. Test Levi Truewhitt Court Clk.

Geo. Fordice proved his Rights for importation of George Fordice and his wife Mary; George Fordice, Jr., and his wife Sarah, and Hannah Fordice. (no date)

p. 147
   The Petition of John Symons sheweth that he hath right to 50 acres of Land for the Importation of himself. (no date)

Pamticoe the 4th of August 1702. These are to Certlfie whome it may Concerne that John Bird assigned over unto Francis Garganus in open Court held at Mr. Barrows the fourth day of August 5 Rites of Transportation into this Government (viz.) John Bird 2 Passages Ann Bird Eliza Smith John Smith. Test Levi Truewhitt Ct. Clk.

p. 148
   Rights for Walter Tanner, John Williamson Ricad. Johnson. (no date)

p. 153
   Head Rights.

[Editor's note: "On the back of a paper bearing date 1695, the following items appear"]

Jo. Walker and his wife Eliza Walker and [*blank*] and her 3 husbands Wm. Lambert Nicholess Brightman, Zachary Jerkin, Wm. Wilkison in one warrant by Chew. Jo. Walters hired Servant for himself.
Edward Bloxam and his wife Ann and her child Wm. Sutur desires the proof of their rights, by Pollock, James Harlow's rights for 15 last March hee came into the country, Edwd. Jarviss desires rights for 4 persons to be sent by Porter, Wm. Hooker for 6 rights by Major Swann.

Vol. III, No. 2. Records of Albemarle County, Edenton Court House, p. 244
   To the Honorable Generall Court, The Humble Petition of Simon Knight praying to prove 2 Rts. himself and Eliz. his daughter, and shall Pray I do declare in the presence of God and under the penallty of perjury Declare that these Rts. do properly belong to me and that no Land has been taken up for the Same by me nor Manner of porpose to the best of my Knowledge. Simon Knight.

[Editor's note: "'The General Court' was held at the House of Thomas White 24th day of September, 1694."]

To the Honorable Court—The Humble petition of Joseph Chowne Shewing that he hath Rts. Viz., Edwd. Dickison, Thos. Smith, Joshua Evins, Jno. Cowerly, Joseph Babb, Jos. Chown 3 times transportation, Jno. Ellis Ready to prove and Cravs Certificate and shall pray. Joseph Chowne. (no date)

p. 246
To the Honorable the Genll. Court—Samuel Swann Sheweth that he hath Right to 640 acres of Land for the Importation of 13 persons Into this Country (Videlicet) Samuel Swann and Sarah his wife, William Samuel, Sampson, Henry and Tho. Swann, Eliza Hunt, Tom Mary, Hanryah, Elizabeth and Jane Negroes. Samuel Swann.

[Editor's note: "The above paper antedates 1694."]

p. 249
Leon Loften's Rights.
    To the Honorable the Governor and Council, Leon Loften Shew: That he hath imported Leo. Loftin and Eliz. Loften which he is ready to prove and craves a certificate. Leon Loften.
    Proved by his Oath. W. Glover. (no date)

p. 250
John Porter's Rights.
    John Porter Sheweth—John Porter desires to prove wrights for Importation of nineteen persons into this Governmentt Viz. him self his wife and fower children and thirteen negroes from Pennsylvania here and hee shall etc. I John Porter doe declare in the presence of God and under the penalty of perjury that I nor any other person for me or by my deseir proved any of the above wrights till this time.

                                                    John Porter. (no date)

Albemarle. To the Honorable Court.
    Wm. Plater humbly Sheweth that he hath right to 200 Acrs of Land by the importation of Wm. Plater, Martha, Grace and Thomas Plater for which he Craves certificate and he shall pray etc. (no date)

p. 256
N. Carolina—ss. To the Generall Court.
Anthony Alexander humbly Sheweth that he hath right to 200 acres of Land by the Importation of himselfe Ann his wife, Anthony his son and Jno. Mason his servant which he is ready to prove and prays a Cert. and shall pray. W. Glover Cl. Cur.

[Editor's note indicates that Anthony Alexander settled in Albemarle County before 1700.]

p. 275
Rights for Sam Parsons, Richd. Simpson, David Jones, John Turner, Wm. Harris, James Robinson, Isaack Little and Jeremiah Tocinson. (no date)

p. 276
Rights for Richd. Burtonshall, Walter Green, Mary Cobb, John Nowell, Jane Simmons, Richd. Jarvis, Bessie and Harry negroes. (no date)

p. 282
In the Honorable Court, The Humble petition of Wm. Hutchinson showing that he hath 14 Rights, viz., Moses Whittaker twice Imported, Fra. Elliss twice Imported, Wan Thomas twice, Jno. Gray, Jno. Oliver, Wm. Hutchinson 4 times Imported, Jno. Lambeth, Tho. Cowlisle. Read to pro and Craves Cert. and shall pray etc.

Wm. Hutchinson.
(General Court 1718)

Vol. III, No. 3. Record of Perquimans Precinct Court, Office of the Register of Deeds, at Hertford, N.C., p. 439

Jane Byer proved Rites for nine persons transported Into this county whose names ar under wreten and Asigned to timothy Cleare vis. his selfe, Richard Byer, Lawrence Nogell, Jane Byer, Robert Boge, William Boge, Margaret Boge, William Moore, James Loadman. Timothy Clare proves on write for his wife, Elizabeth. Charles Mackdaniel proved two rits for the transportation of two persons into this county whose names are underwritten vis. his selfe, Elizabeth, his wife.

Vera copa p. John
Stepney, Clk.
(Apr. 1696)

Secretary of State Records, Land Grant Record Books, Volume 83A, 1701-1704, State Archives, Division of Archives and History, Raleigh.

front of p. (200) [page number printed on reverse side of page:] (fragment) for the importation of Thomas Stanly his Wife and his Daughter Robt. Duglice Fra. Williss Manuel Elbee Jos. Ellis his Wife Mary Elliss Laurence Creet his Wife and Daughter

Thos. Clark, 640 a., Chowan Precinct, 10 July 1701. Survey 23 Oct. 1697. for the Importation of Jno. Willson Robt. Willson twice Jno. Gillcrest W. Hambleton Peter Bassett his Wife his Child Agness Willowby her Child Tho. Clark his wife 1 negro

Tho. Clark, 270 a., Chowan Precinct, 10 July 1701. Survey 24 Oct. 1697. for the Importation of Tho. Husk, Tho. Mercey Tho. Harlo Mary Harlo Mary Harlo Jno. Harlo

p. (200)
Thomas Clark, 503 a., Chowan Precinct, 10 July 1701. Survey 24 Oct. 1697.

For Importation of Wm. Meazle Mary Meazle Geo. Jones An Mathews Pat Raverly Moricce Conivane Alexandr. Jordan Wm. Neal Charles Wier Assignment by Geo. Mathews

front p. (199)
William Waters, 140 a., Chowan Precinct, 16 July 1701. Survey n.d. Warrant (150 a.) 11 June 1697.
For Importation of Jno. Varnham Eliz. Stone Heliner Talbut by Assignment of Jno. Daviss as maring the relict of Varnham to Jno. Cannon whose Relict the abovsaid hath maried

Tho. Garrett, 411 a., Chowan Precinct, 14 Sept. 1701. Warrant (400 a.) 12 Aug. 1694. Survey 26 Apr. 1699.
by Importation of Tho. Garrett Senior Bethia Garrett Tho. Garrett Junior Rich. Malpass Bethia Garrett
By Assignment of N. Chevin: Wm. Hickman Jno. Deane
By Assignment of Jno. Jones (viz.) David Lewis

p. (199)

Wm. Glover, 280 a., Perquimans Precinct, 14 October 1701. Warrant (800 a.) 11 Janr. 1696. Survey n.d.

Wm. Glover Mary Glover Charlesworth Glover Jos. Glover Wm. Davis Eliz. Davis Jno. Overton Jos. Pitts

front of p. (198)

Henry King, 302 a., Chowan Precinct, 16 Sept. 1701. Warrant to James Damerill Oct. 10 1698 (800 a.) who assigns warrant to N. Chevin. N. Chevin assigns "over 6 of these Rights to Mr. Henry King."

persons names Wm. Jones Wm. Stevens Wm. Neal James Jones Eliz. Evens Wm. Rigg

Thomas Spivie, 316 a., Chowan precinct, 16 Sept. 1701. Warrant (640 a.) to Nath. Chevin 9 Apr. 1700; Chevin assigns to Tho. Spivie. Survey n.d.

Persons names Jno. Ash Jno. Ashbee Tho. Parker Eliner Ash Abraham Jones Sarah Jones

p. (198)

Benjamin Blanshard, 455 a., Chowan Precinct, 16 Oct. 1701. Warrant (450 a.) to John King 23 July 1700. Assigns to Benjamin Blanchard 12 Sept. 1700.

Survey n.d.

persons Names Imported Jno. King Sarah King Eliz. King Jno. Skipper Marlin Denitt Mary Ellitt Jno. Ellitt Wm. Sturkee Abraham Jones

Henry Norman, 150 a., Perquimans Precinct, 15 Oct. 1701. Warrant (400 a.) 10 Sept. 1698. Survey 15 Sept. 1698.

persons names Imported Henry Norman Mary his Wife Andrew Ross Mary Thomas James Ross Jno. Semons Geo. Maidds last 4 Rights still Due

p. (193) 197

Tho. Marks, 550 a., Chowan Precinct, 2 Feb. 1702/3. Warrant (550 a.) 10 May 1677. Survey n.d.

Persons Names Tho. Dorothy Eliz. Thos. Jno. Marks Wm. White Tho. Allen And By Assignment of Nath. Chevin assignee of Owin Daniel viz. Jno. Abraham Sarah Jones Thomas Daniel

p. 196
> James Harlo, 216 a., Chowan Precinct, 9 June 1701/2. Warrant to Jno. Jones (350 a.) 9 Mar. 1693, assigned to James Harlo. Names with warrant: Rich. Williams Ann his Wife David Lewis Jno. Eliz. Jno. William Jones. [p. (193) 197: Warrant to James Harlo (750 a.) July 3 1695. Survey n.d.]

p. (195) left
> Nathanl. Nicolls and Jos. Sutton Junior, 421 a., Perquimans Precinct, [20] June 1703. Warrant (450 a.) n.d. Survey n.d.
> for the Transportation of Jos. Sutton Delivrance his Wife Jonas a Negro James Grimes Eliner Grimes Eliner Ash Jno. Worly Ann Creed Isaac Welch

Ezekiel Maudlin, 300 a., Perquimans Precinct, 20 June 1703. Warrant (300 a.) n.d. Survey n.d. Ezekiel Maudlin Hanah Edward Maudlin Sanders an Indian Sarah a Negro Benjamin Archer

p. (195) right
Geo. Sutton, 344 a., Perquimans Precinct, n.d. Warrant (564 a.) n.d. Survey 25 July 1697.
> for the Transportation of Geo. Sutton his Wife Nath. Sutton Joseph Sutton Sarah Sutton Deborah Sutton by assignment of Jno. Whidby Nath. Sutton Rich. Corbett Jone his Wife Sarah a Negro and 70 acrs Due on Whidbyes Warrant Dated the 7th feb. 1693 and allso 44 Acrs Due to Geo. Sutton by warrant Assigned from Jenkin Williams Dated the 22 of Aprill 1694.

p. (194)
Jno. Anderson, 209 a., Perquimans Precinct, n.d. Warrant to Stephen Manwareing n.d. Survey made over to Jno. Anderson 23 Nov. 1697.
> Names of the Rights Edw. Berry Andrew Kinsly Jno. Deadman Robt. Brightwell Alice Brightwell.

p. 193
Thomas Ottiway, 208 a., n. side of Perquimans River, n.d. Warrant (250 a.) n.d. Survey 1 Sept. 1697.
> persons Names Viz. Tho. Ottiway Jane Ottiway Judith Morgan Wm. Hughs Eliza. Ottiway

front of p. (192)

Saml. Barns, 300 a., Curatuck Precinct, n.d. Warrant (300 a.) n.d. Transportation of Jno. Pickett Saml. Barns Susan his Wife Jno. Minikin Mabell his Wife and Mary his Wife

William Woodly, 131 a., Chowan Precinct, n.d. Warrant (200 a.) n.d. by assignment of Wm. Mansell Wm. Mansell Mary his wife Saml. Bayly Experience Bayly

p. (192)
 Coll. William Wilkison, 400 a., Perquimans Precinct, June 1703. Warrant (400 a.) to Jonathan Bateman n.d. [signed: Harvey, Akehurst, Laker, Swann]. Survey 15 July 1696. Assigns to Wilkison. Jonathan Bateman Jno. Bateman 2 Indians 1 mallatto Tho. Broom Tho. Ottiway Abraham Ellis

front of p. (191)
 George Lutton, 130 a., Chowan Precinct, 16 May 1703.
 Warrant n.d. [signed: Walker, Swann, Tomes, Pollock, Glover]. Survey (130 a.) 1 May 1703.
 persons Imported Geo. Lutton Eliner Wm. Katherine Lutton

Thomas Babb, 210 a., Chowan Precinct, 2 Mar. 1703. Warrant n.d. [signed: Walker, Swann, Tomes, Pollock, Glover].
Tho. Babb twice Imported passig of Nath. Chevin Tho. Cassall Wm. Early Jno. Grey

p. (191)
George Kinserly, 175 a., Perquimans Precinct, 13 Jan. 1702/3. Warrant (250 a.) n.d. [signed: Harvey, Laker, Tomes, Pollock, Akehurst]. Survey (175 a.) n.d.
Persons names Geo. Kinserly Eliz. his wife Mary and Eliz. his Daughters

front of p. (190)
 John Shaw, 175 a., Perquimans Precinct, 16 May 1702.
 Warrant (100 a.) n.d. [signed: Walker, Tomes, Pollock, Glover]. Survey (75 a.) n.d.
 By assignment of the Honorable Major Swann two Negroes Named Dick and Will

p. (190)
 Capt. Thos. Luten, 126 a., Chowan Precinct, 13 May 1703.

Warrant (174 a.) n.d. [signed: Ludwell, Harvey, Tomes, Laker, Akehurst].
Survey (126 a.) 6 Oct. 1697.
Ducken Campbell Israel Shepherd Elinor Wardell

front of p. 189
Thomas Houghton, 52 a., Chowan Precinct, "called by the Name of Drummond Point," 30 Mar. 1704. Warrant (650 a.) n.d. [signed: Harvey, Lakar, Tomes, Pollock, Akehurst] Survey (52 a.) 15 Apr. 1699. Survey (196 a.) n.d.
Ruth Lakar by assignment of Mr. Benjamin Laker

p. 189
Thomas Houghton, 196 a., precinct unspecified, 30 Mar. 1704.
Persons Names Joseph Trowell Honer Trowell John George Edward George

Survey for Henry Creeck (490 a.) assigned by Matthew Williamson.
Survey (300 a.) and (150 a.) assigned by Wm. Temple and remainder by warrant of his own, 30 Mar. 1697. [See p. 186 front for grant]

front of p. (188)
[continued from bottom p. (184)] 30 Mar. 1704.
Persons Names Videlicet Henry Butler, Robert Robins, Besse Negro, Sarah Negro, Lawrence Arnold, Anne Collyer, Elizabeth Rebour

p. (188)
Thomas Messer, 80 a., between Little River and Perquimans River, 13 Mar. 1704. Warrant (400 a.) to John Holfort, 13 Mar. 1693. Survey assigned to Messer 6 Nov. 1699. Survey (80 a.) 15 Nov. 1697.
Persons transported videlicet Rowland Williams Old Will A Negroe

front of p. 186
Henry Creech, 490 a., at "Irlington on the head of Arrawood Creek" n.e. side Pasquotank River, 30 Mar. 1704. [See p. 189 for survey]
Persons Names videlicet Roger Martin Francis Williamson twice transported Matthew Williamson
Richd. Jones Mary Jones assign'd by Matthew Williamson John Cally Wm. Powell John Powell

p. 186
John Mackeele, 125 a., Pasquotank Precinct, 30 Mar. 1704.

Warrant (125 a.) n.d. [signed: Harvey, Akehurst, Tomes, Walker].
Survey (125 a.) 20 July 1698.
Persons Names videlicet
James Hund John Pink and his wife assign'd by Wm. Glover
Assignee of James Mills

front of p. 185
John Browne, 261 a., Pasquotank Precinct, 30 Mar. 1704. No
warrant, survey.
Persons Names videlicet
John Dye, and Jane his wife, Hannah Dye, Trustrum Brookes, John
Browne

front of p. (184)
Christopher Nicholson, 122 a., n.w. side head of Suttons Creek
Swamp, 30 Mar. 1704. Warrant (122 a.) n. d. [signed: Robt. Daniell,
Swann, Tomes, Glover].
Persons Names videlicet
Hestor, Tom, Dye, Three Negroes assigned by Tho. Snoden
assignee of Governor Daniell

p. (184)
Francis Pricklove, 165 a., Perquimans Precinct, 30 Mar. 1704. No
warrant, survey.
Persons Names videlicet
Samuel Pricklove Senior Samuel Pricklove Junior James Freeman
Rose A Maid Servant

Samuel Pricklove, 400 a., Perquimans Precinct, [continued p. (188) front]

p. 176
John Anderson, 640 a., Perquimans Precinct, 24 June 1704. Survey
(500 a.) and (140 a.) assigned by Jno. Willoughby, 20 Nov. 1697.
for the Importation of
Wm. Dennis Johannah Dennis Humphry Willis Eliz. his wife Mary
Willis Alexander Moore Alexander Oliver Charles Hews Katherine
McDaniell Tho. Evins Wm. Roe Abel Morris Andrew Turner

front of p. 175
Archibald Holmes, 543 a., Perquimans Precinct, 24 June 1704.
Warrant (543 a.) 5 May 1703. Survey (543 a.) 10 May 1703.

for the Importation of
Wm. Johnson, Edward Sawyer, Lawrence Crate, Ralph Arnold,
Robt. Whelptone, John Roberts, and five Negroes assignd by Tho.
Snoden

**Secretary of State Records, Land Grant Record Books, Volume
96A, 1708-1713, State Archives, Division of Archives and
History, Raleigh.**

p. 27 [upper left corner:]
Major Generall Thos. Pollock, 640 a., Chowan Precinct, 26 Feb.
1711/12.
Warrant (1700 a.) 31 Mar. 1711.
Warrant (1700 a.) "Due to him by Importation of 34 persons" n.d.
[signed: Hyde, Glover, Sanderson, Chevin, Boyd].
Rights 18 Switzers
himself and 2 sons not alphabited
Wm. Maul Edw. Bonwick 11 Negros viz.
London Joe Tom Betty Jenny Tatte Pompey Tom Scipio Bowman
and Moll

p. 32 (reverse)
Thos. Gilbert, 540 a., Chowan Precinct, 5 Mar. 1711/12. Warrant
to Edward Williams (640 a.) "due for Importation" n.d. [signed:
Swann, Danll., Glover, Foster].
Wm. Story Nehe. Jeffries Wm. Sprat Cor benington Wm. Biggs
Rob. Danll. John Tidmash Wm. Parker Nich. Jones Tho. Barnet
Sam Jones John Isles (Giles?) Ezekell hartshorn
Survey for Gilbert (245 a.) n.d.

p. 48 (reverse)
Richard Ballance, 832 a., Currituck Precinct, 2 Dec. 1712. Warrant
(832 a.) n.d. Survey returned (832 a.) n.d., Thos. Swann, deputy
surveyor. Persons Imported are Will Nuton his wife and 4 Chldren
Richd. Ballance and Geo. Lumley his wife and Child (daughter) 7
rights were purchased to an Order of Council (n.d.).

p. 49
Thos. Brint, 153 a., Currituck Precinct, 2 Dec. 1712. Warrant (153 a.)
n.d. Survey returned (153 a.) n.d., Thos. Swann, deputy surveyor.
Persons Imported are Tho. Brint Senior Alice his wife and Charles Brint

p. 51

Jno. Nosaye, 264 a., in fork of No. West River, 2 Dec. 1712. Warrant (264 a.) n.d. Survey returned (264 a.) n.d., Thos. Swann, deputy surveyor.

Persons Imported are

Thos. Swann Thos. Wallis Jona. Chase Sam Eley (Ely) Jno. Webster Ste. (Stephen) Swaine

p. 51 (reverse)

Henry Woodhouse, 326 a., Currituck Precinct, 2 Dec. 1712. Warrant (326 a.) 25 Oct. 1712. Survey returned (326 a.) n.d., Thos. Swann, deputy surveyor.

persons imported are

Thos. Brent Senior Alice his wife Cha. Brent Jno. Brent Eliza. Brent Alice Brent Junior Thos. Brent Junior

p. 52

Thos. Taylor, 447 a., No. East side of North River, 2 Dec. 1712. Warrant (447 a.) n.d. Survey returned (447 a.) n.d., Thos. Swann, deputy surveyor.

Persons Imported are

Jno. Wallis Senior and his wife Jno. Wallis Junior Wm. Wallis Toney, Jeffery, Phillip and Bess Negros

p. 53

Samll. Jones, 120 a., Currituck Precinct, 2 Dec. 1712. Warrant (150 a.) n.d. Survey returned (120 a.) n.d., Thos. Swann, deputy surveyor.

persons Imported are

Luke Neale Wm. Bateman Richd. Turbell

p. 53 (reverse)

Capt. Richd. Sanderson Junior, 570 a., Currituck Precinct, called Duse Quarter, 2 Dec. 1712. Warrant (570 a.) 25 Oct. 1712. Survey returned (570 a.) n.d., Thos. Swann, deputy surveyor.

Persons Imported are

Samll. Alderson Mary Hutson Jno. Bright Henry Bright Ja. Bright Symon Bright Jno. Hester Eliz. Tranter Jno. Tranter Henry Lake Thos. Platt

p. 55 (reverse)

Joseph Sanderson, 105 a., called Jack Grandy's Island, Currituck Precinct, 2 Dec. 1712. Survey returned (105 a.) n.d., Thos. Swann deputy surveyor.

persons Imported are

Robt. Harman Eliz. his wife Anne Harman his Daughter

p. 56

Joseph Sanderson, 750 a. and 16 pole, Currituck Precinct, 2 Dec. 1712. Warrant (750 a.) 20 May 1712. Survey returned (750 a. and 16 pole) n.d., Thos. Swann deputy surveyor.

persons Imported are

Jos. Ward and Mary his wife two boys, Eliz. Johnson two Negros, Thos. Wallis, Josia (Jona.?) Chase Sam Ely Jno. Webster Jno. Berry Ja. Filbrick Nath. Lock Rob. Canon

p. 57 (reverse)

Luke White 175 a. and 33 pole, Currituck Precinct, 2 Dec. 1712. Warrant (175 a.) 25 Oct. 1712. Survey returned (175 a. and 33 pole) n.d. [deputy surveyor not given].

persons Imported are

Mary Bright Jno. Bright Junior Anne Lake Dorothy Whitehurst

p. 61

Robt. Lowry, 622 a., Albemarle County, 1 Dec 1712. Warrant (622 a.) 20 Sept. 1711. Survey returned 25 June 1712.

Persons Imported are

Jos. Jesup Margt. Jessup Hasiah Hutson Ann Hutson Wm. Hutson Sarah Hutson Ja. Hutson Jno. Brotherwood Wm. Norris Susanah Norris Samll. Norris and Geo. Walker

p. 91 (reverse)

Griffin Jones, (640 a.), "in the Forke of pascotank," 2 Feb. 1712/13. Warrant (640 a.) 9 Jan. 1711/12. Survey (640 a.) 5 Feb. 1711/12.

Persons Imported are

himself and wife Jane his Sister Mary Jones, Judith Jones three Negroes Fra. Browne Mary (Marg?) Brown Margt. Brown Fra. Owden and Ed. Ranige

p. 92

Rt. Hicks, 80 a., Chowan Precinct, 4 Feb. 1713/14.

Warrant (100 a.) to Nico. Blackman, 24 Apr. 1707. Survey (80 a.) n.d., per Thos. Luten. "On the Backside of the Platt is Indos'd as followeth." assignment by Nico. Blackman and wife Alice to Thos. Williams, 29 Dec. 1712. Assignment by Thos. Williams to Rt. Hicks, 29 Dec. 1713/14.

Persons Imported are Nico. Blackman Thos. Morgan

p. 94

Wm. Waymouth, 376 a., on the "main Swamp of Nobbs Crook Creek," 1 Apr. 1712. Warrant (400 a.) 1 Mar. 1711/12. Survey (376 a.) 30 Mar. 1712.

Persons Imported are Pasquo Bartlett Senior Pasquo Bartlett Junior Ann Bartlett Mary Bartlett Eliza. Bartlett Alexr. Lefteare Jonas Waterman and Corn. Comiskee

p. 94 (reverse)

Foster Jervis, 315 a., Currituck Precinct, 10 Mar. 1713/14. Warrant (315 a.) n.d. Survey (315 a.) 15 Oct. 1701.

Persons Imported are Tho. Love Senior Grace his wife Tho. Love Junior Mary Love others purchased pursuant to order of Councill.

p. 95

Henry Pendleton, 300 a., s.w. side Pasquotank River, 9 Mar. 1713/14.

Warrant (300 a.) to Thos. Kirke, 11 July 1694. Survey (300 a.) 28 July 1698.

"On the back of the platt of the above Land is indorsed as followeth."

Assignment by Thos. Kirke and wife Sarah to Henry Pendleton, 20 July 1700.

Persons Imported are Thos. Kirke and Eliza his wife each twice Imported.

Eliza Kirke Ann Kirke

p. 97

John Upton, 655 a., Albemarle County, 23 Mar. 1713/14.
Warrant (655 a.) 15 Oct. 1712. Survey (655 a.) 17 Feb. 1712/13.
Persons Imported are Cornelius Tully, Jane Tully, Thos. Tully, Mary Tully, Thos. Wharton, Ann Wharton, Edwd. Wharton, Mary Wharton, Jno. Casey, Mary Casey, Jno. Smithson Eliz. Smithson, and Mary Smithson.

p. 114
Henry Bradly, 640 a., on the West Shore of Chowan, 27 Aug. 1714.
Warrant (640 a.) 29 Aug. 1712. Survey (640 a.) 29 Nov. 1712.
Henry Bradly Kath. Bradly Kath. Bradly Junior Rt. Bradly Josph.
Bradly Waltr. Konrell Chas. Merritt Ellenr. Meritt Jno. Merritt
Michll. Merritt Chas. Merritt Junior Jno. Early Mary Early

p. 117 (reverse)
Tho's. Dockton, 550 a., "on the great Pocoson at the heads of
Pequimons and other Rivers," 27 Aug. 1714. Warrant (550 a.) 11
Jan. 1711/12. Survey (550 a.) 14 Mar. 1711/12.
Jno. Brown Thos. Sickley Mary Sickley Mary Sickley Junior Mary
Downs Rd. Welch Honour Welch Wm. Goslin(?) Jams. Perrish
Mary Parish Indian man Tom.

p. 118
Capt. Wm. Ludford, 430 a., "on Alegator Creek " 27 Aug. 1714.
Warrant (430 a.) 1 Mar. 1711/12. Survey (430 a.) 4 Apr. 1712.
Josph. Knight Susanah Knight Susanah Knight Junior Josph.
Knight Junior Alexr. Bengall Eliz. Bengall Ann Vinyard Alice
Bengall Jno. Hosea.

p. 120
Jno. Hutson, 80 a., Perquimans Precinct, 27 Aug. 1714.
Warrant (80 a.) 1 Feb. 1711/12. Survey (80 a.) 11 Mar. 1711/12.
Edwd. Clerk Junior
Mary Clerk Junior

p. 123 (reverse)
Petr. Parker, 260 a., on N.E. shore of Chowan, 27 Aug. 1714. Warrant
(260 a.) 11 Feb. 1711/12. Survey (260 a.) 11 Mar. 1712. Jno. Roberts
Mary Roberts Mary Roberts Junior Ann Roberts Jno. Roberts Junior.

p. 130 (reverse)
Thos. Parker, 387 a., Chowan Precinct, 30 Aug. 1714.
Warrant (387 a.) 21 Apr. 1713. Survey (387 a.) 1 Oct. 1713. Thos.
Parker Jane Parker Petr. Parker Mary Parker Martha Parker Thos.
Parker Sarah Parker Jno. Parker

**Secretary of State Records, Land Grant Record Books, Volume
111-B, 1715-1719, State Archives, Division of Archives and
History, Raleigh.**

p. (1)

Henry Gibson, 300 a., Currituck Precinct, 9 Oct. 1716.
Warrant (300 a.), 26 Nov. 1715. Survey (300 a .) 10 Dec. 1715.
Rights etc.
Eliza. Forman Grace Winn Wm. Winn Edwd. Winn Mary Winn
Samll. Winn

p. (2): Benja. Bennett, 186 a. Currituck Precinct 9 Oct. 1716.
Warrant (200 a.) 1 Oct. 1715. Survey (186 a.) 10 Dec. 1715.
Rights Videlicet
Alexandr. Garganus Mary Garganus Catherine Ditto Sarah Ditto

p. (3)

Samll. Ballance, 130 a., Currituck Precinct, 9 Oct. 1716.
Warrant (130 a.) 4 Oct. 1715. Survey (130 a.) 10 Dec. 1715.
Rights (Videlicet)
Anne Redeing Emuling redeing

p. (5)

Edward Poyner, 54 a. and 32 poles, "being 2 Islands comonly called
by the name of the Bohemia Islands," 9 Oct. 1716. Warrant (60 a.)
10 Oct. 1715.
Survey (54 a.) 10 Dec. 1715.
Rite (Videlicet)
John HandCock

p. (6)

Wm. Ross, 134 a., Currituck Precinct, 9 Oct. 1716.
Warrant (130 a.) 4 Oct. 1715. Survey (134 a.) 17 Dec. 1715.
Rights (Videlicet)
Mary Van Senior Mary Van Junior

p. (7)

Wm. Lury, 655 a., Currituck Precinct, 9 Oct. 1716.
Warrant (655 a.) 4 Oct. 1715. Survey (655 a.) 10 Dec. 1715.
Rights (Videlicet)
Wm. Lury Dinah Lury Thos. Lury Dinah Lury Junior Vandermur
Lury Henry Slad Junior Mathias Tyse Mathias Copes Peter Floyd
Thos. Chick Simon Fosque Rachel Fosque Wm. Parker

p. (8)

James Newby, 144 a., "in the forck of little river," 10 Sept. 1716.
  Warrant (144 a.) 16 July 1715. Survey (144 a.) 12 Oct. 1715.
  Rights Videlicet
  John Cooper Anne Cooper Wm. Cooper his Son

p. (9)
Benjamin Bennett, 83 a., Currituck Precinct, 9 Oct. 1716.
  Warrant (83 a.) 10 Oct. 1715. Survey (83 a.) 19 Dec. 1715.
  Right Videlicet
  Henry Reading

p. 32
Robt. Harrison, 200 a., n.e. side Pasquotank River, 20 Sept. 1716.
  Warrant (200 a.) to Cornelius Jones, 1 Apr. 1697. Survey (200 a.) 28
  Apr. 1697. Assignment by Cornelius Jones and wife Eliza to Robert
  Harrison, 6 Mar. 1713/14.
  Rights are
  Robt. Harrison his wife and two Sonns.

p. 35
Danl. Maccoy, 300 a., Currituck Precinct, 16 Oct. 1716.
  Warrant (900 a.) 12 May 1700. Survey (300 a.) 24 June 1700.
  rights are
  Danl. Maccoy Christian his wife Christian his Daugher Danl.
  Macfashon "2ce" & Sarah Warrill

p. 84
Joseph Glaister, 134 a., precinct unspecified, 20 Nov. 1716.
  Warrant (500 a.) 29 Apr. 1705. Survey (138 a.)—2 surveys, 1 for 134
  a. and 1 for 4 a., n.d., Wm. Norris deputy surveyor.
  Rights (Videlicet)
  Jos. Glaister and his Two Daughters Ruth and Sarah

p. 95
John Woodhouse, 190 a., precinct unspecified, 19 Dec. 1716.
  Warrant (190 a.) 1 May 1715. Survey (190 a.), 3 May 1715.
  Rights Videlicet
  David Depee Wm. and Dorothy Winn Eliz. Forman

p. 96
John Perkins, 209 a., precinct unspecified, 19 Dec. 1716.

Warrant (209 a.), 14 Apr. 1715. Survey (209 a.) 1 Oct. 1715.
Rights Videlicet
Robert Tucker Mary Tucker Robert Tucker Junior and one Child

p. 97
Philip Talksey, 200 a., n.e. side Pasquotank River, 19 Dec. 1716.
Warrant (200 a.) 1 Dec. 1697. Survey (200 a.) 3 Dec. 1697.
Rights Videlicet
Mary Sarah Anne and Elizabeth Talksey

pp. 98-99
Philip Talksey, 80 a., n.e. side Pasquotank River, 10 Dec. 1716.
Warrant (80 a.) to George Griffin, 9 Mar. 1699. Survey (80 a.) 19
Mar. 1699/700.
Assignment by George Griffin and wife Elizabeth to Philip
Talksey, 7 Feb. 1704/5.
Proved Pasquotank Precinct Court 17 Apr. 1705.
Rights Videlicet
Two Negroes

p. 102
John Northern, 220 a., precinct unspecified, 19 Dec. 1716.
Warrant (220 a.) 5 Oct. 1715. Survey (220 a.) 15 Oct. 1715.
Rights videlicet
Andrew Wilson Senior Anne Wilson Andrew Wilson Junior and
one Child the rest purchas't

p. 105
John Barber, 352 a. and 12 pole, precinct unspecified, 19 Dec. 1716.
Warrant (352 a., 12 pole) 9 Oct. 1716. Survey (352 a., 12 pole) 17 Oct.
1716.
Rights videlicet
Lemuel Winn John Bright Simon Alderson Junior
Henry Slade Junior Hector Dunby Jno. Wormington Eliz. Linton

p. 106:
Joseph Sanderson, 97 a. and 12 pole, precinct unspecified, 19 Dec. 1716.
Warrant (97 a., 12 pole) 15 Oct. 1715. Survey C97 a., 12 pole) 20
Oct. 1715.
Rights Videlicet
Joseph and Elizabeth Sanderson

p. 109
David Ambros, 175 a. and 12 pole, precinct unspecified, 19 Dec. 1716.
  Warrant (175 a., 12 pole) 5 Oct. 1715. Survey (175 a., 12 pole) 16
  Oct. 1715.
  Rights Videlicet
  Anne and Mary Reading Marmaduke Etheredge Senior
  Elizabeth Etheredge

p. 116
Thomas Swan, 122 a., Pasquotank Precinct, [*blank*] 1716.
  Warrant (122 a.) 17 Nov. 1714. Survey 16 Nov. 1708.
  Rights Videlicet
  Henry Lawley and his Wife

**Secretary of State Records, Land Grant Record Books, Volume
111-C, 1713-1716, State Archives, Division of Archives and
History, Raleigh.**

p. (8)
Benjn. Blanchard, 176 a., Chowan Precinct, 4 Sept. 1714.
  Warrant (850 a.) 18 Feb. 1703. Survey (176 a.) 18 Feb. 1703.
  Benjn., Katherine, Aaron, Ephrm., and Judah Blanchard Fras.
  Samll. and Sarah Parker Jno. Stallians, Jno. and Thos. Spivy, Wm.
  Hill Rogr. Spring Moses Hill Jams. Redick Jno. Campbell Thos.
  Phillips Wm. Thompson.

p. (9)
Fras. Roundtree, 312 a., Chowan Precinct, 4 Sept. 1714.
  Warrant (500 a.) 16 Feb. 1703. No survey.
  Wm. Nellson, Fras. Rebecca, Thos. and Ann Roundtree
  Thos. Brooks, Robt. Coleman, Wm. Alsbury Jno. Barnham, Mary
  Bowers.

p. (15)
  Jno. Scott, 129 a., Pasquotank Precinct, 4 Sept. 1714. Warrant (640
  a.) 16 Dec. 1709. Survey (129 a.) 1 Feb. 1709/10. Alexdr. Spence
  Jams. Spence Eliza. Spence.

p. (17)
Stephen Scott, 230 a., Pasquotank Precinct, 4 Sept. 1714.
  Warrant (400 a.) to Wm. Reed, 22 Aug. 1698. Survey (230 a.) 22
  Nov. 1698.

Assignment by Wm. Reed and wife Christian to Josph. Jordan, Octr. 24th 1701.

Assignment Josph. Jordan and wife Filia Christi to Patrick Queadley, 21 Jan.

1706/7. Assignment Patrick Queadley and wife Kath. to Stephn. Scott, 8 Mar. 1706/7.

Ann Mayo 2 Transports

Edwd. Mayo Junior Jno. Brown Fras. Benken, Prudence Cornes, Moses and Rose Negros

Assign'd per Mr. Edwd. Mayo.

p. (19)

Geog. Morby, 380 a., Chowan Precinct, 15 Apr. 1714.
Warrant (380 a.) 12 July 1712. Survey 5 Dec. 1713.
Geog. and Katherine Morby Eliz. Jones Thos. Jayoe Eliz. Hartshorn, Mary Gaff
Jno. and Mary Roberts.

p. (21)

Jno. Minner, 264 a., Chowan Precinct, [*blank*] Apr. 1714. Warrant (264 a.) 21 Apr. 1713. Survey 8 Mar. 1713/14.
Jno., Eliza. Christian, Willm. Henry and Mary Minner

p. (22)

Geog. Wins, 420 a., Chowan Precinct, [*blank*] Apr. 1714.
Warrant (420 a.) 21 Apr. 1713. Survey 9 Mar. 1713/14.
Wm. Hutcheson Senior Wm. Hutcheson Junior Rd. Parker, Thos. Parker, Moses Ely Thos. Dew Geog. S[?]ier (Sciner?) Jona. Begley

p. (29)

Abrm. Blewlett, 640 a., Chowan Precinct, [*blank*] Apr. 1714.
Warrant (640 a.) 21 Apr. 1713. Survey, n.d., Wm. Maule deputy surveyor.
Henry Smith, Rd. Arnelof Rd. Williamson, Jno. Weathers Wm. Thomas, Hanah Harris Chas. Backet, Ann Beckett Wm. Moore Thos. Sheckley Mary Sheckly Rd. Welch Honour Welch.

p. (47)

Josph. Sparnon, 234 a., Pasquotank Precinct, 4 Apr. 1714. Warrant (234 a.) 30 July 1711. Survey 4 Apr. 1710.
Griffeth and Mary Jones Jane Gotherd Tom and Will negro men.

p. (62)
Edwd. James, 55 a., Pasquotank Precinct, 14 Oct. 1713.
   Warrant (55 a.) to Henry Creech, n.d. Survey 24 Nov. 1704.
   Assigned to Edwd. James 30 Oct. 1710.
   Richd. Farrell Senior

p. (63)
Edwd. James, 295a., Pasquotank Precinct, 14 Oct. 1713.
   Warrant (298 a.), n.d. Survey (298 a.) 23 Sept. 1708.
   Winefred Farrell Rd. Farrell Junior Winifred Farrell Junior Isabel
   Farrell Erasmus Farrell Mary Farrell.

p. (65)
Wm. Cranford, 156 a., Chowan Precinct, 9 Sept. 1714.
   Warrant (300 a.) 5 Nov. 1713. Survey (165 a.) 15 Mar. 1713/14.
   Wm. Katherine, and Eliz. Cranford Mary Floy'd
   1 right Purchas'd of the President

pp. (66-67)
Thos. Hastings, 125 a., Pasquotank Precinct, 9 Sept. 1714.
   Warrant (125 a.) to Edwd. Waad, n.d. Survey, n.d.
   Assignment by Alice Waad, legatee of Edwd. Waad to Jas. McKeel,
   1 Oct. 1695.
   Assignment to Danll. Mckeel, 20 Aug. 1700. [No assignment to
   Thos. Hastings]
   Jams. Hund, Jno. Pink and his Wife

p. 81
Samll. Phelps, 151 a., s.w. side Perquimans River, 9 Sept. 1714.
   Warrant (151 a.) 10 June 1707. Survey 25 Feb. 1709/10.
   Uriah, Mary, and Eliza. Huttson.

p. 87
Jonas Waterman, 16 a., s.w. side Pasquotank River, 22 Nov. 1714.
   Warrant (16 a.) 10 June 1707. Survey 1 Feb. 1709/10.
   Jonas Waterman

p. 90
Rd. French, 200 a., Perquimans Precinct, 22 Nov. 1714. Warrant (200
   a.) 10 June 1707. Survey 23 Aug. 1709.
   Richd. French 2 James Oats 2

p. 105

Wm. Chancey, 174 a., Pasquotank Precinct, 22 Nov. 1714. Warrant
    (174 a.) 3 Apr. 1707. Survey 22 Oct. 1709.
    Jno., Hannah, Mary and Jno. Lewis Junior

p. 108

Fras. Tomes, 340 a., Perquimans Precinct, 22 Nov. 1714.
    Warrant (340 a.) 18 Mar. 1706. Survey 29 Jan. 1709/10.
    Jno. and Eliza. Kimball Aron Johnson Jno. Scarf Jno. Kimball
    Junior Grace Kimball Thos. Joy

p. 128

Wm. Reed, 234 a., "on the Sand banks in Currytuck Precinct," 25
    Nov. 1714. Warrant (234 a.) 30 July 1711.
    Survey 15 Nov. 1712.
    Sand. Bernard Thos. Collis and 3 Servants.

p. 129

Wm. Reed, 161 a., on "Powell's Pointe," 25 Nov. 1714. Warrant (161
    a.) 30 July 1711. Survey 21 Nov. 1712. Edwd. Jane and Andw.
    Bennet

p. 133

Jno. Walker, 259 a., Currituck Precinct, 25 Nov. 1714.
    Warrant (259 a.) 20 Nov. 1711. Survey 1 May 1713.
    Wm. Hanton Wm. Willson Mary Mcfarlan Jno. Mcfarlan Jno.
    Richards.

p. 134

Thos. Bettys, 200 a., Pasquotank Precinct, 25 Nov. 1714. Warrant
    (200 a.) 12 May 1713. Survey 12 May 1713.
    Jer. Hanah, Sarah and Sollomn. Werrington.

p. 135

Jams. Davis, 200 a., Pasquotank Precinct, 25 Nov. 1714. Warrant (200
    a.) 5 Dec. 1713. Survey 7 Feb. 1713/14. David Thomas Mary
    Thomas, Corns. Comeskee Sarah his Wife.

p. 235

Thomas Bray, 516 a., Chowan Precinct, 15 Aug. 1715.
    Warrant (516 a.) to Wm. Predgen 4 Mar. 1799 [*sic*]
    Survey for Wm. Predgen 9 Mar. 1699.

Rights
Wm. Fred. and Wm. Prigin Junior
Anne Eliza. Mary Catherine and Anne Prigin Junior Owen and
Sarah Carter Florence Marow

p. 236
Captain Richd. Sanderson, 600 a., Currituck Precinct, 6 Aug. 1715.
Warrant (700 a.) to Henry Slade 15 Mar. 1693. Survey (299 a.) for
Henry Slade and to Richd. Jesper by assignment by Slade and a
warrant of his own for 600 a.
rights
Jno. Daws Indian
Nan and Sue Tony Sarah Moll Jack Sarah Negro Jno. Jose. Benja.
Samll. Hannah and Wm. Slade

p. 250
Richard Madren, 430 a., Pasquotank Precinct, 1 Oct. 1715. Warrant
(430 a.) 6 Mar. 1712/13. Survey 6 Mar. 1712/13.
Rights
Pat ODaniel Junior Eliz. ODaniel
these four Rights being laid upon 130 acres which was taken up into
a Suvey of 250 a.
Surveyed for Jno. Pierce and by him Sold to Rd. Madren

p. 253
Richd. Sanderson Junior 470 a., on the Sandy Banks, Currituck
Precinct, 6 Aug. 1715. Warrant (440 a.) 4 Sept. 1701. Survey (470
a.) 21 Oct. 1701. Assignment to Mathias Towler "ten of the within
rights" 21 Oct. 1701.
Rights
Wm. Brothers and ux. and 8 children

p. 254
William Stafford, 140 a., Currituck Precinct, 18 Oct. 1.715.
Warrant (140 a.) to Richard Everedge 4 Nov. 1702. Survey for
Richard Everege 27 Nov. 1702.
Rts.
Marmaduke Everedge Junior Barbary Everidge John Everidge

p. 255

Dennis Riordane and wife Sarah, 200 a., Currituck Precinct, 13 Sept. 1715. Warrant (200 a.) to Hector Denby 2 Dec. 1695. Survey for Hector Denby 14 Dec. 1695.
Rights
Dennis Riordane
Derby Owine(?) Eliza. Sterman and another right purchased

p. 263
Caleb Bundy, 40 a., precinct unspecified, 9 Sept. 1714.
Warrant (400 a.) 25 Sept. 1711. Survey 25 Sept. 1711.
Rights
Thos. Studds John Lowden and ux. and Child and 4 others already laid upon a former Survey

p. 288
Wm. Fryley, 460 a., called Mardston house, Chowan Precinct, 19 Jan. 1715/6. Warrant (1000 a.) 27 Mar. 1707. Survey (460 a.) and 640 a.) 10 Jan. 171 [*blank*].
Rights are as follows
Jo. Rogers Cha. Hopton Jno. Browder Hannah Cockram Mary Rogers Jo. Dereham Fra. Dereham Nath. and Jo. Cockeram

p. 289
William Fryley, 640 a., called Mardston house, Chowan Precinct, 19 Jan. 1715/6. [Warrant and survey p. 288.]
Rights as follows
Lydia and Mary Cockeram Magdn. Napkin Jno. James and Henry Fleetwood Mary Henry and Fran. Fleetwood Wm. And Rd. Holoman and Susanah King

p. 290
Thos. Gilbert, 200 a., Chowan Precinct, 19 Jan. 1715/6.
Warrant (200 a.) n.d. [signed: Eden, Pollock, Foster]. Survey 4 Sept. 1714. Robt. Barns Philip Brown Wm. Yetts Thomasell Brown

Colonial Court Records, Land Papers—Wills. 1665-1746, State Archives, Division of Archives and History, Raleigh [CCR 187].

Folder: Headrights 1680, 1694, 1696-1698, 1700-1704. Other undated [Each numbered entry represents an individual document]

#1 Perquimans Precinct Court, 2nd Monday in April 1696. Jan Byer
proved 9 transportation rights and assigned 2 to timethy Clare: hir
Selfe Richard Byer Lawrence Nogell Jan Byer Robart Boge
William Boyd Margret Boyd William Moore James Loadman.
Timothy Clare proved 1 right for his Wife Elisabeth.
Charles Mackdanel proved 2 transportation rights: him selfe
Elisabeth his Wife.

#2 Chowan Precinct Court, 1st Monday in Jan. (year not given—at
house of Capt. Hen. Walker)
Jeremiah Perry: 4 Rts.: himself his wife Jane Phill. Thomas Roger
Jane
Richard Griffin: 3: Elinor Bartlett Jane Bartlett Jane Roundtree
James Ibins(?): 4 Rts.: Eliz. Roundtree Henry thickpeny Senior
Mary his wife Henry Thickpeny Junior
George Chambers: 2 Rts. himself and Ursilla his wife
Christopher Buttler: 2 Rts. by Assignment viz. Timothy Love Mary
Love
Mr. Tho. Blount: 1 Rt. by Assignment one negro woman
[Chowan] Precinct Court, 1 Apr. (year not given—at house of
Haniball Hopkins)
Edward Bayes 5 Rts. viz. himself Mary his wife John Bayes
Elizabeth Bayes Mary Bayes Junior
Jno. Willson his own Right
Lyonell Reading: 2 Rts.: viz. himself and Mary his wife
Henry Lysle: 11 Rts. viz. John Blank Sarah Blank Mathew
Adams Eliner Adams Henry Lysle Jane Lysle Margarett thomas
Thomas Narne Edward Banks Roger Deniss Henry Lisle the
second time

#3 Chowan Precinct Court, 12 Feb. [1694]
George Branch proved 8 rights: himself and his wife William Georg
Elizabeth and Phillis Branch and Margarett Thomas his servant.
Certified.
Assignment by George Branch to Nicholas Crisp 14 May 1694.
(reverse:) Assignment by Nicholas Crisp to thomas Blount 11 Sept.
1695. Assignment by Thomas Blountt to Wm. Glover 5 Mar.
169[7?]

#4 Perquimans Precinct Court, 2nd Monday in Jan. 1696/7.

The petition of William Hutchison includes headright claims for multiple importations of the same person. CCR 187, State Archives.

Copy of probate of headright claims at a sitting of Perquimans Precinct Court in 1696. CCR 187, State Archives.

Thomas Spight proved 10 rights: him selfe Richard Malbone Nich. Perce John Morres Elisabeth Morres John Morres Junior William Morres Mare Morres Nathanel Rauen Fone a Negro

Charles Scot proved 4 rights: himselfe Mary Scot Elisabeth Scot Charles Sot on for his Serveted

Denis Meclenden proved 11 rights: him Selfe Charles Cafen Mary his Wife Margret Dun Dennes Dun Rebecka Carpender Elisabeth Mackclenden Thomas Mackclenden Brient Mackclenden Dennis Meclenden Francis Mackclenden

John Oden proved 6 rights: Him Selfe Ann his Wife Ann his Daughter Jan his Daughter Mary his Daughter Rachel his Daughter Abraham William proved 4 rights: him Selfe Ann his Wife Edward Williames John Williams (reverse:) Each is proved and certified

#5 Albemarle Court. (no date)
Petition of John Symons for his right to 50 a. by importation of himself.
Proved and assigned to Nicho. Symons

#6 Pasquotank Precinct, Rights proved, 19 Aug. 1701
Peter McGregory: 3: himself Letitia his wife and Richd. Be[l]vington Assigned to Tho. Abington and by him [*faded*] to Tho. Boyd.
Cornelius Jones: 9: Eliz. Blakborne Mary Howden Dyana [a] Negro Sarah and Sambo Indyans John Parker Adampsikee a Negro and Wapin a Negro

21 Oct. 1701
Mrs. Ann Pope widdow: 1: Psickee a Negro
Saml. Pikes 3: himself Twice Jane his wife
James Forbush 11: James Forbush Alice his wife; John Forbush; James Forbush junior Eliz. Forbush Thomas Forbush Bayley Forbush Edward forbush Lewis Knight Hester Knight Maria Knight, all assignd to Isaac Guilford
Henry Creech 4: himself Richard Creech Richard Hanson Wm. Clarke.

Jan. Court 1701/2
John Tookes 7: Himself twice Fra. Brittoon John Swann william Tooke James Mckoy Margrett Miller and Assigned to Thomas Abington

Apr. Court 1702
Joseph Peircy 9: himself Ann his wife Eliz. his Second wife Joseph Piercy Susanna Peircy Alice Piercy Sarah [*faded*]

Henry(?) Burtenshell: 11: Richd. Burtenshall Prcilla. his wife Richd. Buttenshall Junior Prcilla. Burtenshall Junior Dorcas Burtenshall David Jones Mary Jones David Jones Junior Mary Jones Junior Margrett Jones

Eliz. Burtenshall Aug. Court 1702

Richd. Prince 9: himself twice Daniel Swillwant Eliz. his wife Eliz. Lucas Jeremy John Bernard Henry Spring Wm. Write assigned to Tho. Abington

John Pottinger 3: Himself Elitia his wife and Mary Johnson assigned to Isaac Guilford

Oct. Court 1702

Wm. Barnsfeild 10: himself thrice John Shephard Sam. Gayward Thomas Matthews John Robison John Lahay Joyce his wife and Ann their Daughter Assignd to Wm. Reed

Dec. Court 1702

James Fewox 31: Sarah Word Eliz. Word Henry Smith Rachell(?) Smith Mary Smith John Smith Henry Smith Junior Wm. Casewell Fra. Casewell Edith Batcheldr. Edw. Batcheldr. Marke Wheeler Eliz. Weiler Deborah Weler Jane Weiler Daniel Howel Eliz. Howel [*faded*] Howel John Howel Thomas Howel Abraham [*faded*] [*faded*] Smith Rachell Smith Cornelius Dun[*faded*] [*faded*] John Word Thomas Word

(reverse:) Jan. Court 1702/3

Robert(?) Saunders 40: himself [*faded*] Charles Saunders Geo. B[*faded*] [*faded*]yard John Tooke William Tooke James [*faded*] [*faded*] Philip [*faded*] Samuel Hopkins John [*faded*] [*faded*] Negroes Philatia [*faded*] Twice

Edward Phillips Symon [*faded*]

[*faded*] Rouiston(?) 32: himself Four times [*faded*] Peterson four times Henry Tomes John Guiden(?) [*faded*] Wm. Fisher Wm. Chambers twice Wm. W[*faded*] John Mentor John Bayley George [*faded*] Mary Jones Ebenezer Camel and. Too Negroes

James Banks: himself

Feb. Court 1702/3

Daniel Phillips: 3: Negroes assigned to Saml. Bundy

Mar. Court 1702/3

Thomas Passinghum: 1: himself assigned to Soloman Davis
Daniel Rice: 1: Jno. Powel assigned to Soloman Davis
Daniel Phillipps: 3: himself twice and One Negro assigned to Wm. Barcock

July Court 1703

John Smith 4: Himself twice his wife her former Husband
William Rawleson: 3: himself Lawrana(?) his wife Dorothy Newland
Garrett K[*faded*]: 1: Himself

#7 Pasquotank Precinct Rights proved
Orphants Court 19 Aug. 1701
Peter McGregory proved 3 rights: himself Letitia his wife and Richd. Belvington Assigned in Court to Tho. Abington and by him assigned to Tho. Boyd.
Cornelius Jones proved 9 rights: Eliz. Blackborne Mary Howden Dyana a Negro Sarah and Sambo Indyans John Parker Adam Syckee and Wapping Negroes.
Oct. Court held 20 Oct.
Saml. Pike proved 3 rights: himself Twice Jane his wife
John Nash 1: himself
James Forbus proved 11 rights: Himself Alice his wife John Forbus James Forbus Junior Eliz. Forbus Tho. Forbus Bayley Forbus Edward Forbus Lewis Knight Hester Knight Maria Knight and Assigned in Court to Isaac Guilford
John Tooke proved 7 rights: himself twice Francis Brittoon John Swann Wm. Tooke James [*blank*] Margrett [*blank*] And assigned in open Court to Tho. Abington.
Certified by Tho. Abington

#8 Carteret Precinct Court 15 July 1680
Richard Jones 3 freedom rights: Richard Jones Mary his Wife William Jones
Edward German his own Right being a freedome Right
John Sawyer 2 freedom rights and 1 transportation right: John Sawyer Mary his wife Mary Sawyer transported Servant
John Dunn 3 freedom rights: John Dunn Mary his Wife Edward Gelfe
Lodwick Williams 3 freedom rights and 2 transportation rights: Lodwick Williams Hannah Williams Elinor Williams, William Wilson John Jones
Thomas Harrison 3 freedom rights: Thomas Harrison Elizabeth his Wife Elizabeth Harrison
Michael Macdonnell 4 freedom rights: Michaell Macdonnell Jone his wife Mary Frances Mackdonnell
Carteret Rites

Thomas Keile 6 rights: Thomas Keile Mary his Wife 2: being bought
servant Thomas Towers Christopher Lovane Ruth Barnes, Servants
Tho. Price 1: Rite freedome

#9 (No precinct, no date)
Mr. Nixon 323: Rights Isaac Page Amorous his wife Mary
damarons, Elizabeth his daughter and Steven Hancock.
New rights: Zach Nixon Ellinor his wife and Eliz. his wife: Robin
an indian pd. the bill.
Solloman Poole rights: himself and 3 pruved
Timo. Mead 2 wifes on husban Ellinor Brown a daughter
Hen. Travers Saray his wife: Francis Wilmot Sam Morris Jno. King

#10 Pamtecoe Court, 5 Aug. 1702
Elias Elexander Garganus proved 6 rights, 7 July 1702: Elias Elex
Garganus Ann his Wife Robert Garganus Cathirine Garganus
Sarah Garganus Mary Garganus
Levi Truewhitt Court Clk.

#11 grand Court of north Carolina (no date)
Petition of William Maund Senior, having imported himself 4 times, and
having brought in sundry "pasangers and Servants:" Wm. Maund
Senior 4 Emanuel Cleares(?) Philip Bayly Joseph breeding Samuel
Wilson Henry Smith Thomas [*illegible*] Jno. Bryan Wm. Maund Junior
Thomas [*blank*] Samsee(?) a negro Thomas Youngblood one cald
Francis Thomas Lake Robt. Humble in all 17.

#12 (no date) Petition of Georg Whitby to "his honorable court" to
prove rights:
Georg Whitby his 6 children Wm. Bell and his Servant
Georg Bell and wife and child Jno. barrows his wife and 3 children
Francis Linfield and wife and child Jno. Robison Doctor Davison
his wife and 2 Servants Judeth migett and 3 children Samuell green
and wife Jno. Handbury in all 32.

#13 Pasquotank Precinct Court, 18 July 1704.
Edward James proved 3 rights and assigned them to Stephen
Richardson:
himself Eleanor. his wife and Thomas Steward
Wm. Barcock proved 1 right: Symon a Negro

Captain John Hendrick proved 9 rights: Wm. Bealy twice Isaac Chabanas Wm. Wilson Each twice John Sealvis onne Bartholomew Woolf onne himself onne.
A Warrant ordered for Hendrick.

#14 Chowan Precinct
Petition of Gorge Lasiter "dweller in Nancymond County in Verjenia:" transported 5 persons in March 1702: your petishtioner and his son Robert and Thomas Davis Peter Daugherte Joseph Ashlee

#15 To the Generall Court James Damerell prays to prove his right to 800 acres of land by Importation: Wm. Stevens Wm. Keale James Jones Wm. Jones Elez. Evens Wm. Rigg Fred. Jones Jno. Kent Adam Gamball Jno. Wigings Mick. Lynch Joh. Crummell Jacob Stevens Mary Stevens Ann Hughs Thos. Pynor

#16 Currituck Precinct Court, 28 Apr. 1703
Mr. John Prennit proved 2 rights: Hugh Moore and Isaba. Whitehorse

#17 Pamticoe ss. Rights proved in Court 5 July 1697
Mr. Nicholas Tylors rights: nickolas Tylor 2 pasages Katherine Tylor his wife Kallam Tylor Mary Tylor Rose Tylor Ann Tylor William Tylor Katherine Tylor Archbell Maccarell Daniell Cathell Farnyfold Green michall Oneill Senior Deborah his wife michall Oneill junior Deborah Oneill Ann Oneill Daniell Coventon Samuell Coventon: in all 19.

5 July. James Nevill: rights proved in court: James Nevill 2 passages Dorothy nevill his wife Rebecca nevill Richard nevill James neivell John nevell Thomas nevill Nickolas Tylor Francis Garganis Lenard Jones: in all 12.

5 July. John Burton proved 2 rights: Edward Reiland one indian called Frank

4 June. macdanill proved 3 rights: Macdl. 2 pasages John Hogon

5 July. Mr. William Hancok proved 9 rights: William Janson Susana Jonson
Will. Jonson Mr. Frances Jonson Issarell Janson James Theirll Richard Ashworth

Roger Mounteig Susana Mounteig

5 June. Mr. Jhoseph Lecthworth proved 5 rights: Jhoseph Lecthworth
  Sarah Lecthworth his wif Tabitha Lecthworth Susana Edwards
  Charles a negro

#18 Perquimans Precinct Court, 14 Apr. 1702
  These following Rites Proved
  Simond Allderson Rites   50
  Ellener Allderson   50
  Simond Allderson Junior   50
  Mary hittson   50
  Eliz. Allderson   50
  Sarah Allderson   50
  Thomas Platt   <u>50</u>
                                  350
William Price Rts.   50
  Margarett Price   50
  William Wise   <u>50</u>
                                  150
Mark Whealors Rts.   50
  Fransis Whealor   50
  Ann Whealor   50
  Mark Whealor Junior   50
  Fransis Whealor   50
  Luck Whealor   <u>50</u>
                                  300
James Hogg Rites   50
  Ann Hogg   50
  Elexander Lillington   50
  John Badcock   50
  Robert Evinns   <u>50</u>
                                  250
Phillip Howards Rits   50
  Sarah Jones   50
  Morgain Green   50
  Charles Howard   50
  Wm. Howson   50
  Thomas Green.   <u>50</u>
                                  300
Francis Linfeilds Rts.   50
  Mary Linfeild   50

John Linfeild   <u>50</u>
                    150

#19 March 10th 1698/9.
Petition of Thomas Morgine proving 4 rights: himself, the wife of John Jenet dorothy Jenet and two Chilldren.

#20 General Court (no date)
Petition of Jno. Tarkinton proving 5 rights: John Torkington Martha his wife Wm. Torkington Anne Starke Francis Starke

#21 General Court (no date)
Petition of Ann Stewert transporting 6 rights: 4 Negroes one English servant and Argill Symons

#22 General Court (no date)
Petition of Robert Laton showing he is due 500 a. by Importation: himselfe Eliz. his wife James Laton Mary Laton Olive Fee An Laton and from Virginia a 2nd Importation himselfe and wife and Mary Laton and Olive Fee

#23 Petition of Jno. Bird proving 6 rights: himselfe Mathew Anderson Mary his Wife Jno. Bird Junior James Bassford Richard Wiggins (no date)

#24 Petition of James Fewox showing he is due 100 a. by importation of Rich. Batchelor and John Haswell (no date)

#25 General Court (no date)
Petition of Anthony Alexander showing he is due 200 a. by importation of himselfe An his Wife Anthony his son and Jno. Mason his servant.

#26 General Court (no date)
Petition of Rich. Nowell showing he is due 200 a. for proving 4 rights by Importation of Mary West Saml. West Phebe West Will West

#27 Petition of Wm. Hutchison proving 14 rights: Moses Whittaker twice Imported Fra. Elliss twice Imported Wan Thomas twice Imported Jno. Lambeth Tho. Cowlisle Jno. Gray Jno. Oliver Wm. Hutchison 4 time trasported. (no date)

#28 Perquimans Precinct Court, 2nd Tuesday in Apr. 1700.

John Hare Junior proved 3 rights for 3 persons transported: Him Selfe Sarah His Wife Sarah Shadock.

#29 General Court (no date)
Petition of Mr. John Durant showing he is due 100 a. by importation of Sampson Ruth Negros.

Secretary of State Records, Albemarle Book of Warrants and Surveys 1681-1706, State Archives, Division of Archives and History, Raleigh. [S.S. 978.1].

p. 1 : [page numbers used are those in upper right corner] Certificats of Rts. and Albemarle. Mr. Hugh Smithwike, 370 a., for transportation of 7 persons, 7 Sept. 1669.
Mr. Hugh Smithwike Elizabeth his wife Edw. Hugh and Ralph his Son's Eliza. his Daughter and Elizabeth Bembridge. The 4 first transferred into a patent page the 54. The rest put into a warrant.

Chowan Precinct Court, 12 Feb. 1693. Tho. Stacy proved rights:
Tho. Stacy and Rebecca his [wife] John, Tho., Charles, Francis, Mary, and Eliza. Stacy. Certified, warrant given 1 May 1694.

Perquimans Precinct Court, 2nd Monday in April 1694.
Alexander [Lillington] proved 2 rights: himselfe as being out of the Country in new England one for Robrt. Eives a freeman "that died at my house."
Assignment by Alexr. Lilling[ton] to James Hog, 20 Apr. 1694

Albemarle. John Sturg[eon], [*torn*] hundred and fifty a., for transportation of [his] sons, 30 March 1680.
John Sturgeon, Mary his late wife, Francis his wife, John Smith, Heneretta Smith, CorNelius Cornel, Joseph Cornell, Alexander Cornell, and Cornelius Jones, but four rights due on this Warrant. Five of the rights belong to orphans of Cornelius Cornell [*torn*] himselfe and Francis his Wife Joseph and Alexander his sons and Cornelius [*torn*] were proved before Collonel Jenkins by the said Cornell. Assignment to Major Alexander Lillington four hundred and [*torn*] a. granted to Jno. Sturgeon deceased, 30 Mar. 1680.
The same being due the subscriber in the right of Francis [*torn*] wife unto Jno. Sturgeon deceased all the orphans of Cornelius Cornell [*torn*] being likewise deceased. Witness my hand this [*torn*] a warrant given according to assignment [*torn*]

p. 1: (reverse) Old Warrants
Perquimans Precinct Court, 2nd Monday in Apr. 1694. Benjamin Gidion proved 3 transportation rights: Benja. Gidion two and Johanna his wife. Warrant given.

Albemarle. Palatine Court, 1 Aug. 1692. James Thigpen proved his right to 200 a. by importation of James Thigpen and Elizabeth his wife and James and John his sons. Certified, warrant given 22 Apr. 1694.

Albemarle ss. Palatine Court, 1 Aug. 1692. Henry Creech petitions to prove rights: Tho. Harrison and Elizabeth his wife and Elizabeth Harrison their Daughter Benjamin Pain Henry Creech Joice Creech. Certified, warrant given 22 Apr. 1694.

Perquimans Precinct Court, 2nd Monday in Apr. 1694. Will. Jones proved one Right for his transportation into this County. Certified. Assignment by Willm. Jones to Saml. Nicolson 16 Apr. 1695. This right put into a warrant of Saml. Nicolsons.

Albemarle ss. Andrew Walwood, 300 a., for transportation of 6 persons, 29 Mar. 1680.
Andrew Walwood, Mary his wife, One right by [*torn*]r. Stephens gift, Robt. Weeks, Tho. Tirvile, Wm. Dale.

Albemarle. George Spowers, 100 a., for transportation of 2 persons, [*torn*] March 1680.
George Spowers and Joan his wife.

Albemarle. Darby Sexton, 300 a., for transportation of 6 persons, 29 Mar. [*torn*] Darby Sexton Dorathy his wife Edw. German, Tho. French

Mr. John Philpot proved 8 rights: [*torn*], Will. Hughs, John Atkins, Andrew Jones, Tho. King, John Griffen, [*torn*], Rich. Plater. Certified 18 Apr. [*torn*]

p. 2: Certificats of Rights
Juliana Taylor proved 10 rights: Henry Hudson, Mary Hudson [*torn*] Hudson, John Taylor, Anne Taylor, James Watson, John Blith, [*torn*] a Negroe, Sanders an Indian, Juliana Taylor.

Willm. Boge proved 1 right: himself assigned to Antho. [*torn*]

Willm. Gardner proved 4 rights: Wm. Gardner Elizabeth his w[ife] John Gardner Sarah Gardner.

Daniel Snooks proved 3 rights: Danl. Snook Margt. Snook Robt. Sn[ook]. Warrant given for these and one assigned by Wallingford.

John Clarke proved 2 rights: one for his transportation and one for his freedom.

John Whitby proved 3 rights: Rich. Torbet and Jone his wife Sarah a Ne[gro]. Put in Geo. Suttons Warrant.

Saml. Pricklove proved 4 rights: Saml. Pricklove Senior Saml. Pricklove junior James Freeman Rose a maid servant.

Tho. George proved 3 rights: Tho. Gouge Sarah his wife Robt. Gouge. Warrant given for 150 a.

Robt. Beasley proved 4 rights: James Beasley Peter Jones A[torn] Mary Lacy and by the said Beasley assigned to Mr. Tho. Leper and a w[arrant] according to assignment.

Francis Cofen proved 3 rights: Francis Cofen John Thurston Margt. [torn].

Rich. Chaston proved 2 rights: Anne his wife and Daniel his son. 12 Apr. 1694.

Caleb Callaway proved 2 rights: as Executor to Stephen Hencock [torn] use of the heires whose names are under written Stephen Hancock and his wife.

Wm. Mansell proved 2 rights: one for himselfe and Mary his wife. Warrant given for these and 2 assigned by J. Stepney 13 July 16[torn]. Assignment to Stephen Hancock and Margrett [torn] Barrow insted of two borrowed of him for the Childrens use. 10 Apr. 1694.

All the above written rights proved at pequimonds Court [torn] Munday in April 1694 Certifyed by John Stepney Clerk Court

Perquimans Precinct Court, 2nd Monday in Apr. 1694.

John Stepney proved 11 transportation rights: John Stepney, and
   Marcy Stepney [*torn*] Grace Baley, John Bayley, Wm. Bayley
   junior, Saml. Bayley, Exper[ience] [*torn*] Jane Bayley, Sarah Bayley,
   Mercy Bayley.
   Assignment by John Stepney of two [rights] 1[2] Apr. 169[4] and
   three rights more assigned [*torn*] 13 July [*torn*].

p.2 (reverse): Warrants.
   James Hog proved 3 rights: James Hog, An Hog, John Badcock

Saml. Charles proved 2 rights: Gashom Wodales, Mary Fishyard.
   Warrant given.

Peter Pavell proved 7 rights: Four for himselfe and his wife [*torn*]
   Pavel And three for Will. Jetterton junior viz. Wm. Tetterton
   Mary Hall and [*torn*] W[hite].
   Two Warrants Given one to Peter Pavell for the first four the other
   to Wm. [*torn*] for the three last, 25 Apr. 1694.

Elizabeth Evens proved 5 rights: Rich. Evins, Elizabeth Evens Jo[*torn*]
   [*torn*]fington, Jean Arnel, Tho. Corbet. Assignment by Elizabeth Evins
   of Tho. Corbett's right to Benj. Gidion, 9 Apr. 1694.

Wm. Long proved 1 right: for him Selfe.

John Hopkins proved 6 rights: Sarah Hopkins two, Johanah Kinkard two
   Sarah Kinkard two. Warrant given for these and two old warrants.

John Flowers proved 5 rights: John flowers Susan Flowers Rich. Flowers
   John Flowers junior Mary Stag. Warrant given 14 July 1694.

Tho. Nicols proved 9 rights: Tho. Nicols, Eliza. his wife, [*faded*] his
   Daughter, Sarah Nicols, John Banister, Tho. Davis, John Wells,
   Rob[t]. Hooper, Elizabeth hooper.
   Assignment by Tho. Nicols of 4 rights, Tho. Davis, John Wells,
   Robt. Hooper, Elizabeth Hooper, to Benja. Gidion.
   Assignment by Thomas Nicols of 5 rights, Tho. Nicols, Elizabeth
   Nicols, Elizabeth Nicols, Sarah Nicols, John Banister, to Eliza.
   Evins, 9 Apr. 1694.

[John] Foster proved 2 rights: John Foster, Anne his wife. Warrant
   given 4 Sept. 1694.

[George] Ames proved 4 rights: Geo. Ames Susan Ames Edw. George Sarah [*faded*]

[*torn*]h Johnson proved 16 rights: Lawrence Gonsalvo two, John Johnson [T]ho. Gonsalvo two, Peter Jones, Lawrence Gonsalvo junior, Abraham Willi[ams] [*torn*] Johnson two, Christopher Morton, Peter a French man, Peter [*faded*] [*torn*] [*faded*] Robt. Tester, Twelve of these rights are assigned to [*faded*] [*torn*]. Warrant given. [*faded*] rights Peter Jones Senior Peter [*torn*] Warrant given for [*illegible*] and 2 assigned from [*torn*] Person proved one right [*torn*]

p. 3: Certificats of Rights and
Albemarle. John Hopkins, one hundred and [*torn*] a., for transportation of 2 persons, 29 May 1680.
John Hopkins, Valentine Barton.

Albemarle. Rd. Arnold, 200 a., for transportation of 4 persons, 30 Mar. 1680.
Rich. Arnold Abigail his wife Rich. Arnold junior Jane his Daughter Assignment by Rich. Arnold with the "Consent of Abigail my wife" to Antho. Walters, 2 Sept. 1680. Assignment by Antho. Walters to John Hopkins, 2 Mar. 1681/2.

Albemarle. [*torn*] Vos, 170 a., for transportation of 3 persons, 29 Mar. 1680. Rich. Bentley Jane his wife and Mary his Daughter.

Perquimans Precinct Court, 2nd Monday in Apr. 1694
Andrew Ros proved 4 rights: Andrew Ros, Mary Rosse [*torn*] James Rosse, And assigned them to John Parish

Richard Darlin proved 2 rights: Rich. Darlin Elizabeth Darlin

[Tho.] Stephens proved 3 rights: Tho. Steph[ens] [*torn*] Warrant given 1 Aug. [*torn*]

p. 3 (reverse): Old Warrants
Albemarle. [Robt.] Harman, 150 a., for transportation of 3 persons, 30 Mar. 1680. Robt. Harmon Eliza. his Wife An his daughter transport Rights Warrant given for these and one right viz. Zacha. Nixon assigned by W[*torn*]

Henderson Walker, petition for proving rights: Timothy Burton Leah Thomas John Williams Leonard Burton two Negros Jno. Hawkins Alice his Mother Tho. Hawkins [*torn*] Jno. Morgan Margarett Drake Tho. Hawkins Elizabeth Hawkins her [*torn*] and Sarah Hawkins.

Chowan Precinct Court, 1 Apr. 1694. Henderson Walker proved above rights

Chowan Precinct Court, 1 Apr. 1694. Nicholas Daw proved 4 rights: [*torn*] Michell, Rich. Thompson, Wm. Camell and Nicholas Daw Assignment by Nicholas Daw to Henderson Walker, 2 Apr. 1694.

Chowan Precinct Court, 12 Feb. 1693, James Cooper proved 4 rights: Peter Basset M[*torn*] Basset An Basset Adam Basset Assignment by James Cooper to Henderson Walker, 2 Apr. 1694. Warrant to Henderson Walker for above rights except one right viz. Nicho. Daw reserved for John Be[*torn*], 2 Apr. 1694.

Stephen Manwaring proved 12 rights: R[*torn*] [*torn*]inton, Edw. Davis, Charles Marram, Geo. Loveday, Mary Mancell, Alexander Speed, [*torn*] [*torn*]ter, James Smith, Francis Salem, Tho. Evens Senior, Tho. Evins junior, John Dunston. Certified 14 Mar. 1693. Warrant given 16 M[arch] 1693.

Caleb Callaway proved 4 rights: his owne and three more: Wm. Hening Andrew Hening Elizabeth H[ening]. Certified 17 Mar. 1693. Warrant given for this and two rights assigned by John Barrows to John Henco [*torn*]

p. 4: Old Warrants
Jenkin Wil[liams] proves right for himself, 7 Feb. 1693.

Wm. Bartlest has proved five rights: [Wm.] Bartlest Senior Elizabeth Bartlest Wm. Bartlest junior, Tho. Bartlest Michael Bartlest. Certified 7 Feb. 1693/4. Warrant 5 M[arch]

Jno. Northcoat proved seven Rights: Henry Clay Senior, Mary Clay, Henry Clay junior, Priscilla Clay, two Servants, Joshua Hepworth, Jer. White, Jno. Northcoat, three of these Rts. are sold to Hannah Gosby. Certified 7 Feb. 1693/4. Warrant 5 M[arch]

Anthony Dawson proved rights for himselfe and Jno. Chapman: Antho. Dawson, Wm. Chapman. Certified 7 Feb. 1693/4. Warrant 10 Sept. 1694.

Tho. Lepper proved ten: Tho. Kent, Anne his wife, Sarah Kent, Rebecca Kent, Anne Kent junior, Jno. Tho., [torn] Browne, Wm. Brickstone, Tho. Lepper, Nicolas Robison. Certified 7 Feb. 1693/4. Warrant 28 March 1694.

Jno. Barrows proved by importation: Robt. Tester, Symon Smith and a negroe named Jan[e]. Certified 7 Feb. 1693/4. The first two assigned to John Hancoke.

Tho. Pearce proved Nine rights: Tho. Pearce, Jno. Perce, Susana Perce, Dorathy Pearce, Mary Pearce, Mary Bridges, Jno. Wilkison, John Pearce Ruth Pearce. Certified 7 Feb. 1693/4. Warrant 26 March.

Tho. Harloe proved four: Tho. Harloe Mary Harloe Mary Harloe Jno. Harloe. Certified 7 Feb. 1693/4. Warrant 13 July 1694.

Christophr. Butler proved five rights: Christophr. Butler his wife and two children and a negro Girle. Certified 7 Feb. 1693/4.

p. 4 (reverse): Certificats of Rights and
Jno. Durant proved: [Jno. Duran]t, Sarah Durant one servant named Judith. Certified 7 Feb. [1693/4].

Wm. Godfrey proved five rights: Prudence Hallum, Jno. Hallum, Elizabeth Hallum, Wm. Godfrey Sarah Godfrey. Certified 7 Feb. 1693/4. Warrant March.

James Fewox proved 8 rights: James Fewox, Anne Fewox, Robt. Fewox, Edith Batchellor, James Wilson, Anne W[ilson] Alice Wilson Jno. Wilson.
Certified 7 Feb. 1693/4. Warrant to Jno. Belman for [torn] a warrant for the rest to [torn]

Albemarle. Jno. Edlin, 100 a. for transportation of two persons, 30 Mar. 1680. Jno. Edlin, Sarah his wife.
Assignment from Jno. Edlin (Edling) to Jno. Lacy of Berkeley Precinct, 8 July 1680.

Albemarle. Wm. Charles, 220 a. for transportation of four persons, 21 Apr. 1669.

Wm. Charles Abigail his wife Win, his Son Eliz. his daughter.

Warrant Given To Jane Charles grand daughter to the above written

W. Charles [torn] acres for the two above written Warrants 28 Mar. 1694.

p. 5: Old Warrants

[Torn] Jno. Gray, Tabitha his wife, Jno. Gray J[unior] [torn] 7 Feb. 1693/4.

Turloe Fee proved 2 rights: Turloe Fee, Danl. Fee. Certified 7 Feb. 1693/4. Warrant Given.

Jno. Mason proved 5 rights: Morg[an] [torn] [torn] his wife and 2 children and a hired man named Jno. Haws. Certified 7 Feb. 1693/4. A warrant Given.

Wm. Butler proved 2 rights: Wm. Butler, Diana Butler. Certified 7 Feb. 1693/4. A warrant given.

Patrick Henley proved 22 rights, Pasquotank: Jno. Culpepper, Jno. Robison, Yacko and Grace 2 negroes, Valentine Byrd, Sarah Byrde, Betty, Bes, Mingo, and Tom, 4 Negroes, Andrew, Yampo, Marea and [torn] negroes, Anne Farmer, Patrick Henley, Mary Henley, his wife, Mary Henley, [torn], Betty a negroe, my wife Sarah Henley, Margret Byrde. Certified 7 [torn] 1693/4. A warrant Given.

Mr. Jno. Hawkins proved 5 rights, Pasquotank: Jno. Hawkins, Sarah his wife, 2 negroes, John Cabbidge. Certified 7 Feb. 1693/4.

Stephen Vincent entered 3 rights, Pasquotank: Stephen Vincent "for being twice transported him selfe," and his Wife Mary Vincent. Certified 7 Feb. 1693/4. A warrant Given.

Wm. Jones proved 2 rights, Pasquotank: himselfe and his wife. Certified 7 Feb. [1693/4]. A warrant Given.

p. 5 (reverse): Certificats of Rights and

Edmund Roe Junior proved 2 rights, Pasquotank: Edmund Roe and Anne his wife. Certified 12 Feb. 1693/4. A warrant given.

Henry Keeton proved 2 rights, Pasquotank: Henry Keeton and Mary his wife. Certified 12 Feb. 1693/4.

Albemarle. Capt. [Ralph] Fletcher, 220 a., for transportation of four persons, 29 March 1680.
Ralph Fletcher Eliza. his wife Jacob Cozens Sarah Negroe

Albemarle. Ralph Fletcher, 400 a., for transportation of Nine persons, 30 March 1680.
Tho. Cullen, Sarah his wife Jno. and Rich, his Sons, Sarah, Anne, Mary, Christian, and Martha his Daughters being transportation Rights and becomes due to Fletcher as being assigned by Tho. Cullen [*torn*] Sir Wm. Berkley and from Berkley by his [*torn*] Jno. Culpeper to governor Carteret, and by Carteret's attorney Capt. Craford Esqr., to Ralph Coates, and by Coates to Fletcher.

Albemarle. Henry White, o[ne] [hun]dred and ten acres for transportation of two persons, 5 Oct. 1670.
Henry White as a servant and Mary his wife
Assignment by Henry White to Ralph Fletcher

p. 6: Old Warrants
Caleb Callaway entered 4 rights: Danl. Pembrooke, Tho. Merret, an Indian Boy, [*torn*]thure Long. Certified 7 Feb. 1693.
Warrant given 27 March 1694.

Hannah Gosby proved 9 rights: John Gosby, Jno. Anderson, Jno. Kensey, Rich. Waterlow, Katherine Kensey, Jane Anderson, and three hands bought from Jno. Northcoat, Namely, Joseph Hepworth, Jer. White and Henry Clay Senior. Certified 7 Feb. 1693/4.

Rich. Nowell proved 9 rights: Rich. Nowell, Jane Nowell, Jno. Smith, Elinor. Nowell, Charles Taylor, Geo[rge] Taylor, Mary Tayler, Oliver Nowell, Alice Nowell. Certified 7 Feb. 1693/4. Assigned to Jno. Tomlins.

George Dear proved 10 rights: Ja[ne] Pritchet, and Jno. Dear, and by Hannah Harrison, Edw. Harrison, Hannah Harrison, Joseph Williams. Wm. Fyan, Hannah Fyan Mercy Fyan Eliz. Fyan Lidia Harrison. Certified 7 Feb. 1693/4. And entered into his Warrant.

Tymothy Clare entered 4 rights: Tymothy Clare, Francis Belchamp, Edm. Redman, R[ich.] Fox. Certified 7 Feb. 1693.

Rich. Fox proved 4 rights: Rich. Fox, George Fox, Wm. Fox, Mary Fox. Certified 7 Feb. 1693/4.

p. 6 (reverse): Certificats of Rights and
[*Torn*] proved 6 rights: Christopher Nicols, Hannah his wife, Deliverance Sutton, Saml. Nicolson, [*torn*] Symons, Hannah Nicolson. Certified 7 Feb. 1693/4. Assigned to Hanah Gosby. A warrant given.

George Young proved 3 rights: [*torn*] Forster, Perthesia Forster and Geo. Young. Certified 7 Feb. [1693/4].

Charles Mackdaniel proved 4 rights: Charles Mackdaniel Elizabeth Mackdaniel Tho. Wallingford Sam[*torn*]. Certified 7 Feb. 1693/4. A warrant Given.

Wm. Lacy proved 9 rights: [*torn*] Rous, Jno. Rouse, Mary Rouse, Martha Rouse, Wm. Lacy Senior, Grace Lacy, [*torn*], Jane Davis, Wm. Lacy junior. Certified 7 Feb. 1693/4. A warrant given to Wm. Lacy for [*torn*] last the Rest assigned to Martha Rouse 31 March 1694 and by her to Rich. [*torn*]

James Loadman proved 3 rights: Hubbert Lambert Joan Buyard and James Loadman. Certified [*torn*] Feb. 1693/4. A warrant given.

Stephen Manwaring proved 9 rights: Edw. Berry, Andrew Kinsey, Jno. Deadman, Robt. Brightwell Senior, Alice Brightwell, Robt. Brightwell junior, Rich Parker, Jno. Cast[leton], Stephen Manwaring. Certified 7 Feb. 1693/4.

Tho. Hossold proved 5 rights: Himself twice transported, Mary Hossold, Tho. Hossold junior Thomas Snowden. Certified 7 Feb. 1693/4. A warrant given.

Jno. Bentley entered by importation 7 rights: Rich Bentley, Jane Bentley Mary B[entley] Sarah Bentley a negro Boy a negro woman, an Indian Boy. Certified 7 Feb. 1693/4. A warrant given 20 Mar. 1694.

Roger Snell by importation 5 rights: Roger Snell Rebecca Snell J[*torn*] [*torn*]

p. 7: (fragment) Assignment by James Johnson to Robt. Beasley of 4 persons, 9 Oct. 1690.

[*Torn*] Arch. Grior Peter Grey. Warrant given to Robt. Beasley and assigned to Rich. Cheston.

Albemarle. Mr. William Wilkison, 400 a., for transportation of 8 persons into Albemarle County, 29 [*torn*] 1680.
the persons viz. James Nokes, Margrett his Wife Mr. Tho. Stamp John Stamp Wm. Preston Dunkin Cambell Israel Shephard Elinor. Wardell These becoming due to Ambrose Stephens as Marying the Relect of Nokes and to Mr. More by Mariage of the same and to Wm. Wilkison as purchased from More the said Estate. A warrant Given to Tho. Luten as Marying the Relect of John [*torn*] (Currer?). Assignment of rights by Wm. Wilkison to Mr. John Currer, 17 Oct. 1681.

Albemarle. John Lacy, 310 a., for transportation of 6 persons, [*torn*] March 1680.
John Lacy and by assignment of John Edling two rights viz. John Edling and Sarah his wife and by assignment of Ralph Coates 3 rights viz. Young Mary Negro Assigned by Capt. Wm. Craford in a warrant of Coates James Hunter and Elizab. Randall all transport Rights to be laid on the Land by [*torn*]rked on or near the head of Yapim Creeke. A warrant Given to Robt. Beasley by assignment of Tho. Lepper for above rights except Edling and his wife.

Albemarle. Roger Cheston's orphans, 500 a., for transportation of 10 persons, 30 Jan. 1680.
Roger Cheston Senior, Eliz. his wife, Roger Cheston, junior John Cheston sons, Eliz., Martha, Mary, Archibell, Hanah, and Sarah Cheston Daughters. 4 first rights belong to Robt. Inkenson, the rest to Jo[*torn*] 26 Mar. 1694.

p. 7 (reverse): Old Warrants
Mrs. An Durant proved 8 rights: John Stimson, Dick, Abraham, Maria, Peter, Grace, Maria Junior, and Harry. Certified 10 Mar. [*torn*].

Jno. Archdale esqr. proved by attorney Danl. Akehurst 14 rights:

John Archdale, Mary Archdale, An Archdale, Henry Lax John Zachary [*torn*] wife, John Zachary junior, Freeth Tingle, Benj. Elderkin, Tho. Hunt, Jos. King, Francis Elias (Eliot?), Mary More, Tho. Davis. Certified 10 Mar. 1693.

Danl. Akehurst Esqr. proved 5 rights: Danl. Akehurst, Phili. Christ. Akehurst, Shelba a Negroe, John Emps, and Rose his Daughter. Certified 10 Mar. 1693.

Wm. Allen proved 7 rights by Mordicay Bowden and 2 more rights without warrant: Rebecca Tuly, Tho. Tuly, Mary Tuly, and Mercy Tuly, John Tuly, Eliza. Tuly, and Six [*torn*] Mordica Bowden, and Wm. Johnson, More Wm. Allen, Tho. Beal, a molatta named Robin. Certified and warrant given 14 Mar. 1693.

Col. Willm. Wilkison proved 28 rights: Wm. Wilkison, Tho. Gillam An Walker, Mary North, James Barton, Robt. News, Robt. Pike, Francis [*torn*] Tho. Pilips, Tho. Barton, Charles Jones, Wm. Elfeck, Hester Pope, John Ingram, Bes, Will, [*torn*] Jack, Deborah, Franke, Mingo, Robin, Kent, Sambo, Coffe, Jack, Cutto, Bettee. Certified 14 Mar. 1693/4. First 10 transcribed in his Pa[tent] for 500 a. Warrant given for remaining 18 20 Mar. 1694.

Albemarle. Willm. Jacson, 150 a., for transportation of 3 persons, 29 Mar. 1680.
Wm. Jacson Eliza. his Wife a negro woman named Nell.

James Johnson, April 7th 1690, 4 persons: James Johnson, Rachel Johnson his Wife [*torn*] his sons

p. 8: Old Warrants
(fragment) Andrew, Jack, Peg, Mol Marea, Tom, Mingo, Sandy. Certified 8 [*torn*] 1693 and warrant given same day.

Mathew Kelly entered 11 rights: Mathew Kelly [*torn*] his wife, Two Indians one man and one woman, Gilbert Goodall, his wife Magd[alen] John Newby, and wife, James Newby, John Newby junior. Certified [*torn*] Mar. 1693 and warrant given 10 Mar. [1693].

Tho. Attoway proved 5 rights: Tho. Attoway [*torn*] Morgan Wm. Hughs Eliza. Attoway Jean Attoway. Certified 7 Mar. [1693] and warrant given 13 Mar. 1693.

James Morgan 2 rights: his owne and his wife and four more bought from Wm. Vos: Roger [*torn*] Jno. Wilkeson, John Stamp and his wife Jean Vos. Certified and warrant given 10 [*torn*] 1693.

Rich. Nowell proved 5 rights: Rich. Nowell Elinor. his wife, Alice Nowell, Sarah Taylor, Geo. Taylor. Certified 15 [*torn*] 1693.

Diana Holford proved 3 rights: Diana Holford [torn] Snowden and one servant made named Elizabeth. Certified 12 Mar. 16[93].

Albemarle. Willm. Owen and John Holford, 250 a., for transportation of 5 persons, 29 Mar. 1680.
John Halford Will. Owens Rowland Williams old Will Negroe and George Negroe the last two by assignment from Ralph Coates which were assigned him by Capt. Craford esqr. as Attorney of Peter Carterett esqr. A warrant including the above [*torn*] this old warrant Given to Jno. Hol[ford] [*torn*] 13 Mar. 1693.

Palatine Court, 1 Aug. 1692. Henderson Walker, petition to prove his rights:
John Crew Elizabeth Crew [Eliza]beth his daughter. Assigns rights to George [*torn*].

p. 8 (reverse): Certificats of Rts. and
Robt. Taylor proved 9 rights: Robt. Taylor for himselfe Two Rights and one for his wife, a Negro called Betty a Negro girl called Willoby Tho. Barret a negro man Named Manuell Jno. Mathews An Taylor and four Rights by an old warrant whose names are under the said warrant. Danl. Frizell, 200 a., for transportation of 4 persons, [*torn*] Feb. 1679.
Danl. Frizell, Margrett his wife Alex. Gordon and David Wilson. Assignment by Danl. Frissell to Griffen Rawrence or his heirs. Assignment by Mary Lawrence to Robt. Taylor, 22 Oct. 1685. Warrant to Robt. Taylor 9 Mar. 1693.
Tho. Vandermulin proved 5 rights: Joseph an Indian Jack, Mingo, and Sarah Negroes, Ralph Matham. Certified [*torn*] March 1693.

Albemarle. Mr. Lewis Vandermulen, 330 a., for transportation of 6 persons, 10 May 1670.
Danl. Dekelly, Nico. Hart, David James, [*torn*]sia a Negro woman Temperance and [*torn*] negro women.

Albemarle. Mr. Lewis Vandermulen, 410 a., for transportation of 7 persons, 10 Mar. 1670.
[L]ambert, Grace his wife, [*torn*] his Son, Rachell his Daughter [*torn*] [*torn*]h March, Robert [torn]

p. 9
Mr. Tho. Pollok proved 12 rights: Saml. Stephens, Edw. Telwell, Robt. Boon, John Michell, Laurence Gonsalvo Peter Ashley, Aaron Louverige, Stephen Lewis, Mary a woman, Ashline the more, Anthony the Negroe, Peter Price. Certified 17 Mar. 1693.

Mr. Tho. Pollock, proved 12 rights: Wm. Strange, Johana a Negro, and her Child, Mr. Robt. West, Jno. Robison, Elizab. his wife, Saml. Blake, John Lumbrosier, Job Robison, Eliz. Robison, Robt. West, Robt. West. Certified 17 Mar. 1693.

Mr. Tho. Pollok proved 13 rights: Robt. West junior, Sarah West, Mary West, Francis West, Rebecca West, Jno. West, Benja. West, Deb. West and five Indians. Certified 17 Mar. 1693.

Mr. Tho. Pollok proved 13 rights: Eliz. West, Jno. Robison, Tho. Pollock, James Pollock, Martha Pollock, Peter Cornelius, and Eight Negro's.
Certified 17 Mar. 1693 and 4 warrants containing the rights in the 4 above certificates given 19 Mar., Registered 20 Mar. 1693.

Tho. Tweddy proved 3 rights: Tho. Tweddy and Elizab. Tweddy his wife and Elizab. Tweddy his daughter. Certified, warrant given 13 Mar. 1693.

John Willoughby proved 4 rights: John Willoughby and his wife Deborah and two Children. Certified 9 Mar. 1693, warrant given 13 Mar. 1693.

Jno. Kelly proved 4 rights: Jno. Kelly [*torn*] his wife one Child and Neale Kenny. Certified 14 Mar. 1693, warrant given 14 Mar. 1693.

Tho. Relfe proved 14 rights: Tho. Kent Senior Mary Butler, Two Rights Tho. Relfe, Jane Barnes, Tho. Towers, Christopr. Langhorne, Three Negro's, James Keneshell, Wm. Dickison, Jno. Humphres, Danl. Barnes. Certified and warrant given 14 Mar. 1693.

Luke Hamond proved 4 rights: Jno. Hamond [Sa]rah Hamond Luke Hamond and Sarah Hamond. Certified 15 Mar. 16[93].
Esau Albertson proved rights: [*torn*]

p. 9 (reverse)
(fragment) Tho. Jacson, John Dellaway, Sam. an Indian, John an Indian, Mary an Indian, B[*torn*] Mol and Indian, Marea a Negro, Michael a Negroe, Grace a Negro, Tom a Negroe, Hanah a Negroe, Bridjet a Negro, Peter a negro, Mingo a Negro, Jack a negro, Dick a Negro, Sarah a Negroe. Certified 14 Mar. 1693, warrant given 16 Mar. 1693.

Henry Slade proved 12 rights: Jno. Daws, an Indian Named Nan, one named Sue Tony a negroe, Sarah, Mol, Jack, and Sarah, Jno. Slade, Joseph Slade, Benj. Slade, Saml. Slade, Hannah Slade, Wm. Slade. Certified 15 Mar. 1693.

Mr. Tho. Pollok proved 9 rights: Wm. Braid, Lidia Braid, Eliza Palmer, Tho. Palmer, Tymothy Callaham, John Holdbetch, Maria a Negro, Archibell Grei[r] Robt. Stanford. Certified 19 March 1693.

Jonathan Bateman proved 20 rights: Johanathan Bateman, Margret his wife, Jona. Bateman, Jno. Bateman, Robt. Davis, Rich Williams, Eliza. Williams, Saml. Pool, Henr. Butler, Robt. Robins, Johanah Robins, A negro woman named Bes, a Negroe Girle named Sarah, Laurence Arnold, An Collier, Eliz. Arnold, Rebecca Arnold, Jno. Arnold, John Williams, Eliza. Williams. Certified 9 Mar. 1693, warrant given 19th and registered 20th [March 1693].

Mr. Will. Collins proved 10 rights, Pasquotank Precinct: John Felton Jno. Wilson, a Negro man belonging to Jno. Felton, Robt. Tredw[ell] Rich. Plater, Nichols. Allgood, Sambo, and Tom, Wm. Collins, and Tho. Woodley.
Certified 3 Feb. 1693, warrant 19th and registered 20th [*torn*] 1693.

Mr. Rich. Pope proved 13 rights, Pasquotank Precinct: Rich. Pope, Jno. Macmarro, Two Negro's, Wm. Indicott, One Negro to Mr. Hunt, one to Mr. Symonds, One to Mr. Jacson, one to Mr. Durant, one to Jno. Whitby, Will. Jones, Stephen Richison, and one woman servant to Wm. Steel. Certified 3 Feb. 1693. Warrant 19th, registered 20th Mar. 1693.

Robt. Beasley proved 6 rights: Robt. Beasly Sarah Beasly, Johanah Beasly, Rich. Cheston, Sarah Cheston, James Beasley. Certified 7 Feb. 1693. Warrant 13th, registered [*torn*] Mar. 1693.

p. 10: Certific[ats] and
Edw. Wilson proved 6 rights: Edw. Wilson, Wm. Vincent, Mary Vincent, Anne Vincent, Wm. Vincent, junior, Jno. Vincent junior. Certified 9 Mar. 1693. Warrant 28 Mar. 1694.

Henry Gorin entered his own right. Certified 10 Mar. 1693. Assigned to James Fewox and entered into his warrant 4 Sept. [1693].

Mrs. Susanah Heartley proved 22 rights: Francis Heartley, Susanah Heartley, Henry Gallaway, Jno. Clark, George Clarke, Tho. Clarke Humphrey Leg, Mary Collier, Eliza. Spry, Judith Spry, Sambo, and Doll, Hannah, A Negro Sambo, Bes, Negros John Frenchman, Paul a Frenchman, Peter a Dutchman Hanah Danvers, Two English Boys called by the Names of Simon, Brandy Bes and Katharine Spelman. Certified 9 Mar. 1693. Warrant given.

John Fendall proved 18 rights: Josias Fendall, Mary his wife, Josias Fendall, junior, Mary Fendall, Jno. Fendall, Robt. Fendall, Henry Fendall, George Swan, Zachariah Gillam, Jno. Harbot, Mary Taylor, Abra. Hansford, Danl. Graham, Josias Fendall, George Cammell, John Fendall, Peter Small, Robt. Fendall. Certified 10 Mar. 1693. Warrant given for the 13 first.

Rich. Ruks proved 4 rights: Rich. Rucks Mary Rucks Eliza. Rucks and Tho. Rucks. Certified and warrant given 10 Mar. 1693.

Jno. Jones proved 3 rights: Rich. Williams Anne his wife David Lewis Certified 7 Mar. 1693.
More proved in Court on a second importation: John Jones his wife Eliz., Jno. Jones [*torn*] Willm. Jones, and warrant given 9 Mar. 1693.

Edw. Smithwike proved 8 rights: John Phene, Katherine Haskins, Margeret Colman, An Gregory, Saml. Bottomley, Nichol. Gent, Mary Philips, Andrew Kensley. Certified 8 Mar. 1693, warrant given 9 Mar. 1693.

Jno. Porter junior in [*torn*] of his father John Porter Senior proved rights: John Porter senior, John Porter junior Mary [*torn*] Children, Twelve [*torn*]

p. 10 (reverse): Old Warrants
(fragment) Charles Carter Tho. White Will. Morris. Certified 16 Mar. 1693, warrant given.

Albert. Albertson junior proved 2 rights: Albert Albertson and his wife. Certified 9 Mar. 1693, warrant given 15 Mar. 1693.

Jno. Parish proved 4 rights: Tho. Jacobs An Jacobs Mary Jacobs, Jno. Hufton. Certified 9 Mar. 1693.

Jno. Parish proved 6 rights: Joshua Scott his wife and one Child his two sisters Tho. Rabley. Certified and warrant given 16 Mar. 1693.

Edw. Mayo proved 11 rights: Zachery Nixon, L[*torn*] Keeton, Edw. London, Jno. King, Wm. Bread Joseph a servant man, John Davis, Griffen Wa[*torn*] Ellinor a servant woman, John Nixons wife, Robt. Griffen. Certified [*torn*] and assigned to Mr. Will. Glover. The first assigned to Robt. Harmon and assigned back to W. Glover by Harmon.

Rich. Harris proved 6 rights: Rich. Harris, Susan Harris Richardson Harris, Eliz. Harris, Mary harris, Barbary Doge Cadasho a Negro. Certified and warrant given 15 Mar. 1693.

Jno. Godfrey proved 6 rights: Francis Godfrey, Jane his wife, Frances Godfrey, his daughter, Wm. Godfrey his Son, [*torn*] Godfrey, Tho. Robts., Hanah Sheephooke, a servant Elizab. Lilley, one Negroe woman two children, Dor. Cully, and Moiale Perry, Mathew Wilson, John Temple, Brid[*torn*] one Molatta, Child, Wm. Bloomfeild, Tho. Hotkins, John Sinclare, Eliz. his [wife] four rights belonging to my wife one negroe man called Luke.
Certified 10 Mar. 1693, warrant given 14 Mar. 1693.

Susan Harris proved 3 rights: Susan [*torn*] Jno. Deadman Louis Dennis. Certified 10 Mar. 1693, warrant given to Jno. Harris.

Rich. Williamson entered rights: John Mi[*torn*] [*torn*] an Indian and himselfe. Certified [*torn*].

p. 11

Albemarle. Tho. Symons, 400 a., for transportation of 8 persons, 5 Feb. [1693]
[Tho.] Symons, Mary Symons, Wm. Symons, Rebecca Symons, Eliz. Symons, Jer. Symons, Mary Symons, [a] negroe boy named Will.

Tho. Symons proved 11 rights: Tho. Symons, Sarah Watts, one negroe Tuck one negroe Tony one negro Girle named Sarah, Ruth Pinder, Timothy Pindar, Wm. Elworthy John Dollaw[torn] [Geo]rge Fisher and wife Deborah.
Certified 3 Feb. 1693.

Assignment by Tho. Symons to Jeremiah Symons of 3 rights: John Dellower George Fisher Deborah Fisher, 5 Feb. 1693/4.

Jeremiah Symons proved 5 rights: Jeremiah Symons, Jonathan Taylor, Andrew MackLewer, a ne[gro] girle named Nan, a negroe boy named Jack. Certified 3 Jan. [1693], warrant given.

Joseph Comander proved 6 rights: Joseph Comandr., and his wife, Wm. Take, J[faded] [torn] sister, Tho. Welch, Andrew Dennis. Certified 3 Jan. 1693, warrant given.

Albemarle. Jno. Bolton, 250 a., for transportation of 5 persons, 5 Feb. 1679. John Per.dleton Henry Pendleton, Mathew Pendleton, John Bolton, Elizabeth his wife. Warrant given to Humphry Bolton.

p. 11 (reverse)

Danl. Akehurst entered 15 rights: Danl. Akehurst, Jno. Hawkins, and wife Saml. Moore, Rich. Clarke, Rich. Care, Jer. Harmon, Geo. Moore, Alex. Goden, Anne Quinton, Tho. Kirke, Jane a negroe, Wm. Guy, Mary Akehurst, a negroe named Jack. Certified 3 Jan. 1693.

Perquimans. Tymothy Clare proved 3 rights: himself his wife Mary, and Wm. Carman. 6 Jan. 1690.

Perquimans. Peter Gray entered into county 4 persons for which land is due but has never been taken up. Peter Gray his wife Mary his Sons Francis and Peter Gray. 7 April 1690.

Peter Grey proved rights: for himselfe being transported twice. Certified 7 Feb. 1693 and for one Right given him by Jno. Tweegar being proved alsoe.

Edw. Mayo proved 13 rights: Edw. Mayo Senior, Edw. Mayo Junior Sarah [May]o, Anne Mayo, Elizabeth Mayo, 3 negroes, Jno. Nixon, Em Nixon, [*torn*], Affrica Pike, Saml. Pike. Certified 7 Feb. 1693/4.

Susan Harris proved 3 rights: Susan [*torn*] Jno. Deadman Louis Dennis. Certified 10 Mar. 1693, warrant given to Jno. Harris.

Rich. Williamson entered rights: John Mi[*torn*] [*torn*] an Indian and himselfe. Certified [*torn*].

p. 12: Certificats and Rts.
(continued from bottom of p. 12 reverse)
[*torn*] Jennings Esqr. Martha his wife [*torn*] Jennings and Annis Jennings Ralph Garnet and Margret Garnet. 30 Mar. 1680.

Albemarle. Willm. Jennings esqr., 200 a., for transportation of 4 persons, 29 Mar. 1680.
Nathanl. Nichols An Grant Willm. Garner a servant boy named Robt. A maid servant named Jone a negro man named Sambo

Joseph Sparnon proved 6 rights: Joseph Sparnon, Alice Sparnon, Robt. Morgan Mary [P?]ency, An Jacson, Joseph Jacson. Certified [no date]. These Rights are assigned over by Joseph Sparnon to Wm. Jennings.

Albemarle. Wm. Johnson, 250 a., for transportation of 5 persons, 30 Mar. 1680.

Wm. Johnson Mary his wife John Rolfe and Mary Rolfe and Mary an Indian Woman.

Albemarle. Patrick Bayley, 100 a., for transportation of 2 persons, 29 Mar. 1680.
Patrick Bayley Lucy his Wife
A new warrant Given to Wm. Gennins for the abovewritten [*torn*] two old warrants This last being assigned to the abovementioned Wm. J[ennings] [*torn*] Said Jennings hath maried.

p. 12 (reverse): Old Warrants
Albemarle. Mr. Lewis Vandermulen, 730 a., for transportation of 13
  persons, 21 Apr. 1669.
  Mr. Lewis Vandermulen, Eliza. his wife, John Nicolson, Saml.
  Sergant, Morgin Watkins, Tho. and John Vandermulen, his sons
  Jane and Mary Vandermulin his daughters, Wm. Lerry, John More,
  Simon Alderson, and Mary Lookley.
  New warrant given for these 3 old warrants and certificate [*torn*]
  March 1693.

Albemarle. Henry White, 100 a., for transportation of 2 persons, 29
  Mar. 1680.
  Jno. Morrison a Negro woman Named Jone
  Assignment by Henry White to John [*blank*] 11 Mar. 1693.

John Tomlins proved 3 rights: John Tomlins, Wm. Bartlet senior Wm.
  Bartlet junior. Certified 15 Mar. 1693.

Mr. John Jennings proved rights: Tho. Robison three Negroes by
  Names Betty Dick and Jack and by three old Warrants eighteen
  rights certified [no date].

Albemarle. John Jennings, 400 a., for transportation of 8 persons, 5
  Feb. 1679.
  Doctor Tho. Relfe twice transported Dorathy his wife, Tho. Relfe
  junior, John More, Willm. Gardiner John Jennings and Willm. Relfe

Albemarle. Wm. Gennings esqr., 300 a., for transportation of 6
  persons (continued top of p. 12)

p. 13: Old Warrants
Albemarle. Tho. harris, 300 a., for transportation of 5 persons, 21
  Apr. 1669.
  Tho. Harris, Diana Harris Edw. Remington Saml. a Servant bought
  of Mr. Secretary and Wm. Hogpen assigned by Jno. Vines.

Albemarle. Tho. Harris, 300 a., for transportation of 5 persons, 21
  Apr. 1669.
  Jno. Moore and his wife, Rich. Felton Alice his wife and Tho.
  Symons these were assigned by Jno. Vines. A warrant given to John
  heris.

Albemarle. Willm. Bundy, 170 a., for transportation of 3 persons, 7 [*torn*] 1669.
Wm. Bundy Eliza. his wife Mary Bundy his Daughter

Perquimans. Jno. Whitby proved 6 rights by importation: Negro Jack, Honora an Irish woman, Edw. Pratt, Negro Toby, Negro Judith, and himselfe, 6 Jan. 1693. Warrant given.

Albemarle. Albert Albertson, 400 a., for transportation of 8 persons, 30 Mar. 1680.
Albert Alberson, Mary his wife Albert and Esaw his sonnes Susannah, and Hannah his daughters Jno. Gosby, and Mary Gosby.
A new warrant Granted and Registered 7 Feb. 1693/4.

p. 13 (reverse): Certificats of Rights, and
Caleb Bundy proved 13 rights: Edw. Jones, Danl. Johson, Tho. Hilton, Saml. Skinner Josiah Evins Wm. Jordan Humphrey Pung A Negroe named Luke. Certified 3 Jan. 1693, registered 27 Feb. 1693.

Albemarle. Tho. Macky, 150 a., for transportation of 3 persons, 29 Mar. 1680. Tho. Macky Eliz. his wife Wm. Symson
Registered 27 Feb. 1693.

Mr. Patrick Bayly proved 7 rights: Patrick Bayley Lucy Harvy a negroe woman Margeret Hamleton Two Rights, Jno. Hudson Symon Daxter. Certified 7 Feb. 169[3]. Registered and warrant given 3 Mar. 1693.

Jno. Buntin proved 5 rights out of this petition of Mr. Wm. Duckenfeild and Mr. Wm. Dukenfeild has proved other three Rights being Eight Rights:

Jno. Buntin Alice his wife Joseph Holbrook Wm. Peers Tho. Woodward these five belong to Buntin, Jno. Ares Joseph Simpson Edw. Standing, these three by Mr. Duckenfeild. Certified 6 Mar. 1693. Registered and warrant given.

Benjamin Lakar, one right: Peter Thisle. Certified 16 Mar. 1693/4. Registered and warrant given 16 Mar. 1693.

Margery White proved 11 rights: Rich. Williams, Margery his wife, Sarah, Anne, Nichol. Wise, James Gad, Rich. Robison, Alexander Murrey, Ralph Whiting, Willm. Warde, Wm. White. Certified 15 Mar. 1693. Registered and warrant given 27 Mar. 1694.

Tho. Harvy esq. proved 23 rights: Nicl. Hunt, Adam Camill, Patrick Bayley, David Wilson, Margeret Tus[on] (may be continued top of p. 9 reverse)

p. 14: Old Warrants
Chowan Precinct, first Monday in April 1694. These Rights fol[low]ing was Proved and Certificates ordered by the Court viz.

By Jno. Wheatley three Rights being himselfe his wife and Jno. Harris.

By Anne Stuart Nine Rights viz. Jno. Cropley, Anne Cropley, Mary Cropley, Anne Cropley Junior, Elizabeth Cropley, Jno. Vines, James Fisher, Wm. Darby, Jno. Darby, and a warrant given 27 August.

By Arthure Carleton 7 rights viz. Elizabeth Block Senior, Mary Block Elizabeth Block Junior Jno. Block Jam. Block, Sarah Block, and Arthure Carleton, And the three first assigned to James Fisher. And Warrant Given for the Rest.

By Arthure Carleton three Rights Tho. Cutlet, Katherine Cutlet, Alex. Cutlet four of Carletons Rights assigned to Francis Wells

By Rich. Bartett two rights proved viz. Elizabeth Roundtree and Mary Bartlett.

By Joan Brethett three Rights viz. Ralph Wilkison Robt. Glasgoe Eliz. Glasgoe

By Rich. Griffen four rights viz. Rich. Bartlet Ellinor Bartlet Joan Round[tree] and Richard Griffen

James Blount three rights viz. James Blount Jno. Blount Elizabeth Blount. One put into his Warrant the Other two assigned to Mr. Thomas Blount.

By Nicolas Symons his owne right proved and entered into his Warrant 4 Sept.

By order of Court Cotten Robison have a certificate for the rights proved by Anthoney Walteras and George Miles.

By Edw. Stanley two rights proved viz. his owne and Roger Middleton.

By Wm. Harrison two Rights viz. An Harrison Wm. Harrison Assigned to Argill Simonds and Wm. Given.

By Elizabeth Ward three Rights viz. Jno. Maniweathers Rice Ward and Nicolls Brightman.
Assignment by Eliza. Ward of these 3 rights "to my son Edw. Smithwike" 25 May 1694
And entered into a warrant with other rights of the said Smithwike

By Lewis Williams 9 rights proved viz. Lewis Williams, Senior Lewis Williams junior, Eliz. Williams twice transported, An Williams, Anthony Williams, Johana Williams, Katherine Williams, Edw. Redman.

Tho. Green his owne Right proved And assigned to Mr. Tho. Blount

Edward Murrey his owne Right proved

p. 14 (reverse)
By Mary Harrison 4 Rts. viz. Jno. Harrison Eliz. Harrison, Mary and Wm. Harrison

By James Evins his owne right and Abigail his wife proved.

By Mr. Edw. Smithwike 3 rights proved viz. John Shearin Lidia Shearin and Mary Shearin her daughter. These are a second transportation and entered into Smithwikes Warrant

Albemarle ss. Palatine Court 20 Sept. 1692.
Tho. Blount proved 7 rights viz. Tho. Blount Christian Blount Joshua Hepworth Elizabeth Green and three Negroes.

Mr. Tho. Blount proved 3 rights: Humphrey Leg and two Negroes. Chowan Precinct Court 12 Feb. 1693. Certifed.

James Cooper proved 4 rights: himselfe Christian Elizabeth and Jane Cooper. Chowan Precinct Court 12 Feb. 1693. Certified.

Assignment by James Cooper of 4 abovewritten rights to Mr.
Tho. Blount, 2 Apr. 1694.

Albemarle. James Blount Junior, 100 a., for transportation of 2
persons 29 Mar. 1680.
Edw. Roe Junior and Jno. Chantrey
Assignment by James Blount to Tho. Blount 2 Apr. 1694.

Albemarle. Tho. Blount, 500 a., for transportation of 10 persons 29
Mar. 1680. James Blount Ursula Rodgers James Blount junior
Eliz. his wife Jno. Blount Jno. Currier Edw. Roe his [*torn*]
Nightingale and two Children not baptized.

p. 15: Old Warrants
Albemarle. Henry Slade, 60 a., for transportation of 1 person, 7 Sept.
1669. Henry Slade
Assignment by Henry Slade to George Harris 16 Mar. 1693/4.

Henry Slade proved 5 rights: Wm. Leverige senior Temporance his
Wife Wm. Leverige junior, Hanah Leverige Jacob Carver.
Certified 17 Mar. 1693.
Assignment by Henry Slade to George Harris

George Harris proved 5 rights by purchase from James Williams,
Pasquotank Precinct: Phillis Williamson, An Grande Diana
Williamson, and Christo. Williamson, and James Williamson.
Certified 15 Mar. 1693.

Geo. Harris proved 12 rights: Tho. Page, his Wife, and three Children,
Eliz. Powell, Mary Empson, J[*torn*] Harris, and his wife, Wm.
Stuart, Jno. Hall, Thomas Empson. Warrant given 11 July 1694.

Ralph Coates, 500 a., for transportation of 10 persons into Albemarle
County, [*blank*] March 1680.
Ralph Coats, Robt. Wallis, Rich. Briggs, Samll. Gotee, A servant
boy named Philip, Jno. Noe, Rich. Vincent, Eliz. Smith, Michael
Wilson
This warrant was passed 17 Apr. 1694 to Tho. Twiddy "being 9
rights."
Warrant given 11 July.

Mrs. Elizabeth Hunt proved 5 rights: Elizabeth Hunt, Anthony Hatch, [*torn*] Henry Gilliard, Christian James. Certified 20 Apr. 1694. Warrant given 11 July.

Wm. Bundy proved 1 right: himself (no date)

p. 15 (reverse): Certificat of Rt. and
Arnold White proved 5 rights: Arnold White Mary White and three Negros. Certified 20 Apr. 1694. Warrant given 11 July

Tho. King proved 1 right: himself (no date)

Rowland Buckley proved 7 rights: himselfe two times transported Ellinor his wife, Rowland Buckley junior, Wm. Winbury, Mathew Stricklin, and Mary Buckley. Certified 20 Apr. 1694. Warrant given 11 July.

Tho. Towers proved 7 rights: Tho. Towers two times for himselfe and two times for his wife: being transported in, Mary Towers, Margrt. Burley, and Charles Thomas. Certified 20 Apr. 1694.
Warrant given 11 July.

Ralph Gardnet proved 4 rights: himselfe Giles Dowlear Henry Gilliard Sarah Hatton and two more bought from Edw. Roe junior Namely Emund Roe Eliz. Roe. Certified 20 Apr. 1694. Pasquotank.

Albemarle. Ralph Garnet, 100 a., for transportation of 2 persons, 5 Feb. 1679. Ralph Garnet Joana his wife. Warrant given 11 July.

Robt. Moline by his wife proved 4 rights: himselfe Ellinor his wife Jno. Vaughan, and a Negroe James. Certified 20 Apr. 1694. Warrant given 11 July.

John Bornsby Senior proved 10 rights: himselfe, Sarah his wife, Wm. Croney, Jno. Bornsby junior Tho. Borneby, Wm. Borneby, Miles Borneby, Jno. Newman, Jno. Cammell, Jno. Morgan. Certified 20 Apr. 1694. Warrant given 11 July.

Mr. Jno. Hawkins proved 2 rights: himselfe whose name is upon Record being Nathanl. Lawson and one for Barbary Middleton. Certified 20 Apr. 1694. Nathaniel Lawson was two times transported which is Three rights to Mr. Hawkins. Warrant given 11 July. Pasquotank.

p. 16: Old Warrants

Jno. Stamp proved 3 rights: John Stamp Joan Stamp and Tho. Stamp. Certified 20 Apr. 1694. Warrant given 11 July. Pasquotank.

Rich. Pope proved 3 rights: himselfe and his wife twice transported. Certified 20 Apr. 1694. Warrant given 11 July. Pasquotank.

John Rapier 2 rights: himselfe and one for Wm. Hogpen and two bought from Saml. Welst. Certified. Warrant given 11 July. Pasquotank.

Jno. Browne 1 right: himselfe (no date)

Wm. Carteret 3 transportation for himselfe. Warrant given 11 July.

Wm. Jones proved 4 rights: Wm. Princ Sarah Princ Jane Princ and Wm. Prince. Certified 20 Apr. 1694. Pasquotank. Assigned from Eliz. Mowberry. Warrant given 11 July.

David Prichard Senior proved 6 rights: himselfe, Sarah Prichard, David Prichard junior Tho. Prichard, Hugh Prichard, Jno. Motley, and two from Rich. Madrom Namely Eliz. Madram and An Madram. Certified 20 Apr. 1694. Warrant given 11 July. Pasquotank.

Wm. Rawlison proved 4 rights: Wm. Rawlison Eliz. Rawlison Wm. Rawlison junior and Eliz. Dunston. Certified 20 Apr. 1694. Warrant given 11 July. Pasquotank.

Tho. Kirke proved 6 rights: himselfe two times transported and his wife two times transported Eliz. Kirke, and An Kirke. Certified 20 Apr. 1694. Warrant given 11 July. Pasquotank.

Wm. Bornby proved 7 rights: Tony, Boatswain, Negroes a white woman Named Ellinor Sarah Hamond Wm. Bornby Mr. Henley's Wife and Mother. Certified 20 Apr. 1694. Warrant given 11 July. Pasquotank.

Saml. West proved 10 rights and sold all but two whose names are upon Record which are his owne two rights for being two times transported. (no date)

Henry Pendleton proved 2 rights: himselfe and Elizabeth [*torn*]. Warrant given 11 July.

p. 16 (reverse): Certificats of Rts. and

Cornelius Jones proved 9 rights: John Scarbrough Mary Scarbrough and two children Cornelius Jones Eliz. Jones Abraham Watkins and two rights for Simon Rice. Certified 20 Apr. 1694. Warrant given 11 July. Pasquotank.

Charles Jones has bought of Eliz. Mowbery six Right which he must have a warrant for: Robt. Hambleton, Laurence Bras, Black Charles, Wm. Hill, Jno. Jones, and Hugh Jones. Certified 20 Apr. 1694. Warrant given for these with 6 more in fol. 32.

Albemarle. Tho. Carteret, 400 a., for transportation of 8 persons, 29 Mar. 1680.
Tho. Carteret Mary his wife John Carteret Wm. Carteret Edw. Foster Jno. Callinoe James Perrishaw Peter Dardino.

Tho. Carteret proved 4 rights: Wm. Bentley Charles Haley Grace Carteret and Tho. Carteret. Certified 2 Apr. 1694. Warrant given.

Chowan Precinct. George Miles proved 3 rights: himselfe Margerett his wife and Danl. Cox. 1 Jan. 1679.

Anthoney Walteras "at the same time" proved 11 rights: himselfe Rebecca Walters, Wm. Walters, Katherine Walters, Jno. Jackson, Elinor Jackson, Rebecca Jackson, Joseph Danl., Sarah Jacson, alias Danl. Katherine Danl., and Tho. Sharpman, allowed to Cotton Robison.

Jane Robison, wife of Cotton Robison, proved 9 rights in Shaftesbury Precinct Court, 1 Jan. 1679: Jno. Battle Senior, Philip Battle Saml. Newtook Jno. Micke Margarett Harwell Jane Robison and Cotten Robison.

Saml. Davis proved 14 rights: Wm. Hall, Eliz. Hall, Sarah Hall, Tony a Negroe, Jack, and Margrett Negroes, Samuel Davis, Eliz. Davis, Tho. Gregory, Rich. Gregory, Eliz. Gregory, Eliz. Davis two times transported An Davis. Certified 20 Apr. 1694. Warrant given.

James Davis proved 4 rights: Willm. Davis James Davis Wm. Whitehorne Phebe Pindar. Certified 20 Apr. 1694. Warrant given for 200 a. Pasquotank.

p. 17: Old Warrants

Abraham Tooke proved 2 rights: himselfe and one from Michael Mackdaniel. Certified 20 Feb. 1694. Warrant given for 100 a. Pasquotank.

Bryan Fitspatrick proved 3 rights: Bryan Fitspatrick Cornelius his son Jno. Griffen. Certified 20 Apr. 1694. Warrant given for 150 a. Pasquotank.

Jno. Wilson proved 2 transportations for himselfe and 5 from Edmund Clancey: James Kinsello Danl. Camwell Mathew Witherit Rich. Flowers Francis Merret. Certified 20 Apr. 1694. Warrant given for 350 a. Pasquotank.

George Powers proved 2 rights: Jno. Prince and Sarah his wife and from Edmund Clancy 6 rights: Jno. Wilks, Francis Sympson, Rich. Tillmarch, his wife, and two Children. Certified 20 Apr. 1694. Warrant given for 400 a. Pasquotank.

Jno. Mason proved 6 rights: Morgan Rice Jno. Morgan Tho. Cobb Sarah Mason the other two sould to Rich. Crag. Certified 20 Apr. 1694. Warrant given for 200 a. Pasquotank.

Jno. Jones proved 4 rights: Jno. Jones Sarah Davis Susan Jones Eliz. Jones. Certified 20 Apr. 1694. Warrant given for 200 a. Pasquotank.

Mathew Williamson proved 6 rights: Roger Martin Francis Williamson, twice transported, Mathew Williamson, Rich. Jones, Mary Jones. Certified 20 Apr. 1694. Warrant given for 300 a.

Rich. Madram proved 5 rights: Rich. Madram Eliz. his daughter Eliz. his wife An Daldrige and Anne Madram two of which are sold to David Prichard Senior. Certified 20 Apr. 1694. Warrant given. Pasquotank.

Mrs. Mary Clark, widow, proved 11 rights: Jno. Clark, Sarah Hattan, Tho. White Jam[es] Jeny, Jack, Tom, Sambo, Toby, Maria, and Dick. Certified 20 Apr. 1694. Warrant given for 550 a. Pasquotank.

Elizabeth Mowbery proved 15 rights: Wm. Westerman, Saml. Barnes, Edw. Cham[bers] [Elizabeth] Mowbery for her selfe twice transported, Wm. Jones Senior, Wm. Jones Junior, three [*torn*] transported these first Nine rights shee hath given to her son Wm. Jones and must [*torn*] the warrant with his owne rights Robt. Hamleton, Laurence Bras, Black Charles, Wm. [*torn*] Jno. Jones, Hugh Jones, these six are sold to Charles Jones. Certified 20 [Apr.] 1694. Pasquotank.

p. 17 (reverse): Warrants for Survey of Land
Albemarle. Ralph Fletcher, 780 a., for transportation of 15 persons, 17 Feb. 1693.
The persons names, viz.
Ralph Fletcher, Eliz. his wife Jacob Cozens Sarah, a negroe, Tho. Cullen, Sarah his wife, Jno. and Rich, his Sons Sarah, Anne, Mary, Christian, and Martha his Daughters, Henry White Mary his wife. the last 11 due to Fletcher by assignment.

Albemarle. Tymothy Clare, 250 a., for transportation of 5 persons, 17 Feb. 1693.
The persons names viz.
Tym. Clare Francis Belchamp Wm. Redman Rich. Fox, Wm. Carman. Assignment by Tym. Cleare to Patrick Canaday 17 Feb. 1693.

Albemarle. Rich. Fox, 200 a., for transportation of 4 persons, 17 Feb. 1693.
persons names. Rich. Fox, Geo. Fox Wm. Fox, Mary Fox. Surveyed and returned 4 May 1694.

p. 18
Albemarle. Humphrey Bolton, 250 a., for transportation of 5 persons, 6 Feb. 1693.
The persons names. Jno. Bolton Eliz. his wife Tho. Pendleton Henr. Pendleton Math. Pendleton. Surveyed and returned 19 Feb. 1693/4.
15 Feb. 1693 Survey for Humphrey Bolton, 250 a., Pasquotank Precinct.
Registered 26 Feb. 1693.

Albemarle. Joseph Commandr., 300 a., for transportation of 6 persons, 6 Feb. 1693.
Joseph Commander, Dorathy his wife Wm. Tuke Johannah Tuke Tho. Welsh, Andrew Dennis.
Survey and return 19 Feb. 1[693] for 97 a.

14 Feb. 1693 Survey for Mr. Joseph Commander, 97 a., Pasquotank Precinct.
Registered 26 Feb. 1693.

p. 18 (reverse): Warrants and Surveys
Albemarle. Jeremiah Symons, 400 a., for transportation of 8 persons, 7 Feb. 1693.
The persons names viz. Jeremiah Symons, Jonathan Taylor, Andrew Macklewer, Nan a Negroe, Jack a Negroe, John Dellaware, Geo. Fisher, Deb. Fisher. Survey and return 19 Feb. 1693/4 for 158 a.
10 Feb. 1693 Survey for Jeremiah Symons, 158 a., Pasquotank Precinct.
Registered 27 Feb. 1693.

Albemarle. Tho. Macky, 150 a., for transportation of 3 persons, 7 Feb. 1693.
The persons names viz. Tho. Macky Bridget his wife Wm. Symson Survey and return 19 Feb. 1693 for 150 a.
15 Feb. 1693 Survey for Tho. Macky, 150 a., Pasquotank.
Registered 27 Feb. 1693.

Albemarle. Tho. Symons, 400 a., for transportation of 8 persons, 6 Feb. 1693/4.
Tho. Symons Sarah Watts, Negro Jack Negro Tony Negro Sarah, Ruth Pender Tymothy Pender [*torn*]n Elworthy.

p. 19
Assignment by Tho. Symons to Caleb Bundy one right out of this warrant and alsoe to Ruth Pender her owne right, 17 Dec. 1693/4.

Albemarle. Survey and return, 296 a., 19 Feb. 1693/4.
10 Feb. 1693 Survey for Tho. Symons, 96 a., Pasquotank Precinct.
11 Feb. 1693 Survey for Tho. Symons, 200 a., Pasquotank Precinct.
Registered 27 Feb. 1693.

Albemarle. Caleb Bundy, 450 a., for transportation of 9 persons, 7 Feb. 1693. The names. Edw. Jones Danl. Johnson Tho. Hilton Saml. Skinner Josiah Elworthy Evins Wm. Jordan Humphrey Bung a negro named Luke W. Survey 415 a., "in three several Tracts:" 175 a. for Caleb Bundy, 130 a. for Wm. Bundy, and 110 a. for Saml. Bundy, 19 Feb. 1693.

16 Feb. 1693 Survey for Wm. Bundy, 130 a., Pasquotank Precinct.
16 Feb. 1693 Survey for Caleb Bundy, 175 a., Pasquotank Precinct.
17 Feb. 1693 Survey for Saml. Bundy, 110 a., Pasquotank Precinct.
Registered 28 Feb. 1693.

p. 19 (reverse): Warrants and Surveys
Albemarle. Hanah Gosby, 500 a., for transportation of 10 persons, 7
Feb. 1693/4.
The names John Gosby, John Anderson, John Kinsey, Rich.
Walterland, Katherine Kinsey, Jane Anderson, Stephen
Hempworth, Jer. White, Henry Clay, [Han]nah Nicholson.
Registered 4 Apr. 1694.

p. 20
Albemarle. Survey and return for Hanah Gosby, widow, 500 a., 24
Feb. 1693/4.
21 Feb. 1693 Survey for Hanah Gosby, widow, 500 a.
Survey and return for Patrick Canaday, 210 a., 27 Feb. 1693/4.
24 Feb. 1693/4 Survey for Patrick Canaday, 210 a., on Perquimans
River.

Albemarle. Francis Tomes, 510 a., for transportation of 10 persons, 1
Jan. 1693.
Mary Tomes, Mary Fitsgarret, a servant, Joseph Ashley, Charles,
Two Indians three Negrose Eliz. a servant
Assignment by Francis Tomes to Timothy Ceare 7 Nov. 1693.
Survey and return for Tymothy Clare, 473 a., 26 Feb. 1693.
24 Feb. 1693 Survey for tymothy Clare, 473 a., on Perquimans River.

Albemarle. John Bentley, 350 a., for transportation of 7 persons, 26
Mar. 1694.
The persons viz. Rich. Bentley, Jane Bentley, Mary Bentley, Sarah
Bentley, a Negro boy, a Negro Woman, an Indian boy Assignment
by John Bentley to John Spelman 27 Mar. 1694. Survey and return
for John Spelman, 350 a., 29 Mar. 1694.
29 Mar. 1694 Survey for Jno. Spelman, 350 a., Perquimans Precinct.

p. 20 (reverse): Warrants and Surveys
Albemarle. Roger Snell, 250 a., for transportation of 5 persons, 26
Mar. 1694.

The persons viz. Roger Snell Mary Snell Rebecca Snell John Snell Waltr. Chase
Survey and return for Roger Snell, 250 a., 28 Mar. 1694.
28 Mar. 1694 Survey for Roger Snell, 250 a., s. of Perquimans River.

Albemarle. Thomas Harvy esqr., 640 a., for transportation of 13 persons, 5 Jan. 16[94].
The names of the persons Tho. Harvy, Heckto Maria, Tom, Peter, Nick, Maria, Nick, Betty, Negros, Elizabeth Jordan, Katherine Gardinr., a servant named William, a servant named Elinor
Survey for Tho. Harvy esqr. 631 a., 28 Mar. 1694.
28 Mar. 1694 Survey for Tho. Harvy esqr., 631 a., s. of Perquimans River.

p. 21
Albemarle. Alexander Lillington, 1050 a., for transportation of 21 persons, 5 Jan. 1693.
Tho. James, Sarah James, Joseph James, John James, Sarah James, Edw. Wilson, Alexandr. Lillington, Sarah Lillington, Elizabeth Lillington, John James, Joseph James, Eliz. Willis, Wm. Dickins, Mary Walker, peter Person, Mary Greatbach, George, Baccas Hanah, Bes, Moll Survey and return for Major Alexander Lillington, 640 a., 30 Mar. 1694. 30 Mar. 1694 Survey for Major Alexander Lillington, 640 a., Perquimans Precinct.

Albemarle. Alexander Lillington, 300 a., for transportation of 6 persons, 5 Jan. 1693.
Tho. Stanford, Eliza. Stanford, John Stanford, Ellinor Stanford, Mary Stanford, Sarah Stanford. These rights were assigned to Alexander Lillington by Tho. Stanford
Survey and return for Major Lillington, 640 a., 410 a. due upon the Remainder of the Rights in the above warrant, 31 Mar. 1694.
31 Mar. 1694 Survey for Major Alexander Lillington, 640 a., Perquimans Precinct.

p. 21 (reverse): Warrants and Surveys
Albemarle. Caleb Callaway, 250 a., for transportation of 5 persons, 5 Jan. 1693.
Caleb Callaway, Eliza. his wife Willm. Hughs Edw. Benit and his wife.

These two latter rights wear assigned over to Caleb Callaway by Edw. Benit.

2 Apr. 1694 Survey and return for Mr. Caleb Callaway, 250 a.

2 Apr. 1694 Survey for Mr. Caleb Callaway, 250 a., Perquimans Precinct.

27 March 1694 Survey for Mr. Benjamin Lakar, 538 a., Perquimans Precinct. Survey and return for Benjamin Lakar esqr., 138 a., 27 Apr. 1694.

Albemarle. Benjamin Lakar, 800 a., for transportation of 16 persons, 5 Jan. 1693.

Benj. Lakar, Eliz. Lakars, Benj. Lakar junior, Eliz. Lakar, Sarah Lakar, Lydia Lakar, Ruth Lakar, Deborah Lakar, Mingo, and his wife, and two Children, Wm. Ros, Francisco a Negro, Joan Lakar, Maria a Negro.

p. 22

Albemarle. Tho. [Lepper], 500 a., for transportation of 10 persons, 28 Mar. 1694.

The persons viz. Tho. Kent, An his wife, Sarah Kent, Rebecca Kent, An Kent junior, John Thomas, Willm. Browne, Wm. Brickston, Tho. Lepper, Nicholas Robison

Survey and return for Mr. Tho. Lepper, 470 a., 2 Apr. 1694.

2 Apr. 1694 Survey for Mr. Tho. Lepper, 470 a., Perquimans Precinct.

Albemarle. Jane Charles, 300 a., for transportation of 6 persons, 28 Mar. 1694.

John Edlin, Sarah his wife, Wm. Charles, Abigail his wife, Wm. his son, Elizabeth his daughter

Survey and return for Jane Charles, 287 a., 3 Apr. 1694. And what remaines in this warrant is assigned to John Wyate 5 Apr. 1694.

3 Apr. 1694 Survey for Jane Charles, 287 a., s. of w. branch Yawpim Creek.

p. 22 (reverse)

[Albemarle.] John Wyate, 293 a., for transportation of 5 persons, 5 Apr. 1694.

The persons viz. Wm. Wyate, deborah and Rebecca his wife, Mary
Pearcy, Joan an Irish woman, and forty three acres assigned by
Tho. Lepper out of his and Jane Charles's Warrant.
Survey and return for John Wyate, 288 a., 5 Apr. 1694.
5 Apr. 1694 Survey for John Wyate, 288 a., Perquimans Precinct.

Albemarle. Robt. Harmon, 200 a., for transportation of 4 persons, 31
Mar. 1694.
The persons viz. Robt. Harmon Elizabeth Harmon by an old
warrant and Zachary Nixon assigned by W. Glover assignee of Mr.
Edw. Mayo.
Survey and return for Robt. Harmon, 92 a., 6 Apr. [1694].
6 Apr. 1694 Survey for Robt. Harmon, 92 a., Perquimans Precinct.

p. 23: Surveys
Albemarle. Tho. Pearce, 450 a., for transportation of 9 persons, 26
Mar. 1694.
The persons viz. Tho. Pearce John Pearce, Susan Pearce, Dorathy
Pearce, Mary Pearce, Mary Bridges, John Wilkison, John Pearce,
Ruth Pearce.
Assignment by Tho. Peirce of the 3 last rights to John Pearce
6 Apr. 1694 Survey and return for Thomas Peirce, 300 a., 6 Apr.
1694.
6 Apr. 1694 Survey for Tho. Pearce, 300 a., Perquimans Precinct.

Albemarle. John [Ches]ton, 300 a., for transportation of 6 persons,
[*torn*] Mar. 1694.
The persons viz. Eliz. Cheston, Martha, Mary, Archibel, Hanah,
and Sarah, Cheston.
Survey and return for John Cheston, 300 a., [*torn*] Apr. 1694.
[*torn*] Apr. 1694 Survey for John Cheston, 300 a., Perquimans
Precinct.

p. 23 (reverse): Warrants and Surveys
Albemarle. Ro[bert] Beasley, 300 a., for transportation of 6 persons,
13 Mar. 1693/4.
The names of the persons viz. Robt. Beasley, Sarah Beasley, James
Beasley, Johana Beasley, Rich. Cheston, Sarah Cheston
Survey and return for Robert Beasley, 282 a., 10 Apr. 1694.
10 Apr. 1694 Survey for Robert Beasley, 28[2] a., on Perquimans
River.

Albemarle. Wm. Lacy, 250 a., for transportation of 5 persons, 31 Mar. [1694].
The persons viz. Wm. Lacy senior Grace Lacy John Davis Jane Davis Wm. Lacy junior.
Survey and return for Wm. Lacy, 250 a., 12 Apr. 1694.
13 Apr. 1694 Survey for Wm. Lacy, 250 a., on Perquimans River.

p. 24
[Albemarle. Peter Grey,] [*torn*], for transportation of 7 persons, 3 Mar. 1693.
The persons viz. Peter Grey trasported 3 times and his Wife his sons francis and Thomas. John Tweeger assigned by the said tweeger.
Assignment by Peter Grey of the 3 last rights to Jane Bayard, 11 Apr. 1694.
Survey and return for Peter Grey, 200 a., 11 Apr. 1694.
11 Apr. 1694 Survey for Peter Grey, 200 a., on Perquimans River.

Albemarle ss. Charles Macdaniel, 200 a., for transportation of 4 persons, 3 Mar. 1693.
The persons names viz. Charles MacDaniel Eliz. Macdaniel Tho. Wallingford Saml. Powell
Survey and return for Charles Macdaniell, 143 a., 13 Apr. 1694.
13 Apr. 1694 Survey for Charles Macdaniell, 143 a., on Perquimans River.

Albemarle, Robt. Beasley, 200 a., for transportation of 4 persons, 31 Mar. 1694.
[The] persons viz. James Johnson, Rachell Johnson, his wife Wm. Johnson, James Johnson junior
Assignment by Robt. Beasley to Rich. Cheston, 31 Mar. 1694.

p. 24 (reverse): Warrants and Surveys
Assignment by Rich. Cheston of "two of the last" to Jane Bayard, 12 Apr. 1694.

Albemarle. Rich. Cheston, 100 a., for transportation of 2 persons, 12 Apr. 1694.
The persons viz. Anne Cheston Danl. Cheston.
Survey for Rich. Cheston, 200 a., 100 a. by within warrant and 100 a. by assignment of warrant for 200 a. to Cheston by Robt. Beasley, 14 Apr. 1694.

14 Apr. 1694 survey for Rich. Cheston, 200 a., on Perquimans River.

Albemarle ss. Willm. Butler, 100 a., for transportation of 2 persons, 16 Mar. 1694.
Wm. Butler Diana Butler.
Assignment by Wm. Butler to Jane Buyard, 11 Apr. 1694.
Survey for Jane Bayard, 366 a., 100 a. by this warrant and 100 a. by assignment of 2 rights by Rich. Cheston out of a warrant for 200 a. assigned him by Robt. Beasley, and 15[0] a. by assignment of 3 rights by Peter Grey's warrant, and [16] a. more by assignment of Patrick Canady, 40 a. due him, by him assigned to Bayard, 12 [*torn*].
12 Apr. 1694 Survey for Jane Bayard Widow, 366 a., on Perquimans River.

p. 25
Albemarle ss. James Morgan, 300 a., for transportation of 6 persons, 10 Mar. 1693.
The person viz. James Morgan and his Wife and Four assigned by Wm. Vos viz. Roger White John Wilkison John Stamp Joan Vos.
Survey and return for James Morgan, 300 a., 5 May 1694.

p. 25 (reverse): Warrants and Surveys
Albemarle. John Whitby, 300 a., for transportation of 6 persons, 7 Feb. 1693/4.
The Names viz. Jno. Whitby, Jack a Negroe, Honora an Irish woman, Edward Pratt, Toby, and Judith Negroes.
Survey and return for John Whitby, 230 a., 9 May 1694.

Albemarle. Robert Beasley, 200 a., for transportation of 4 persons, 1 Mar. 1694.
The persons viz. John Lacy Mary a Negroe James Hunter and Eliz. Randall assigned by Tho. Lepper out of an old warrant.
Survey and return for Robt. Beasley, 218 a., 200 a. by within warrant and 18 a. remaining due to him on a former warrant for 300 a., 3 May 1694.

Albemarle. Saml. Nicolson, 300 a., for transportation of 6 persons, 23 Apr. 169[4].
Wm. Jones Christopher Nicolson hanah his Wife Deliverance Sutton Saml. Nicolson Francis Symons.

Survey and return for Saml. Nicolson, 300 a., 7 May 1694.

p. 26
Albemarle. Anthony Haskett, 400 a., for transportation of 8 persons, 12 Apr. 1694.
    The persons Anthony Haskett Anthony Haskett junior John Gray Tabitha Gray Jno. Gray junior Tho. Gray Jahu Gray and by assignment of Wm. Bogue one right viz. Wm. Bogue.
    Assignment by Anthony Haskett of 4 of the last rights to Wm. Bogue, 13 Apr. 1694.
    Survey and return for Willm. Bogue, 200 a., 13 Apr. 1694.
    Assignment by Anthony Haskett of 3 of these rights to Nicolas Symons, 30 Apr. 1693. Entered in Symons' warrant 4 Sept. viz. Anthony Haskett Senior John Grey Tabitha Grey
    Assignment by Anthony Haskett of 1 of these rights to Robt. Frasor, 2 May 1694. Which is put into Frasor's warrant 10 Aug. 1694 viz. Anthony Haskett.

Albemarle ss. James Loadman, 150 a., for transportation of 3 persons, 13 Mar. 1693.
    Hubbard Lambert Jane Byard James Loadman.
    Survey and return for James Loadman, 143 a., 13 Apr. 1694.

p. 26 (reverse): Warrants and Return's.
Albemarle ss. Albert Albertson, 400 a., for transportation of 8 persons, 7 Feb. 1693.
    The persons Names Albert Albertson, Mary his Wife, Albert and Esaw his sons, Susanah and Hanah his daughters, John Gosby, and Mary Gosby Survey for Albert Albertson, 290 a., 8 May 1694.

Albemarle. Daniel Akehurst esqr., 500 a., for transportation of 10 persons, 6 Feb. 1693.
    The persons names viz. John Hawkins, and his wife, Saml. More, Rich. Clerk, Rich. Car, Jerem. Harmon, George More, Alex. Goden, Anne Quinton, Tho. Kirke.
    Assignment by Daniel Akehurst to Robt. Wilson, 16 Feb. 1693/4.
    Assignment by Robert Wilson of all rights but Tho. Kirke "unto my son Isaak Wilson," 16 Feb. 1693/4.
    "Upon further consideration I doe assigne the right of Tho. Kirk alsoe.

    Robert Wilson."

Survey and return for Isaac Wilson, 490 a., 30 Apr. 1694.

Albemarle. James Thigpen, 200 a., for transportation of 4 persons, 12 Apr. 1694.
The Persons viz. James Thigpen, Eliza. Thigpen, James Thigpen junior, and John Thigpen
Assignment by James Thigpen to David Sherwood, 30 Apr. 1694.

p. 27
Albemarle ss. Mr. John Durant, 150 a., for transportation of 3 persons, 3 Mar. 1693.
The persons names viz. John Durant Sarah Durant a servant named Judith.
Assignment by John Durant to David Sherwood, 6 Mar. 1693.
Survey and return for David Sherwood, 350 a., 150 a. by this warrant and 200 a. by warrant assigned by James Thigpen to Sherwood, 2 May 1694.

Albemarle ss. Capt. Ralph Fletcher, 780 a., for transportation of 15 persons, 17 Feb. 1693.
The persons Names viz. Ralphe Fletcher, Eliza. his wife, Jacob Cozens, Sarah a Negroe, Tho. Cullen, Sarah his wife, Jno., and Rich, his sons, Sarah, Anne, Mary, Cristian, and Martha his daughters, Henry White, Mary his wife, the eleven last being due to the said Fletcher by assignment.
Survey and return for Ralphe Fletcher, 370 a., 10 May 1694.
Assignment by Ralphe Fletcher of 6 rights to Jenkin Williams, 10 May 1694.
Survey and return for Jenkin Williams, 317 a., 11 May 1694.
Assignment by Ralph Fletcher of remaining 93 a. to George Sutton, 11 May 1694.

p. 27 (reverse)
Albemarle. Jenkin Williams, 50 a., for transportation of 1 person, 22 Apr. 1694.
The person viz. Jenkin Williams.
Assignment by Jenkin Williams to George Sutton, 11 May 1694.
Survey for George Sutton, 99 a., 6 a. by this warrant and 93 a. assigned by Capt. Fletcher, 12 May 1694.

Albemarle. Laurence Gonsalvo, 560 a., for transportation of 12 persons, 16 June 1694.

Laurence Gonsalvo John Johnson Tho. Gonsalvo Sarah Johnson each twice transported Peter Jones, Laurence Gonsalvo junior, Abraham Williams, Xpopher Morton, all by assignement From Sarah Johnson.

Albemarle ss. Survey and return for Laurence Gonsalvo, 560 a., 25 June 1694.

p. 28

Albemarle. Richard Oliver, 350 a., for transportation of 7 persons, 29 Mar. 1680.

Rich. Oliver, Alice his wife, Sarah, An, Mary, Feelix, and Margeret his daughter

Assignment by Richard Oliver, Shaftesbury Precinct, to Edw. Smithwike, 4 Oct. 1681.

Survey and return for Edw. Smithwike, 350 a.

p. 28 (reverse)

Certificats of Rts. for Land

John Wade proved 12 rights: Jno. Wade two times Jane Wade Two servants Christopher Waymouth Senior a servant woman Christopher Waymouth Junior two transportations Susan Waymouth Susan Waymouth and Wm. Short. Certified 20 Apr. 1694. Warrant given for 600 a. Pasquotank.

Wm. Collins proved 5 rights: Wm. Collins, Alice Collins, his wife Tho. Collins, James Collins, and Wm. Collins. Certified 20 Apr. 1694. Warrant given for 250 a.

Mr. Martin proved 5 rights: Walter Darby, Danl. Mackeele, two Negroes and Peter Fur. Certified 20 Apr. 1694. Warrant given for 250 a. Pasquotank.

Isaac Dellaware proved 3 rights: Isaac Dellaware Francis Dellaware Epraim Coates. Certified 20 Apr. 1694. Warrant given for 150 a. Pasquotank.

Henry Palin junior proved 3 rights: Henry Palin and his wife and Dick a Negroe. Certified 20 Apr. 1694. Warrant given for 150 a. Pasquotank.

Robt. Lowry proved 7 rights: Robt. Lowry Hanah Lowry Michaell Perry and four rights purchasd from Saml. West and his wife each twice transported. Certified 20 Apr. 1694. Pasquotank.

Mathew Kelly proved 5 rights: Cornelius Gowin and two transportations for himselfe, the other two sold to Rich. Crag. Certified 20 Apr. 1694. Warrant given for 150 a. Pasquotank.

Charles Bolt proved 3 rights: Charles Bolt and Eliz. his Wife and his son Geo. Kemp. Certified 20 Apr. 1694. Warrant given for 150 a.

Henry White proved 9 rights: Henry White senior, an White, Rich. Rodes, John Taylor, Rich. Fowler, Henry White junior, Mary White, Harbert Opoene, Toby a Negroe. Certified 20 Apr. 1694. Warrant given for 450 a. Pasquotank.

Augustine Scarbrough proved 9 rights: Austin Scarbrough, An Scarbrough, Mary Scarbrough An Richeson Peter Mayfeild Wm. Boyd John Barber Robt. Park[es] and George Scarbrough. Certified 20 Apr. 1694. Warrant given for 450 a. Pasquotank.

p. 29
Peter Furre proved 4 rights: Peter Furre Katherine Furre Margeret and Mary Furre. Certified 20 Apr. 1694. Warrant given for 200 a. Pasquotank.

Rich. Cragg proved 13 rights: two Rights for himselfe namely Rich. Crag, and James Armstrong, and from Robt. Cock Hanah Farmer and Wm. Sandeford, And from Edmund Clancy Namely Wm. White, Wm. Sympson, Jona Taylor, John Lacy, John Anthony, From Mathew Kelly two rights Cornelius Gowin and James Cowin and from Jno. Mason two rights Sarah Mason and Eliz. Cob. Certified 20 Apr. 1694. Warrant given for 650 a. Pasquotank.

Robt. Cock proved 6 rights: Robt. Cock Anne Cock Tho. Morris Wm. Morris the other two to Rich. Crag. Certified 20 Apr. 1694. Warrant given for 300 a. Pasquotank.

Tho. Symons proved 4 rights for Eliza. Coates as being her Guardian: James Coates James Mackmurren Jane Mackmurrin Wm. Walkins. Certified 20 Apr. 1694. Warrant given for 200 a.

John Tomlinson proved 7 rights: two Rights for himselfe being twice transported and five rights bought of Mr. Geo. Muschamp Namely Barbery Middleton Danl. Ophee James a Negroe and Mr. Muschamp being twice transported. Certified 20 Apr. 1694. Warrant given for 350 a. Pasquotank.

Mr. Geo. Muschamp proved 11 rights: Jane Cliff James Wrexam Edmund Cliffe Barbery Angle Turloe Fee Danl. Fee the other 5 sold to John Tomlinson. Certified 20 Apr. 1694. Warrant given for 600 a. Pasquotank.

Elizabeth Dunston proved 12 rights: Peleg Dunston, Mathew Scot, Sara Scot, Elizabeth Scot, Eliza. Dunston, Aaron Loverige, Nathaniell Edgecome, Wm. Hickman, Ellinor Hobbet, Tho. Anderson, Eliz. Deane, John Deane. Certified 20 Apr. 1694. Warrant given for 600 a. Pasquotank.

Charles Taylor proved 7 rights: Geo. Taylor, Ellinor Taylor, Geo. Taylor junior, Margery Taylor, Lomock Taylor, Charles Taylor, and Charles Taylor his Freedom Right. Certified 20 Apr. 1694. Warrant given for 350 a. Pasquotank.

Danl. Philips proved 6 rights: Michael Mackdaniel Joan his Wife Mary Mackdaniel Francis Mackdanl. Rich. Kemp and Rich. Foster. Certified 20 Apr. 1694. Warrant given for 300 a. Pasquotank.

Eliz. Boursby proved 12 rights: John Robison senior Eliz. his Wife John Lumbrosier John Robison junior Job Robison, Eliz. Robison, Saml. Blackwell, Mercy Jones, Tho. Jones, Mercy Relfe, John Relph, and Mercy Relph. Certified 20 Apr. 1694. Warrant given according to assignment. Pasquotank.

p. 29 (reverse): Certificats of Rights
Wm. Jacson Senior proved 2 rights: Robt. Bonane and Isaak Skinner. Certified 20 Apr. 1694. Pasquotank.

Wm. Jacson junior proved 8 rights: three rights for himselfe and two bought from Saml. West Namely John Watts Jane his wife Sarah Jacson and Phebe Davis two times transported. Certified 20 Apr. 1694. Warrant given for 250 a. Pasquotank.

Willm. Turner proved 7 rights: Wm. Turner, Ruth Turner, Katherine Turner, Ruth Watkins, Henry Platt, two rights and John Lawrence. Certified 20 Apr. 1694. Warrant given. Pasquotank.

Chowan Precinct Court, 2 July 1694. Mr. Tho. Garrat proved 5 rights: Tho. Garrat Senior, Bethia Garret, Tho. Garret junior, Bethia Garret, Rich. Malepass. Warrant given for 250 a.

Chowan Precinct Court, 1st Monday in July 1694. Joseph Chew proved 4 rights: Joseph Chew, Elizabeth his wife, his daughter Elizabeth, and his Daughter Sarah. Warrant given 11 July 1694.

Chowan Precinct Court, 1st Monday in July 1694. Willm. Walters proved 3 rights: John Canon Senior John Canon junior and Alice Canon. Certificate ordered and warrant given.

Chowan Precinct Court, 1st Monday in July 1694. Lewis Williams proved 4 rights: Tho. Stanbridge his wife Mary his daughter Mary Stanbridge and David Blake.

Shaftesbury Precinct Court, 4 Mar. 1679/80. Robert Jones proved 4 rights: himselfe Eliz. His Wife Jorganan Jones Roger Adams Assignment by Robt. Jones to Cotton Robbison, 14 May 1694.

p. 30
Shaftesbury Precinct Court, 2 Sept. 1680. Willm. Ludford proved 2 rights: himselfe and Anne his wife transportation Rights. Vera Copia from Capt. Hursts returnes.

Willm. Ludford proved 1 right: Henry Lashley, vera Copia from Capt. Hursts returnes.
Assignment by Willm. Ledford of 3 rights to Edward Smithwike, 2 July 1694. Assignment by Edward Smithwike to Jonathan Jones.

Shaftesbury Precinct Court, 5 Feb. 1679. David Jones proved 3 rights: himselfe Affrica his wife Joana LLewelling Phillip Battle. vera Copia from Capt. Hursts Booke and entered into Jonathan Jones Patent he being son of the said David Jones.

Shaftesbury Precinct Court, 1 Jan. 1679. Robt. Warberton proved 5 rights: himselfe Eliz. his wife John Warberton his son Mary

Warberton and Eliz. his daughters. Vera Copia from Capt. Hurts returnes.

Albemarle. Assignment by Cotton Robison to Robt. Warberton, 21 Dec. 1681.

Albemarle. Edward Smithwike, 200 a., for transportation of 4 persons, 29 Mar. 1680.
Edw. Smithwike Eliz. his wife John Shearing Eliz. Shearing
Warrant and survey being lost, Smithwike obtained an order for his Patent, then in court produced and found other rights belonging to his father, Mr. Hugh Smithwike, and new warrant given, including all rights due to Smithwike.

Perquimans Precinct Court, 2nd Monday in Apr. [1694]. Hanah Hill proved 15 transportation rights: Henry Phelps hanah his Wife John Phelps Jonathan Phelps hanah Phelps junior Robt. Pane James hill Saml. Hill Mary Hill Nathanl. Spivey and his Wife Judith John Spivey Sarah Spivey junior Anne Spivey Jonathan Phelps. Warrant given 14 July 1694.

p. 30 (reverse): Certificats of Rights.
Perquimans Precinct Court, 9 July 1694. Robert Wilson proved one right for John Walbee a freman that died at his house.

Perquimans Precinct Court, 2nd Monday in Apr. 1694. Robt. Wilson proved 8 rights: Robt. Wilson and Anne his Wife Isaack Wilson Sarah Wilson Isaack Wilson and An his Wife David Sherwood and his Wife. Assignment by Robt. Wilson of the 3 last rights to John Pricklow, 14 July 1694.

Perquimans Precinct Court, 9 July 1694. John Pricklow proved 5 transportation rights: himselfe Eliz. his wife Priscilla his Daughter Rachell his Daughter Rebecca Sebrel. Warrant given 14 July 1694.

Albemarle. Paul Latham, 250 a., for transportation of 5 persons, 22 Mar. 1680. Willm. Seares Paul Lathum An his Wife Colbert Grant a Negro Girle named Bes. New warrant given to Eliz. Lathum Daughter of Paul.

Chowan Precinct Court, 2 July 1694. Wm. Grace proved 8 rights: Wm. Grace, and Robt. Hollaway, at a second transportation Wm. Grace, his Wife, and two Daughters Margeret, and Feacy Grace, Sarah Grace, Margeret grace, Eliz. Grace. Certificate ordered. Assignment by Wm. Grace to Thomas Pollock, 10 July 1694.

p. 31
Albemarle. John Hunt, 350 a., for transportation of 7 persons, 1 Feb. 1679. John Hunt, Francis his Wife, Wm. Duks, Alice Norris, an Indian named Harry, Two Indians named Jack and Jersy.

Albemarle. John Hunt, 530 a., by assignment of 6 rights from Mr. Abraham Kimberley deceased to John Harvy deceased and assigned again by Thomas Harvey one of John Harvey's executors to John Hunt in a warrant, and one warrant more by assignment of francis Marwood for 3 rights to Peregreen Maners relict of whom Hunt married and became possessed of the 9 rights, 26 Mar. 1680.
Wm. Bateman, Rich. Curteen, Capt. Nathanl. Batts, Saml. Alford, Geo. Beasley, and Anne Tompson, Francis Marwood, Cypurian, her husband, Giles her son.

Palatine Court, 11 July 1694. Capt. John Hunt proved his right to land by importation of Eliz. his wife, Thomas Drinkwater, Anthony Joy, Mary Mackfarloe, four Negros and John Clarke. Warrant given including the 2 above old warrants.

Palatine Court, 11 July 1694. Rich. Bentley proved his right for his second transportation and assigned it to John Spelman.

Palatine Court, 11 July 1694. John Spelman proved his right to land by importation of John Spelman and Katherine his Wife. Warrant given including above assignment.

Palatine Court, 11 July 1694. Danl. Akehurst proved 4 rights: Philichrista Akehurst her third transportation Pheby a Negro Wm. Duncan Tony an Indian.

Perquimans Precinct Court, 9 July 1694. John Lilly proved 8 rights: John Lilly Senior Eliz. Lilly Jane Lilly Eliz. Johnson John Lilly junior three transportations Hanah Lilly.

p. 31 (reverse): Certificats of Rights.
Rich. Nowell proved 5 rights: George Taylor Loomox Taylor Phebe West Willm. West Saml. West. Warrant given. (no date) [1694]

John Hare proved 5 rights: himselfe Lidia his Wife John Bentley Wm. Orendall Edw. Orendall. [1694]

Wm. Lacy proved 1 right: himselfe [1694]

Jerimiah Brooke proved 8 rights: himselfe, Tho. Mercy Senior, Tho. Mercy, Sarah Mercy, Tho. Stanley, Eliz. his wife, Eliz. Ax, Robt. Duglas. Assignment to George Mathews and 5 by him to Thomas Johnson, the rest put in his warrant.

Robt. Frazer proved 2 rights: himselfe and Anne his Wife. Warrant given for these and 2 others by assignment. 10 Aug. 1694.

Willm. Man proved 4 rights: himselfe Jane Man Tho. Man Sarah Man Warrant given 17 July 1694 for 150 a.

Jean Harbut proved 7 rights: Wm. Harbut, Senior Wm. Harbut Mary Harbut, Jane Harbut, Ellinor Bennit, Robt. Stacy, Edward Boughoe. Warrant given. [1694]

George Ames proved 2 rights: Edw. George and John George. Assigned to Tho. Horton. Entered in Horton's warrant, assigned to Danl. Snoo[k].

Tho. Woolenford proved 1 right: himselfe. Assigned to Danl. Snook.

James Fisher proved 5 rights: himselfe, An Fisher, Mary Graves, James Fisher, Wm. Bentley. Warrant given for these and 3 assigned from Carle[ton].

Rich. Woolerd proved 2 rights: himselfe and Anne Woolerd. Warrant given 17 Sept. 1694.

George Mathewes proved 13 rights: Wm. Dennis, Johanah Dennis, Humphrey Willis, Eliz. his Wife, Mary Willis, Alexander More, Isaak Mello, Alexandr. Oliver, Charles Hues, Catee Mackdaniel, Tho. Evins, Wm. Dennis, on more. Put in his Warrant.

Jerimiah Brooks proved 2 more rights: Eliz. Ax Eliz. Brooks

Willm. Arrington proved 5 rights: Eliz. Oliver, Wm. Arrington, Eliz. Arrington, Sarah Arrington, Henry Gent.

Assigned the last to Robert Frasor.

Joseph Trowell proved 2 rights: Joseph Trowell Honer Trowell. Assigned to Tho. Horton. Entered into Horton's warrant.

Robrt. Inkison proved 3 rights: Sarah Cheeston John Tomson Mary an Indian.

Edward Yarnesey proved his owne right and assigned it to Nicholas Symons. Entered into Semons warrant. 4 Sept. [1694]

Wm. White proved 3 rights: Benjamin Pain Jos. Pain Peter Bassell. Assigned to Nicholas Symons and entered into his warrant. 4 Sept. [1694]

Nicholas Symons proved 1 right: Thomas Page Entered into his warrant 4 Sept. [1694]

p. 32
Willm. Carman proved 2 rights: himselfe and Eliz. his wife [1694]

Chowan Precinct Court, 2 July 1694. Edw. Sap proved 5 rights: Edw. Sap Mary his wife himselfe a second time and Mary and Eliz. his daughter Assigned to Rich. Wollert. Entered into Woolerd's warrant of Sept. 17.

Chowan Precinct Court, 2 July 1694. Dr. Godfrey Spruell proved 8 rights:
Godfrey Spruell Senior, Joana Spruell, Susanah Spruell, Anna Margeritta Spruell, Saml. Spruell, Godfrey Spruell junior, Nicholas Phelps, Sarah Walker.

Benjamin West proved 2 rights: Benjamin West and Francis West and John Morgan and Eliz. Morgan by assignment. Certified 20 Aug. 1694. Warrant given with 2 assignments the same day.

Charles Jones proved 6 rights: Charles Jones, An Jones, Hagar a Negro, John Griffen, Jos. Alford, and wife. Put into Jones's warrant with his purchased rights certified.

Robt. White proved 9 rights: Robert White, Mary White, Vincent White, Robt. White, Cutbert Phelps, Thomas Evins, John Dea[r], Thomas

Jones, and Anne Jones. Certified 18 July 1694. Warrant given 20 Aug. 1694.

John Godfrey for the orphans of Robert Smith proved 4 rights: Robt. Smith Eliz. Smith Sarah Smith Anne Smith Warrant given to Joseph Smith son of Robert Smith.

Albemarle. Anthony Markam, 150 a., for transportation of 3 persons, 29 Mar. 1680.
Anthony Markan Joy Markam her freedom right Joseph Hunt Transport Right

Mr. Anthony Markam proved 5 rights: Walter Darby Danl. Mackeel Two Negros and peter Furre. Certified 20 Apr. 1694 and warrant given.

p. 32 (reverse): Certificats of Rights
Perquimans Precinct Court, 7 Apr. 1690. James Fewox petitioning for the proving of 3 rights: James Fewox Anne his Wife Robert Fewox his son. Warrant given.

Albemarle. Rich. Elkes, 200 a., for transportation of 4 persons, 29 Mar. 1680. Rich. Elks Anne his wife Rich. his Son Margret his daughter Assignment by Ann Stuart to Argell Semmons 4 Sept. 1694. Warrant given 4 Sept. 1694.

Perquimans. Patrick Kenedy making oath in court that he imported 4 persons, for whom no land was taken up. Land due for importation of:
Patrick Kenidy Eliz. his Wife James Lowry and Elizabeth Kenidy his daughter. Apr. Court 1690.
Assignment by Patrick Kenidy to Juliana Taylor 28 Apr. 1690. Assignment by Juliana Taylor to Capt. Anthony Dawson 4 June 1694. Warrant given 10 Sept. with 2 rights.

Court 5 Feb. 1679. Mr. Joseph Chew proved 4 transportation rights: himselfe and his Man Robert Joanes with them guns Poder and Shott answerable to the same Lanslett Harrison his Servant and Eliz. his Wife. Two of them viz. Robert Joanes and Lanslett Harrison put into Mr. Chews warrant, 11 July 1694.

p. 33

Cornelius Lerry proved 6 rights: John Right Eliz. Right Austin Right Mary Right Cornelius Lerry and Mary Lerry. Certified 22 Aug. 1694.

Edmd. Roe Senior proved 2 rights: Edmund Roe and Nightingale his Wife
Assigned to John Burd. Certified 8 Aug. 1694.
Assignment by Danl. Akehurst of one right already proved, Anthony Carroll, to John Burd.

Palatine Court 20 Sept. 1692. John Burd petitioning for rights which were accordingly proved and entered.
John Burd An Burd John Smith An Byrd and Mary Burd. Warrant given.

Danl. Philips proved 1 right assigned to him by Wm. Johnson Namely Eliz. Thomas. Certified 20 Aug. 1694. Assigned to John Jones and put into his warrant.

Wm. Jackson Senior proved 2 rights: Robrt. Bowman and Isack Skinner. Certified 3 Sept. 1694. Warrant given and 16 a. due upon a former survey.

Albemarle. Giles Dolere, 250 a., for transportation of 5 persons, 29 Mar. 1680. Giles dolere Wm. Edgar John McLeen Tho. Jones Trustrum Brookes. These Rights Sould with the Land to Wm. Carterett and placed in his warrant.
Henry Pendleton proved 2 rights: Rich. Cradock and Lawrence Brasse. Certified 21 July 1694.

p. 33 (reverse): Warrants and Surveys.
Albemarle ss. Mr. John Fendall, 650 a., for transportation of 13 persons, 12 June 1694.
The Persons viz. Josiah Fendall, Mary his Wife Josiah Fendall junior, Mary Fendall, John Fendall, Robt. Fendall, Henry Fendall, Geo. Swan, Zachirias Gillam John Harbert, Mary Taylor, Abraham Hansford, Danl. Graham. 13
Survey and return for Mr. John Fendall, 640 a., 20 June 1694.

Albemarle, Willm. Bartlest, 250 a., for transportation of 5 persons, 5 Mar. 1693. The persons viz. Wm. Bartlest senior Eliz. Bartlest Wm. Bartlest junior Tho. Bartlest Michaell Bartlest.

Survey and return for Willm. Bartlest senior for 150 a., 50 a. by one right assigned by Wm. Gascoigne out of warrant granted him 5 March last, 2 July 1694.

Assignment by Wm. Bartlest of 3 rights to James Mills 24 Apr. 1694.

Albemarle ss. John Northcoat, 200 a., for transportation of 4 persons, 5 Mar. 1693. The persons are Henry Clay Senior Mary Clay Hen. Clay junior Pricilla Claye

Survey and return for John Northcoat, 116a., 5 July 1694.

p. 34

Albemarle ss. John Tomlins, 650 a., for transportation of 13 persons, 14 Mar. 1693.

The persons viz. John Tomlins, Wm. Bartlest, Wm. Bartlest junior, by certificate Rich. Nowell, Jane Nowell, Jno. Smith, Ellinor Nowell, Charles Taylor, Geo. Taylor, Mary Taylor, Oliver Nowell, Alice Nowell, Geo. Taylor upon 2d transportation the last ten assigned by Rich. Nowell.

Survey and return for John Tomlins junior, 300 a., 12 July 1694.

Survey and return for Willm. Tomlins, 288 a., 14 July 1694.

p. 34 (reverse): Warrants and Returns.

Albemarle ss. John Parish, 550 a., for transportation of 11 persons, 15 Mar. 1693.

The persons viz. Joshua Scott, and his Wife, and one Child, his two sisters, and Tho. Rabley, Tho. Jacocks, Anne Jacocks, Mary Jacock John Hofton, and John Parish.

Assignment by John Parish to John Hofton of all but 26 a. remaining due to Parish 12 July 1694. The excepted part put into a new Warrant of John Parish's.

Survey and return for John Hofton, 524 a., 17 July 1694.

Albemarle ss. Richard Nowell, 200 a., for transportation of 4 persons, 14 Mar. 1693.

The persons names viz. Alice Nowell, Rich. Nowell, Ellinor Nowell, Sarah Taylor

Survey and return for Rich. Nowell, 400 a., 200 a. by within warrant and 200 a. by another warrant dated 24 Mar. last, 17 July 1694.

Albemarle ss. Rich. Nowell, 250 a., for transportation of 5 persons, 24 Mar. 1694.

The persons Names viz. George Taylor Loomax Taylor Saml. West Wm. West Phebe West

Assignment by Rich. Nowell of 1 right: Phebe West to Tho. Allen, 14 July 1694.

Survey and return for Rich. Nowell, 400 a., 200 a. by within warrant and 200 a. by warrant dated 14 Mar. last, 17 July 1694.

Albemarle ss. Charles Taylor, 350 a., for transportation of 7 persons, 11 July 1694.

The persons viz. Geo. Taylor Ellinor Taylor Geo. Taylor junior Margery Taylor Loomock Taylor Charles Taylor and Charles Taylor his Freedom rt.

Assignment by Charles Taylor of 4 of the last rights and 18 a. to Thomas Allen, 19 July 1694. Warrant given for the said 4 rights and 1 from Nowell.

Survey for Charles Taylor, 132 a., 18 July 1694.

p. 35: Warrants and Returnes

Albemarle. Morgan Thomas, 250 a., for transportation of 5 persons, 5 Mar. 1693.

The persons viz. Morgan Thomas Dorathy his Wife two Children and one servant.

Survey and return for Morgan Thomas, 250 a., 19 July 1694.

p. 35 (reverse)

Albemarle ss. John Pricklove, 400 a., for transportation of 8 persons, 14 July 1694.

The person viz. John Pricklove, Eliz. his Wife Priscilla his Daughter, Rebecca Sebrell, An Wilson, junior, David Sherwood, and his Wife, the three last by assignment from Mr. Robert Wilson.

Survey and return for John Pricklove, 400 a., 7 Aug. 1694.

Albemarle ss. Hanah Hill, 750 a., for transportation of 15 persons, 14 July 1694.

The persons viz. Henry Phelps, Hanah his Wife, Jno. Phelps, Jonath. Phelps, Hanah Phelps junior, Robt. Paine, James Hill, Sam. Hill, Mary Hill, Math. Spivey, Judith his Wife, Jno. Spivey, Sarah Spivey, Anne Spivey, Jonathan Phelps his Freedom.

Assignment by Hanah Hill of the first 6 rights to Jonathan Phelps, 4 Aug. 1694.

Survey and return for Jonathan Phelps, 310 a., 6 Aug. 1694.

Assignment by Hanah Hill of 8 rights to Saml. Phelps, 4 Aug. 1694.

Assignment by Hanah Hill of the last right to Robert Wilson, 4 Aug. 1694.

p. 36

Albemarle ss. Austin Scarbrough, 450 a., for transportation of 9 persons, 11 July 1694.

The persons Austin Scarbrough, Anne Scarbrough, Mary Scarbrough, Anne Richison, Peter Mayfeld, Wm. Boyd, John Barber, Robrt. Parkes, and Geo. Scarbrough.

Survey and return for Augustin Scarbrough, 327 a., 31 July 1694.

Albemarle ss. Stephen Vincent, 150 a., for transportation of 3 persons, 3 Mar. 1693.

The persons viz. him selfe 2 transported and Mary Vincent

Survey and return for Stephen Vincent, 96 a., 2 Aug. 1694.

p. 36 (reverse)

Albemarle ss. Mr. Willm. Temple, 650 a., for transportation of 13 persons, 5 Mar. 1693.

The persons viz. Wm. Temple, Robrt. Temple, Mathew Woolridge, Elmer Berne, Sarah Hammon, Jno. Bishop, Mary Bishop, Mary Bishop, Jno. McDaniel, Eliz. Temple, Tho. Gregory, Eliz. Temple, Rich. Gregory

Survey and return, 191 a., 1 Aug. 1694

Albemarle ss. Wm. Jackson junior, 250 a., for transportation of 5 persons, 11 July 1694.

The persons, Jno. Watts Jane his Wife Sarah Jackson and Phebe Davis two times transported.

Survey and return for Wm. Jackson junior, 312 a., 18 July 1694.

p. 37

Albemarle ss. Robert Wallis, 400 a., for transportation of 8 persons, 5 Jan. 1693.

Robt. Wallis, Eliza. Wallis, Wm. Johnson, Robt. Jones, Thomas Wallis, John Laskins, James and Jonny two Negroes.

Survey and return for Mr. Robert Wallis 30 July 1694.

Albemarle ss. James Davis, 200 a., for transportation of 4 persons, 11 July 1694.
The Persons viz. Wm. Davis, James Davis, Wm. Whitehead, Phebe Pindar
Survey and return for James Davis, 160 a., 2 July 1694.

Albemarle ss. Mathey Kelly, 550 a., for transportation of 11 persons, 10 Mar. 1693.
The persons viz. Mathew Kelly and his Wife Indian Man and Woman Gilbert Goodall and his Wife Magdalen John Newby and his Wife James Newby Jno. Newby junior Eliz. Newby
Survey and return for Mathew Kelly, 360 a., 27 July 1694.

p. 37 (reverse): Warrants for Survey and Returnes.
Albemarle ss. Robert Lowry, 350 a., for transportation of 7 persons, 5 Mar. 1693/4.
The persons viz. Robt. Lowry, Hanah Lowry, Michael Percy and four from Saml. West namely Sam West, and his Wife, twice transported.
Survey and return for Robert Lowry, 260 a., 27 July 1694.

Albemarle ss. Wm. Man, 150 a., for transportation of 3 persons, 27 July 1694.
Jane Man Sarah Man Tho. Man
Survey and return for Wm. Man, 120 a., 26 July 1694.

p. 38
Albemarle ss. Wm. Turner, 350 a., for transportation of 7 persons, 11 July 1694.
The Persons Wm. Turner, Ruth Turner, Katherine Turner, Ruth Watkins, Henry Platt two transportations, John Lawrence.
Survey and return for Wm. Turner, 310 a., 26 July 1694.

Albemarle ss. Thomas Tweddy, 150 a., for transportation of 3 persons, 13 Mar. 1693.
Tho. Tweddy Eliz. Tweddy Eliz. Tweddy his Daughter
Survey for Mr. Tho. Tweddy, 300 a., 150 a. by within warrant and 150 a. by warrant dated 11 July, 25 July 1694.

Albemarle ss. Rich. Craig, 650 a., for transportation of 13 persons, 11 July 1694.

The persons viz. Rich. Craig, James Armestrong, Hanah Farmer, Wm. Sanderson, Wm. White, Wm. Sympson, Jonath. Taylor, John Lacy, Jno. Anthony, Cornelius Gowin, James Gowin, Sarah Mason, Eliz. Cob

Survey and return for Rich. Craig, 500 a., 25 July 1694.

p. 38 (reverse): Warrants for Survey and Returnes.
Albemarle ss. Patrick Bayly, 350 a., for transportation of 7 persons, 2 Mar. 1693.

The persons Names Patrick Bayley, Lucy Harvey, a Negro Woman, Margerett Hambleton two Rts. Jno. Hudson, Symon Daxter.

Survey and return for Patrick Bayley, 221 a., 23 July 1694.

Albemarle ss. Saml. Davis, 650 a., for transportation of 13 persons, 11 July 1694.

The persons viz. Wm. Hall, Eliz. Hall, Sarah Hall, Tony, Jack, and Margeret Negros, Sam Davis, Eliz. Davis, Tho. Gregory, Eliz. Gregory, Rich. Gregory, Eliz. Davis two times, transported. Assignment by Saml. Davis of one of the rights being the first of the within mentioned, 21 July 1694.

Survey and return for Saml. Davis, 95 a., and one for 326 a., 30 July 1694.

p. 39
Albemarle ss. Rich. Ruikes, 200 a., for transportation of 4 persons, 10 Mar. 1693.

The persons viz. Rich. Rookes, Mary Rookes, Eliz. Rookes, Tho. Rookes

Assignment by Rich. Rookes of one right, Eliz. Rookes, to Albert Albertson, 11 July 1694.

Albemarle ss. Jno. Davis, 100 a., for transportation of 2 persons, 13 Mar. 1693/4.

The persons viz. Jno. Morison and a Negroe Woman Named Joan

Survey and return for John Davis, 150 a., 100 a. by this warrant, and 50 a. for one right, Wm. Hall, assigned to him by Saml. Davis, out of a warrant dated 11 July last, 20 [*torn*]

p. 39 (reverse): Warrant for Surveys and Returnes
Albemarle ss. Wm. Godfrey, 250 a., for transportation of 5 persons, 5 Feb. 1693.

The persons viz. Prudence Hallum, John Hallum, Eliz. Hallum, Wm. Godfrey, Sarah Godfrey

Survey and return for Wm. Godfrey, 350 a., 250 a. by this warrant, and 100 a. by two rights, Francis Godfrey and Joan Godfrey, assigned him by John Godfrey from his warrant for 1400 a. dated 14 Mar. 1693, 15 July 1694.

Albemarle ss. Jno. Godfrey, 1400 a., for transportation of 28 persons, 14 Mar. 1693.

Persons Names Francis Godfrey, Joan his Wife, Fr. Godfrey, Wm. Godfrey, Edw. Godfrey, Tho. Roberts, Hanah Sheephook, Eliz. a servant, Lylly a negro Woman and 2 Children Dorathy, Cully, and Moyale, Perry, Mathew Wilson, Jno. Temple, Bridget Bowan, One Malatta Child, Wm. Bloomefeild, Tho. Hoskins, Jno. Skinklar, Eliz. [*torn*] four rights belonging to my Wife One Negroe man Called Lu[*torn*] Survey and return for John Godfrey, 640 a. and 310 a., 4 July 1694.

Assignment by John Godfrey of 2 rights, Francis Godfrey and Joan Godfrey, to Wm. Godfrey, 5 July 1694.

p. 40

Albemarle. Wm. Stewart, 400 a., for transportation of 8 persons, 13 Mar. 1693.

John Williams, Mary his Wife, Will. Williams, John Williams, Wm. Stuart, Eliz. his Wife, Eliz. Nice, and Nichol. Parson

Survey and return for Wm. Stuart, 238 a., 22 June 1694.

Albemarle ss. John Peirce, 300 a., for transportation of 6 persons, 16 June 1694.

Peter Small and the freedom right of John Fendall and Robert Fendall, assigned by John Fendall, and Ruth Peirce, John Peirce, and John Wilkison, assigned by Thomas Peirce.

Survey and return for John Peirce, 300 a., 20 June 1694.

p. 40 (reverse) Warrants for Survey and Returnes

Albemarle ss. Nicholas Semons, 500 a., for transportation of 10 persons, 4 Sept. 1694.

Nicholas Semons Anthony Hasket Senior John Grey Tabitha Grey Benj. Pain Joseph Pain and Peter Bassett and Tho. Page and Edw. Yarnesey and Robert Griffen.

Survey and return for Mr. Nicholas Semons, 360 a., 5 Sept. 1694.
Assignment to Leonard Loften, 40 a., 18 Sept. 1694.

Albemarle ss. Thomas Stacy, 400 a., for transportation of 8 persons, 1 May 1694.
The persons viz. Tho. Stacy, Rebecca Stacy, John, Thomas, Charles, Francis, Mary, and Elizabeth Stacy
Survey and return for Thomas Stacy, 100 a., [*torn*] Sept. 1694.
Survey and return for Jno. Foster, assignee of Thomas Stacy, 200 a., 15 Sept. 1694.
Survey and return for Leonard Loften, assignee of Thomas Stacy, 100 a., and 20 a. as assignee of Nicholas Semmons, 15 Sept. 1694.

p. 41
Albemarle ss. George Dear, 500 a., for transportation of 10 persons, 6 Sept. 1694.
Jane Cretchet, John Dear, Hanah Harrison, Edw. Harrison, Joseph Williams, Wm. Fyan, Hanah Fyan, Mercy Fyan, Eliz. Fyan, Lydia Harrison
Survey and return for Geo. Dear, 124 a.

Albemarle ss. An Stuart junior, 450 a., for transportation of 9 persons, 2[*torn*] Aug. 1694.
John Cropley, An Cropley, Mary Cropley, An Cropley junior, Eliz. Cropley, John Vines, James Fisher, Wm. Darby, John Darby
Survey and return for Vines Copley, assignee of An Stuart junior, 400 a., 7 Sept. 1694.

p. 41 (reverse) Warrants for Survey and Returnes.
Albemarle. George Peircy, 200 a., for transportation of 4 persons, 13 Mar. 1693.
The persons John Crew, Eliz. Crew, Eliz. his daughter, being assigned by Capt. Henderson Walker and George Peircy
Survey and return for George Peircy, 187 a., 12 Sept. 1694.

Albemarle ss. Argill Semons, 400 a., for transportation of 8 persons, 5 Sept. 1694.
Rich. Elkes, An Elkes, Rich. Elks junior, Margrett Elks, Lawrence Keeton, Edw. London, John King, Wm. Bread, the last four assigned by Wm. Glover

Survey and return for Argell Semons, 400 a., 18 Sept. 1694.

p. 42
Albemarle ss. Mr. Edw. Smithwike, 650 a., for transportation of 13 persons, 13 July 1694.
The persons viz. Lydia Shearin, John Sherin, Ralph Smithwike, Elizabeth Smithwike, Eliz. Bembrige, John Shearing, Lydia Shearing, 2d transportation Mary Shearing, Edw. Smithwike, Lydia his Wife, John Manyweathers, Rice Ward, Nicholas brightman.
Assignment by Edward Smithwike of the first 3 rights to George Dear, 12 Sept. 1694.
Assignment by George Dear of the above 3 rights to Anne Simmons, 15 Sept. 1694.
Survey and return for An Simmons, assignee of George Dear, assignee of Edw. Smithwike, 124 a., 13 Sept. 1694.
Survey and return for Edw. Smithwike, 380 a., "in a difference between the said Smithwike and Thomas Gillam," 22 Sept. 1694.

Albemarle ss. Mr. Jno. Hawkins, 350 a., for transportation of 7 persons, 11 July 1694.
The persons viz. Nathaniell Lawson twice transported Alexandr. Gooden by assignement from Joseph Sparnon viz. Mary Peirce, Wm. Jenings Senior Sabiana and Nan
Survey and return for Mr. John Hawkins, 350 a., 31 Aug. 1694.

p. 42 (reverse) Warrants for Survey and Returnes.
Albemarle ss. Wm. Collins, 500 a., for transportation of 10 persons, 19 Mar. 1693.
The names of the Persons viz. John Felton, John Wilson, a negro belonging to John Felton, Robt. Tredwell, Rich. Plater, Nicho. Allgood, Sambo, Tom, Negros Wm. Collins, Tho. Woodley
Survey and return for Mr. Wm. Collins, 500 a., 24 Aug. 1694.

Albemarle ss. Henry Keeton, 200 a., for transportation of 4 persons, 3 Mar. 1693.
Lawrence Keeton Ruth his Wife and a new England Indian due by a former Warrant and Mary Keeton her freedom.
Survey and return for Henry Keeton, 200 a., 18 Aug. 1694.

p. 43

Albemarle ss. henry Pendleton, 300 a., for transportation of 6 persons, 11 July 1694.

The persons viz. Henry Pendleton, Eliz. Carteret, Rich. Cradack, Lawrenc Bras, In the Record proved by Anthony Carell Two namely Eliz. Carrell and a new England Indian.

Survey and return for Henry Pendleton, 300 a., 18 Aug. 1694.

Albemarle ss. William Ro[sse], 600 a., for transportation of 12 persons, 11 July 1694.

The persons viz. Sarah Prince, Jane Prince, Wm. Prince, Wm. Westerman, Saml. Barnes, Edw. Chambers, Elizabeth Mowbery 2 transportations, John truebloud, Agnes trueblood, Mary trueblood a Negro Man Named Will.

Survey and return for John and Amos trueblood, assignees of Wm. Rosse, 600 a., 28 Aug. 1694.

p. 43 (reverse): Warrants for Survey and Returnes

Albemarle ss. Uriah Canon, 350 a., for transportation of 7 persons, 11 July 1694.

The persons Uriah Canon Danl. Howell, and Elizabeth his Wife, John Bishop, his Wife, and one Childe, Jno. Hill

Survey and return for Uriah Cannon and John Bishop, assignee of Cannon, 350 a., 27 Aug. 1694.

Albemarle ss. Wm. Jenings, 650 a., for transportation of 13 persons, 8 Mar. 1693.

The persons viz. Patrick Bayley, Lucy his wife, Joseph Sparnon, Alice Sparnon, Rob. Morgan, An Jackson, Joseph Jackson, Wm. Johnson, Mary Johnson John Relfe, Mary Relfe, and Mary an Indian Woman.

Survey and return for Wm. Jennings Senior and Thomas Johnson, assignee of Jennings, 600 a., 25 Aug. 1694.

p. 44

Albemarle ss. Elizabeth Coates, 200 a., for transportation of 4 persons, 11 July 1694.

The Persons viz. James Coates James McMurrein Jane McMurrein Wm. Watkins.

Survey and return for Elizabeth Coates, 150 a., 30 Oct. 1694.

Albemarle ss. Jno. Hunt, 1300 a., for transportation of 26 persons, 11 July 1694.
  The persons are Elizabeth Hunt, Thomas Drinkwater, Anthony Joy, Mary Mcfarloe, 4 Negroes and Jno. Clerk, Jno. Hunt, francis Hunt Wm. Dukes, Alice Norris, one Indian, and two Negroes, Wm. Bateman, Rich. Curteen, Nathanl. Batts, Saml. Alford, Geo. Beasly, and An tompson, Francis Marford, Cyprian, her husband, Giles her son
  Survey and return for Capt. Jno. Hunt, 450 a., 11 Oct. 1694.

p. 44 (reverse) Certificates of Rts. and Old Warrants
Mr. John Hawkins proved 7 rights: Alxandr. Goodwin and two by assignment from Nathaniel Lawson being to times transported and four from Joseph Sparnon being assigned to him, Mary Pearch Wm. Senior Sabina and Nan

Albemarle. Stephen Scott, 200 a., for transportation of 4 persons, 29 Mar. 1680.
  Step. Scott Sarah his Wife Step. Scott junior, Elinor Scott

Stephen Scott proved 2 rights: himself and one for his Wife Elizabeth. Certified 11 July 1694. Warrant given.

Mr. John West proved 5 rights: Winifrid West John Wades, Pisre Whon Cesar 3 Negros.
  Certified 17 July 1694. One by assignement from Jno. Browne to Mr. Danl. Akehurst namely John Browne, and two Rights assigned out of a Warrant of George Hare namely Henry Slade and Wm. Loverige, and two more out of a Warrant of Charles Boult namely Eliz. Boult and Geo. Kemp.

Albemarle. John and Benjamin West, 200 a., for transportation of 4 persons, 27 Mar. 1680.
  Jno. West, Benj. West, Robt. West and Joseph Calle.
  Warrant given.

Albemarle. Capt. Nathaniel Batts, 120 a., for transportation of 2 persons, 7 Sept. 1669.
  Tho. Cocks Annis Robison. Entered in warrant of Mr. Chew.

p. 45

Rich. Stamp proved 3 rights: John Stamp Tho. Stampe and Joan Stamp and one Right assigned to him by Jno. Lumbrosier Named John Reefe.
Certified 16 Apr. 1694.

Susanah Johnson, at court 1st Monday in Apr., proved 2 rights: by oaths of John Spencer and John Haly. And assigned to George Pearce and warrant given to Geo. Pearce assignee. [1694]

Uriah Canon proved 3 rights: himself and Two by assignement from Danl. Howell Namely Eliz. Howell and Johanah Howell. Certified 22 Aug. 1694. Put into John Bishop's warrant.

Henry Jones proved 4 rights: three Rights for himself being three times transported and one for his Wife.
Certified 1 Sept. 1694. Warrant given.

William Ros proved 7 rights: John trueblood Agnas trueblood Mary Trueblood Wm. Ros John Conden One Negro man Named Wist one Negro Woman Named Hanah
Certified 20 Aug. 1694. Warrant given.

Isaac Rowden proved 5 rights: Ebenezar Plump Robert Daily John Tosh Isaac Rowden and one Negro Man
Certified 17 July 1694. Warrant given.

30 July 1694. Jno. Bishop proved 4 rights: John Bishop his wife and Child and John Hill by assignment
Certified, warrant given.

p. 45 (reverse): Certificats of Rights and Perquimans Precinct Court, 2nd Monday in Oct. 1694
Jonathan Jones proved 1 right: himselfe.

Israell Snell proved 1 right: himselfe and assigned it to Jonathan Jones. Warrant given.

Lawrence Hunt proved 4 rights: Himselfe Eliz. Hunt and Rich. Berry twice imported. Warrant given.

Thomas Nichols proved 5 rights: Martin Cob Wm. Suds Ruth Cob John Lewis Saml. Brookes. Assigned to Danl. Snooke

Tho. Philips proved 3 rights: himselfe Mary his Wife and Peter Middleton and assigned to Danl. Snook.

Rich. Atkins proved 2 rights: himselfe and Eliz. Stuck.

John Hopkins proved 4 rights: Tho. Ralfe Eliz. his Wife Wm. Elfeck Wm. Eliz. Soon.

p. 47 (reverse): Patents
Willm. Wilkison esqr., 500 a., Chowan Precinct, for transportation of 10 persons, 14 Mar. 1693/4.
The persons imported are Wm. Wilkison, Tho. Gillam, An. Walker, Mary North, James Barton, Robt. News, Robt. Pike, Francis Heape, Tho. Pillips, Tho. Browne, in all ten persons.

John Jones, planter, 200 a., Chowan Precinct, for transportation of 4 persons, 14 Mar. 1693/4.
The persons imported are John Jones Elza. Jones John Jones Will Jones.

p. 48: Patents
Albemarle. Saml. Bundy, planter, 110 a., Pasquotank Precinct, for transportation of 3 persons, 20 Apr. 1694.
The persons names viz. Edw. Jones Danl. Johnson and Tho. Hilton being assigned to the abovesaid Saml. Bundy By Caleb Bundy out of his Warrant.

p. 48 (reverse): Patents
Albemarle ss. Tho. Harvey esqr., 631 a., Albemarle County, for transportation of 13 persons, 20 Apr. 1694.
The persons inported viz. Tho. Harvey, Hecto, Maria, Tom, Peter, nick, Maria, Nick, Betty Negroe, Eliz. Jordan, Katherine Gardiner a servant named Willm. a servant named Elinor.

Albemarle ss. Benjamin Lakar esqr., 538 a., Perquimans Precinct, for transportation of 3 persons, 20 Apr. 1694.
The persons Imported are Benjamin Lakar Elizabeth Lakars Benjamin Lakars junior.

Albemarle ss. Major Alexander Lillington, 640 a., Perquimans Precinct, for transportation of 13 persons, 30 Mar. 1694
The persons Imported viz. Tho. James, Sarah James, Joseph James, John James, Sarah James, Edward Wilson, Alexander Lillington, Sarah Lillington, Eliz. Lillington, John James, Joseph James, Eliz. Willis, Wm. Dickins.

p. 49 (reverse): Patents
Albemarle ss. Alexander Lillington esqr., 640 a., Perquimans Precinct, for transportation of 13 persons, 31 Mar. 1694.
The persons imported viz. Mary Walker, Peter Parson, Mary Greatbach, George Baccas, Hanah, Bes, Moll, Tho. Stanford, Eliz. Stanford, John Stanford, Ellinor Stanford, Mary Stanford, Sarah Stanford

Albemarle ss. Caleb Callaway esqr., 250 a., Perquimans Precinct, for transportation of 5 persons, 2 Apr. 1694
The persons Imported viz. Caleb Callaway, Eliz. his wife, Wm. Hughs, Edw. Bennit, and his wife

p. 50
Albemarle ss. John Barrows, Gent, 300 a., Perquimans Precinct, for transportation of 6 persons, 24 Apr. 1694.
John Barrows Sarah Barrows freedom rights Alexander Lillington Caleb Galloway John Barrows Will Hall

p. 50 (reverse): Patents.
Albemarle ss. John Gosby son of Hanah Gosby, widow, 300 a., Perquimans Precinct, for transportation of 6 persons, 1 Mar. 1693/4. The persons imported are John Gosby, John Anderson, John Kinsey, Rich. Waterland, Katherine Kinsey, Jane Anderson

Albemarle ss. Sarah Gosby daughter of Hanah Gosby, widow, 200 a., Perquimans Precinct, for transportation of 4 persons, 1 Mar. 1693/4.
The persons Imported viz. Stephen Hempworth Jer. White Henry Clay Hanah Nicolson.

p. 51: Patents
Albemarle. Tho. Symons, planter, 200 a., Pasquotank Precinct, for transportation of 4 persons, 17 Mar. 1693/4.

This 1702 petition to the justices of Chowan "persink" from a resident of Nansemond County, Virginia, asks for a land grant based on his transportation of five persons "into this Cuntre." CCR 187, State Archives.

Minutes of Chowan Precinct Court, ca. 1700, recording probates of headrights. Several claims were by assignment, one of which was of "one negro woman." A number of them include the statement that one of the rights claimed was for the claimant's wife. CCR 187, State Archives.

The persons Imported viz. Tho. Symons, Sarah Watts, Jack and tony Negroes.

p. 51 (reverse): Patents
Albemarle. Tho. Symons, 96 a., Pasquotank Precinct, for transportation of 2 persons, 1 Apr. 1694.
The persons viz. Ruth Pindar Sarah a Negro

Albemarle. Jerimiah Symons, 158 a., Pasquotank Precinct, for transportation of 4 persons, 1 Apr. 1694.
The persons viz. Jer. Symons, Jonathan Taylor, Andrew Maclewer, Nan a Negro

p. 52: Patents
Albemarle. Jane Charles, 287 a., w. branch of Yawpim Creek, transportation of 6 persons, 1 Apr. 1694.
The persons imported viz. John Edlin, Sarah his wife, Wm. Charles, Abigail his wife, Wm. his Son, Eliz. his Daughter

p. 52 (reverse)
Albemarle ss. Tho. Lepper, 470 a., Perquimans Precinct, for transportation of 10 persons, 1 Apr. 1694.
The persons imported viz. Tho. Kent, An his wife, Sarah Kent, Rebecca Kent, An Kent junior, John Thomas, Wm. Browne, Wm. Brickston, Tho. Lepper Nicols. Robison

Albemarle ss. John Wyate, planter, 288 a., Perquimans Precinct, for transportation of 6 persons, 1 Apr. 1694.
The persons imported viz. Wm. Wyate, Deborah Wyate Rebeca Wyate Mary Pearce and Joan an Irish woman and right to forty three acres assigned by Tho. Lepper

p. 53: Patents.
Albemarle ss. Timothy Cleare, planter, 473 a., on Perquimans River, for transportation of 10 persons, 5 Apr. 1694.
The persons imported viz. Mary Jones, Mary Fitsgarrett, Joseph Etshley a servant Charles two Indians three Negros Eliza. a servant in all ten.

p. 53 (reverse): Patents

Albemarle ss. Peter Grey, planter, 200 a., on Perquimans River, for transportation of 4 persons, 5 Apr. 1694.
The persons Imported viz. Peter Grey transported three times and his Wife

Albemarle. Edw. Smithwike, planter, 200 a., e. branch Mattacomack Creeke, for transportation of 4 persons, 1 Apr. 1694.
Mr. Hugh Smithwike Elizabeth his Wife Edw. and Hugh his sons.

p. 54
Albemarle. Jonathan Jones, planter, 350 a., n. side Mattacomack Creeke, for transportation of 7 persons, 1 Apr. 1694.
The persons imported viz. Willm. Ledford Anne Ledford Henry Lashley David Jones Affrica Jones Johana Flewelling and Philip Battle.

p. 54 (reverse)
Albemarle ss. Willm. Jackson, planter, 234 a., Pasquotank Precinct, for transportation of 5 persons, 16 Mar. 1693/4.
The Persons are Wm. Jackson Eliz. his Wife a Negroe named Nell Robert Bonane Isaak Skiner and the remaining 16 acres entered into his Warrant.

p. 55: Patents.
Albemarle ss. Humphrey Boulton, planter, 250 a., Pasquotank Precinct for transportation of 5 persons, 16 Mar. 1693.
The persons imported are John Boulton Eliz. his Wife Tho. Pendleton Henry Pendleton Mathew Pendleton

p. 55 (reverse)
Albemarle ss. Tho. Mackie, 150 a., Pasquotank Precinct, for transportation of 3 persons, 16 Mar. 1693.
The persons imported are Tho. Mackie Bridgett his Wife, Wm. Sympson

Patents.
Albemarle ss. Willm. Bundy, planter, 130 a., Pasquotank Precinct, for transportation of 3 persons, 2[torn] Apr. 1694.
The persons imported are Saml. Skiner Josiah Evins Wm. Jordan assigned by Caleb Bundy out of his Warrant.

p. 56: Patents.
Albemarle ss. Caleb Bundy, planter, 175 a., Pasquotank Precinct, for transportation of 4 persons, 20 Apr. 1694.
The persons imported are Wm. Jordan Humphrey Bung a negro named Luke and Wm. Elworthy.

p. 56 (reverse): Patents
Albemarle ss. John Spelman, planter, 350 a., Perquimans Precinct, for transportation of 7 persons, [*torn*] Apr. 1694.
The persons imported are Rich. Bentley, Jane Bentley, Mary Bentley, Sarah Bentley, a negre Boy, a Negro Woman, an Indian Boy

p. 57: Patents
Albemarle. Roger Snell, planter, 250 a., s. side Perqumans River, for transportation of persons, 20 Apr. 1694.
The persons Imported are Roger Snell, Mary Snell, Rebecca Snell, John Snell, Walter Chase

p. 57 (reverse): Patents
Albemarle. Robert Harman, planter, 92 a., Perquimans Precinct, for transportation of 2 persons, 20 Apr. 1694.
The persons imported are Robert Harman Elizabeth Harman

Albemarle ss. Thomas Peirce, planter, 300 a., Perquimans Precinct, for transportation of 6 persons, 20 Apr. 1694.
The persons imported are Tho. Peirce, John Peirce, Susan Peirce, Dorathy Peirce, Mary Peirce, Mary Briges

p. 58: Patents
Albemarle ss. John Cheston, planter, 300 a., Perquimans Precinct for transportation of 6 persons, 20 Apr. 1694. The persons Imported are Eliza. Cheston Archibell, Mary, Martha Hanah Sarah Cheston

p. 58 (reverse): Patents
Albemarle ss. Robert Beasly, planter, 282 a., on Perquimans River, for transportation of 6 persons, 1 May 1694.
The persons imported are Robt. Beasley, Sarah Beasley, James Beasley, Johanah Beasley, Rich. Cheston, Sarah Cheston

p. 59: Patents

Albemarle ss. Willm. Lacy, planter, 250 a., on Perquimans River, for transportation of 5 persons, 2 May 1694.
The persons imported are Wm. Lacy Senior, Wm. Lacy junior, Grace Lacy, Jno. Davis, Jane Davis

p. 59 (reverse): Patents for Land
Albemarle. Rich. Chaston, planter, 200 a., on Perquimans River, for transportation of 4 persons, 20 Apr. 1694.
The persons imported are Anne Chaston Danl. Chaston James Johnson Rachel Johnson his Wife.

Albemarle ss. Charles Macdaniell, planter, 143 a., on Perquimans River, for transportation of 3 persons, 1 May 1694.
The persons Imported are Charles Macdaniel, Elizabeth Macdaniel, Tho. Wallingford

p. 60
Albemarle ss. Jane Bayard, widow, 366 a., on Perquimans River, for transportation of 8 persons, 1 May 1694.
The persons Imported are Wm. Butler, Diana Butler, Wm. Johnson, James Johnson junior, Francis Grey, Tho. Grey, John Tweeger, and Wm. Carman for Sixteen acres.

p. 60 (reverse): Patents for land
Albemarle ss. Patrick Canady, planter, on Perquimans River, for transportation of 5 persons, 16 Mar. 1693.
The Persons imported are Timothy Cleare Francis Belchamp Wm. Redman Rich. Fox and Wm. Carman for ten acres the rest assigned to Jane Bayard.

p. 61
Albemarle ss. Richard Fox, planter, 200 a., on Perquimans River, for transportation of 4 persons, 22 May 1694.
The persons imported are Rich. Fox George Fox Wm. Fox Mary Fox

p. 61 (reverse): Patents for land
Albemarle ss. James Morgan, planter, 300 a., Perquimans Precinct, for transportation of 6 persons, 22 May 1694.
The persons Imported are James Morgan, and his Wife, Roger White, John Wilkison, John Stamp, Joan Vosse.

Albemarle ss. John Whitby, planter, 230 a., Perquimans Precinct, for transportation of 5 persons, 22 May, 1694.

The persons Imported are John Whitby Jack a negroe Honora an Irish woman Edw. Prat, Toby a negro.

p. 62

Albemarle ss. Robt. Beasley, planter, 218 a., Perquimans Precinct, for transportation of 1 person for every 50 a., 1 June 1694.

The persons transported are Wm. Lacy, Mary a negroe, James Hunter, Elizabeth Randolph, and the right to Eighteen acres being the remainder of a former warrant in page 24.

p. 62 (reverse)

Albemarle ss. Samuel Nicolson, planter, 300 a., Perquimans Precinct, for transportation of 6 persons, 22 May 1694.

The persons imported are Willm. Jones, Christopher Nicolson, Hanah his wife, Deliverance Sutton, Saml. Nicolson, Francis Symons.

p. 63

Albemarle ss. Willm. Bogue, planter, 200 a., on Perquimans River, for transportation of 4 persons, 1 May 1694.

The persons imported are Wm. Bogue, John Gray junior, Tho. Gray, Jahu Gray

p. 63 (reverse): Patents for land

Albemarle ss. James Loadman, planter, 143 a., on Perquimans River, for transportation of 3 persons, 1 May 1694.

The persons Imported are Hubbert Lambert Jane Bayard James Loadman

Albemarle ss. Albert Albertson, planter, 290 a., Perquimans Precinct, for transportation of 6 persons, 2 May 1694.

The persons Imported are Albert Alberson, Mary his Wife, Albert, and Esau his sons, Susannah, and Hannah his daughters

p. 64

Albemarle ss. Isaac Wilson, planter, 490 a., Perquimans Precinct, for transportation of 10 persons, 22 May 1694.

The persons Imported are John Hawkins, and his Wife, Saml. More, Rich. Clerk, Rich. Car, Jer. Harmon, Geo. More, Alex Goden, Ane Quinton, Tho. Kirke

p. 64 (reverse)
Albemarle ss. David Sherwood, planter, 350 a., Perquimans Precinct,
for transportation of 7 persons, 15 May 1694. The persons
Imported are James Thigpen, Eliza. Thigpen, James Thigpen,
Junior, John Thigpen, John Durant, Sarah Durant, a Servant
Named Judith.

p. 65
Albemarle ss. Capt. Ralph Fletcher, 370 a., on Perquimans River, for
transportation of 7 persons, 15 May 1694.
The persons Imported are Ralph Fletcher, Elizabeth his wife, Jacob
Cozens, Sarah a Negro, Tho. Cullen, Sarah Cullen, John Cullen,
two of which being old rights have 60 accres a patent by vertue of
an old warrant upon the acct. of armes and amunition

p. 65 (reverse): Patents for land
Albemarle ss. Jenkin Williams, planter, 317 a., on Perquimans River,
for transportation of 1 person for every 50 a., 15 May 1694.
The Rights for this land are Henry White Mary his wife Ann Cullen
Mary Cullen Christian Cullen and Martha Cullen and Seventeen
acres patent of the right for Sarah Cullen.

Albemarle ss. George Sutton, planter, 99 a., Perquimans Precinct, for
Rights assigned to him from Capt. Ralph Fletcher and Jenkin
Williams, 22 May 1694.
The rights for this land viz. Ninety three acres upon Rich. Cullen
and Sarah Cullen being all that remanes upon Capt. Fletchers
Warrant for 780 acres and 6 acres upon Jenkin Willms.

p. 66
Albemarle ss. Laurence Gonsalvo, planter, 560 a., Perquimans Precinct,
for transportation of 1 person for every 50 a., 25 June 1694.
The persons Imported are Laurence Gonsalvo John Johnson Tho.
Gonsalvo Sarah Johnson each twice transported Peter Jones
Laurence Gonsalvo junior Abraham Williams and Christopher
Morton.

p. 66 (reverse): Patents of Land.
Albemarle ss. Edward Smithwick, 350 a., Chowan Precinct, for
transportation of 7 persons, 20 July 1694.
The persons Imported are Richard Oliver Alice his Wife Sarah, An,
Mary Feelix and Margeret his Daughters

p. 67

Albemarle ss. John Fendall, planter, 640 a., on Perquimans River, for transportation of 13 persons, 20 July 1694.

The persons Imported are Josiah Fendall, Mary his Wife, Josiah Fendall junior, Mary Fendall, Jno. Fendall, Robt. Fendall, Henry Fendall, Geo. Swan, Zacharias Gillam, John Harbert, Mary Taylor, Abraham Hansford, Danl. Graham

p. 67 (reverse): Patents for Land

Albemarle ss. William Bartlift, planter, 150 a., Perquimans Precinct, for transportation of 3 persons, 23 July 1694.

The persons are Thomas Barclift Michael bartlift and one assigned from Wm. Gascoigne

p. 68

Albemarle ss. John Northcoat, planter, 116 a., Perquimans Precinct, for transportation of 1 person for every 50 a., 23 July 1694.

The persons imported are Henry Clay Senior Mary Clay junior Henry Clay junior

Albemarle ss. John Tomlins junior, 300 a., Perquimans Precinct, for importation of 6 persons, 23 July 1694.

The persons imported are John Tomlins Wm. Bartlift Senior Wm. Bartlift junior Rich. Nowell Jane Nowell John Smith by assignment from John Tomlins Senior.

p. 68 (reverse): Patents for Land

Albemarle ss. Willm. Tomlins, 288 a., Perquimans Precinct, for transportation of 1 person for every 50 a., 23 July 1694. The persons Imported are Ellinor Nowell, Charles Taylor, Geo. Taylor, Mary Taylor, Oliver Nowell, Alice Nowell for the last thirty eight acres these rights assigned to the said Wm. Tomlins by John Tomlins Senior.

p. 69

Albemarle ss. William Wilkison Esqr., 412 a., Chowan Precinct, for transportation of 1 person for every 50 a., 12 Aug. 1694.

The persons Imported are Mingo, Robin, Kent, Frank, Sambo, Coffe, Jack, Cottoe, Betty, Negro's

This patent granted upon return of patent formerly granted to Wm. Wilkison by Gov. Sothell according to an act entitled and act for Old Titles of land in That Case Provided.

p. 69 (reverse)
Albemarle ss. Smithwike Warberton, 300 a., Chowan Precinct, for transportation of 6 persons, 22 Aug. 1694.
The persons Imported are Robert Warberton, Eliz. his Wife, John Warberton, Mary Warberton, and Eliz. Warberton, and Cotton Robison

p. 70
Albemarle ss. John Hofton, planter, 524 a., Perquimans Precinct, for transportation of 1 person for every 50 a., 1. Sept. 1694. The Persons Imported are Joshua Scott, his Wife one Child his two sisters Thomas Rabley, Thomas Jacocks, Anne Jacocks, Mary Jacocks, John Hofton, and twenty four acres for John Parish

p. 70 (reverse): Patents for [Land]
Albemarle ss. Richard Nowell, planter, 400 a., Perquimans Precinct, for transportation of 1 person for every 50 a., 1 Sept. 1694. Alice Nowell Rich. Nowell Ellinor Nowell Sarah Taylor Geo. Taylor Loomox Taylor [*torn*] West Willm. West Imported

p. 71
[Albemarle] ss. Charles Taylor, planter, 132 a., for transportation of 1 person for every 50 a., 1 Sept. 1694.
The persons imported are George Taylor Ellinor Taylor and thirty Two acres for Geo. Taylor junior.

p. 71 (reverse)
Albemarle ss. Morgan Thomas [*torn*], Pasquotank Precinct, for transportation of 1 person for every 50 a., 1 Sept. 1694.
The Persons Imported are Morgan Thomas Dorathy his Wife Two Children and One servant.

p. 72: [Patents] for Land
Albemarle ss. John Peimce, planter, 300 a., Perquimans Precinct, for transportation of 1 person for every [50] a., 1 Sept. 1694. The Persons Imported are Peter Small John Fendall Robert Fendall Ruth Peirce John Peirce John Wilkison

Albemarle ss. Nicholas Semmons, planter, 360 a., Chowan Precinct, for transportation of 1 person for every 50 a., 6 Sept. 1694. The persons Imported are Nicholas Semmons, Anthony Hasket Senior, John Grey, Tabitha Grey, Robert Griffen, Benj. Peirce, Joseph Pain, and ten acres upon Peter Bassett

p. 72 (reverse)
Albemarle ss. Thomas Stacy, planter, 100 a., Chowan Precinct, for transportation of 1 person for every 50 a., 10 Sept. 1694. The persons Imported are Thomas Stacy and Elizabeth Stacy

p. 73
Albemarle ss. John Foster, planter, 200 a., Chowan Precinct, for transportation of 1 person for every 50 a., 15 Sept. 1694. The persons imported are Rebecca, John, Thomas, Charles Stacy

p. 73 (reverse): Patents for Land
Albemarle ss. Leonard Loften, planter, 120 a., Chowan Precinct, for transportation of 1 person for every 50 a., 16 Sept. 1694. The persons Imported are Francis Stacy Mary Stacy and twenty acres upon Peter Bassett

p. 74
Albemarle ss. George Dear, planter, 124 a., Chowan Precinct, for transportation of 1 person for every 50 a., 1 Jan. 1694. The persons Imported are Jane Cretchet John Dear and twenty four acres upon Hanah Harrison.

p. 74 (reverse): Patents for Land
Albemarle ss. Vines Cropley, planter, 400 a., Chowan Precinct, for transportation of 1 person for every 50 a., 1 Jan. 1694. The persons Imported are John Cropley, An Cropley, Mary Cropley, An Cropley junior, Elizabeth Cropley, John Vines, James Fisher, Wm. Darby

p. 75
Albemarle ss. George Peircy, planter, 187 a., Chowan Precinct, for transportation of 1 person for every 50 a., 1 Jan. 1694. The persons Imported are John Crew Elizabeth Crew Eliz. Crew junior and thirty Seaven acres upon Geo. Peircy

p. 75 (reverse): Patents for Land

Albemarle. Argell Semons, planter, 400 a., Chowan Precinct, for transportation of 1 person for every 50 a., 1 Jan. 1694. The persons Imported are Richard Elkes, An Elkes, Rich. Elks junior, Margeret Elks, Lawrence Keeton, Edw. London, John King, Wm. Bread

p. 76

Albemarle ss. Anne Simmons, daughter of Mathew Simmons deceased, 124 a., Chowan Precinct, for transportation of 1 person for every 50 a., 1 Jan. 1694.

The persons imported are Lydia Shearing, John Shearing and twenty four acres upon Ralph Smithwike.

p. 76 (reverse): Patents for Land

Albemarle ss. Edward Smithwike, planter, 380 a., Chowan Precinct, for transportation of 1 person for every 50 a., 1 Jan. 1694. The persons imported are Elizabeth Smithwike, Elizabeth Bembrige, John Shearing, and Lydia Shearing their 2d transportation Mary Shearing, Edward Smithwike, Lydia his wife and thirty acres upon John Manyweathers.

p. 77

Albemarle ss. John Hawkins, planter, 350 a., Pasquotank Precinct, for transportation of 1 person for every 50 a., 1 Jan. 1694. The persons Imported are Nathaniel Lawson, twice transported Alexander Gooden, Mary Peirce Wm. Jenings, Sabiana, and Nan

p. 77 (reverse): Patents for Land

Albemarle ss. Wm. Collins, planter, 500 a., Pasquotank Precinct, for transportation of 1 person for every 50 a., 1 Jan. 1694. The persons Imported are John Felton, John Wilson, a negro belonging to John Felton, Robert Tredwell, Rich. Plater, Nicholas Allgood, Sambo, Tom Negroes, Wm. Collins, Wm. Woodley

p. 78

Albemarle. Henry Keeton, planter, 200 a., Pasquotank Precinct, for transportation of 1 person for every 50 a., 1 Jan. 1694. The Persons imported are Lawrence Keeton Ruth his Wife a new England Indian Mary Keeton her freedom

p. 78 (reverse): Patents for Land

Albemarle ss. Henry Pendleton, planter, 300 a., Pasquotank Precinct, for transportation of 1 person for every 50 a., 1 Jan. 1694. The

Persons Imported are Henry Pendleton, Eliz. Carteret, Rich. Cradduck, Lawrence Bras, Eliz. Carrell, and a New England Indian

p. 79

Albemarle ss. John Trueblood and Amos Trueblood, planters, 600 a., Pasquotank Precinct, for transportation of 1 person for every 50 a., 1 Jan. 1694.

The persons Imported are Sarah Prince Jane Prince Wm. Prince Wm. Westeman Sam Barnes Edw. Chambers Eliz. Mowbery 2 transportations John Trueblood Agnes Trueblood Mary Trueblood A Negro named Will.

p. 79 (reverse): Patents for Land

Albemarle ss. Uriah Cannon and John Bishop, planters, 350 a., Pasquotank Precinct, for transportation of 1 person for every 50 a., 1 Jan. 1694.

The persons Imported viz. Uriah Cannon, Danl. Howell, and Eliz. his Wife, John Bishop, his Wife, and one Child, Jno. Hill.

p. 80

Albemarle ss. Willm. Jenings Senior and Thomas Johnson, planters, 600 a., Pasquotank Precinct, for transportation of 1 person for every 50 a., 1 Jan. 1694.

The persons Imported viz. Patrick Bayley, Lucy his Wife, Joseph Sparnon, Alice Sparnon, Robt. Morgan, An Jackson, Joseph Jackson, Willm. Johnson, Mary Johnson, John Relfe, Mary Relfe, and Mary an Indian Woman

p. 80 (reverse): Patents for Land

Albemarle ss. John Pricklove, planter, 400 a., Perquimans Precinct, for transportation of 1 person for every 50 a., 1 Jan. 1694. The persons Imported viz. John Pricklove, Eliz. his wife, Priscilla, and Rachell his daughters, Rebecca Sebrell, An Wilson junior, David Sherwood, and his wife

p. 81

Albemarle ss. Jonathan Phelps, 310 a., Perquimans Precinct, for transportation of 1 person for every 50 a., 1 Jan. 1694.

The persons Imported are Henry Phelps, hanah his Wife, John Phelps, Hanah Phelps, Hanah Phelps Junior Robert Paine

p. 81 (reverse)

Albemarle ss. Augustine Scarbrough, planter, 327 a., Pasquotank Precinct, for transportation of 1 person for every 50 a., 1 Jan. 1694. The persons Imported are Austin Scarbrough, An Scarbrough, Mary Scarbrough, An Richison, Peter Mayfeild, Wm. Boyd, John barbor, for the last twenty seven acres.

p. 82 (reverse): Patents for Land
Albemarle ss. Stephen Vincent, planter, 96 a., Pasquotank Precinct, for transportation of 1 person for every 50 a., 1 Jan. 1694. The persons Imported are the said Stephen Vincent and forty Acres upon Mary His Wife

p. 83
Albemarle ss. William Temple, planter, 191 a., Pasquotank Precinct, for transportation of 1 person for every 50 a., 1 Jan. 1694. The persons Imported are Willm. Temple Robert Temple Mathew Woolberge and Ellinor Berne for 41 Acres

p. 83 (reverse): Patents for Land
Albemarle ss. Wm. Jackson Junior, planter, 312 a., Perquimans Precinct, for transportation of 1 person for every 50 a., 1 Jan. 1694. The Persons Imported are John Wallis Jane his Wife Sarah Jackson and Phebe Davis 2 times transported.

p. 84
Albemarle ss. Robert Wallis Esqr., 400 a., Pasquotank Precinct, for transportation of 1 person for every 50 a., 1 Jan. 1694. The Persons Imported are Robert Wallis Eliz. Wallis Willm. Johnson Robert Jones Tho. Wallis John Laskin James and Jenny 2 Negros

p. 84 (reverse): Patents for Land
Albemarle ss. James Davis, planter, 160 a., Pasquotank Precinct, for transportation of 1 person for every 50 a., 1 Jan. 1694. The Persons Imported are Wm. Davis James Davis Wm. Whitehead and ten acres on Phebe Pindar

p. 85
Albemarle ss. Mathew Kelly, planter, 360 a., Pasquotank Precinct, for transportation of 1 person for every 50 a., 1 Jan. 1694. The Persons Imported are Mathew Kelly and his Wife, Indian Man and Woman Gilbert Goodall and his Wife Magdalen and ten Acres upon John Newby.

p. 85 (reverse): Patents for Land
Albemarle ss. Robert Lowry, planter, 260 a., Pasquotank Precinct, for
transportation of 1 person for every 50 a., 1 Jan. 1694.
The Persons Imported are Robert Lowry Hanah Lowry Michall
Perry and ten Acres upon Saml. West.

p. 86
Albemarle ss. William Man, planter, 120 a., Perquimans Precinct, for
transportation of 1 person for every 50 a., 1 Jan. 1694. The
persons Imported are Jane Man Sarah Man and twenty Acres for
Thomas Man.

p. 86 (reverse): Patents for Land
Albemarle ss. William Turner, planter, 310 a., Perquimans Precinct,
for transportation of 1 person for every 50 a., 1 Jan. 1694.
The persons Imported are Wm. Turner, Ruth Turner, Katherine
Turner, Ruth Watkins, Henry Platt, twice transported and ten
Acres for John Lawrence.

p. 87
Albemarle ss. Thomas Tweddy, planter, 300 a., Pasquotank Precinct,
for transportation of 1 person for every 50 a., 1 Jan. 1694.
The persons Imported are Thomas Twiddy Eliz. Twiddy and Eliz.
Twiddy his daughter Robert Wallis Rich. Brigs Ralph Coates

p. 87 (reverse): [Patents for] Land.
Albemarle ss. Richard Cragge, planter, 500 a., Pasquotank Precinct,
for transportation of 1 person for every 50 a., 1 Jan. 1694.
The persons Imported are Richard Crag, James Armestrong,
Hanah Farmer, Wm. Sanderson, Wm. White, Wm. Sympson,
Jonathan Taylor, John Lacy, John Anthony, Cornelius Gowin

p. 88
Albemarle ss. Patrick Bayley [planter], 221 a., Pasquotank Precinct,
for transportation of 1 person for every 50 a., 1 Jan. 1694.
The persons Imported are Patrick Bayley Lucy Harvey [*torn*] Negro
Woman Jno. Hudson and [twen]ty one acres for Symon [*torn*]ter.

p. 88 (reverse): Patents for Land
Albemarle ss. Saml. Davis, planter, 95 a., Pasquotank Precinct, for
transportation of 1 person for every 50 a., 1 Jan. 1694. The
Persons Imported are Wm. Hall and 45 Acres for Eliz. hall.

p. 89

Albemarle. Richard Rookes, planter, 150 a., Perquimans Precinct, for transportation of 1 person for every 50 a., 1 Jan. 1694. The Persons Imported are Rich. Rookes Mary Rookes Thomas Rookes

p. 89 (reverse): Patents for Land

Albemarle ss. Willm. Godfrey, planter, 350 a., Perquimans Precinct, for transportation of 1 person for every 50 a., 1 Jan. 1694.

The persons Imported are Prudence Hallum, John Hallum, Elizabeth Hallum, Wm. Godfrey, Sarah Godfrey, Francis Godfrey, Joan Godfrey

p. 90

Albemarle ss. John Davis, planter, 150 a., Pasquotank Precinct, for transportation of 1 person for every 50 a., 1 Jan. 1694. The persons Imported are John Morison, Joan a Negro and Wm. Hall.

p. 90 (reverse): Patents for Land.

Albemarle ss. John Godfrey, Gent, 310 a., Perquimans Precinct, for transportation of 1 person for every 50 a., 1 Jan. 1694. The persons Imported are Frances Godfrey, Wm. Godfrey, Edw. Godfrey, Thomas Roberts, Hanah Sheephooke, Eliz. a Servant and ten Acres upon Lilly a Negroe Woman

p. 91

Albemarle ss. John Godfrey, Gent, 640 a., Perquimans Precinct, for transportation of 1 person for every 50 a., 1 Jan. 1694.

The persons Imported are forty Acres Lilly a Negro Woman two Negro Children, Dorathy, Cully, and Moyale, Perry, Mathew Wilson, John Temple, Brigett Bowman, One Malatta Child Wm. Bloomfeild Thomas Hotkins

p. 91 (reverse): Patents for Land.

Albemarle ss. Samuel Davis, 326 a., Pasquotank Precinct, for transportation of 1 person for every 50 a., 1 Sept. 1694.

The Persons Imported are Sarah Hall, Tony, Jack, and Margret Negros, Saml. Davis Eliz. Davis and five acres to Elizabeth Hall and twenty one Acres for Thomas Gregory

p. 92: Land.

Albemarle ss. Wm. Stewart, planter, 238 a., Perquimans Precinct, for transportation of 1 person for every 50 a., 1 Jan. 1694. The persons Imported: viz. John Williams Mary his Wife Wm. Williams John Williams Wm. Stuart.

p. 92 (reverse)
Albemarle ss. Joseph Commander, planter, 100 a., Perquimans Precinct, for importation of 1 person for every 50 a., 1 Jan. 1694. The persons Imported are Joseph Comandr. and Dorathy his Wife

p. 93
Albemarle ss. Capt. John Hunt, 450 a., Pasquotank Precinct, for transportation of 1 person for every 50 a., 1 Jan. 1694. The Persons Imported are Elizabeth hunt Tho. Drinkewater Antho. Joy Mary Mcfarloe four Negros and Jno. Clerke

p. 93 (reverse): Patents
Albemarle ss. Elizabeth Coates, 150 a., Pasquotank Precinct, for transportation of 1 person for every 50 a., 1 Jan. 1694. The persons Imported are James Coates, James McMurrein, Jane McMurrein

p. 94: Warrants and returnes
Albemarle ss. George Fordice, 250 a., for transportation of 5 persons, 10 Oct. 1694.
The persons viz. Geo. Fordice Geo. Fordice junior Mary Fordice Hanah Fordice
Survey and return for Geo. Fordice, 244 a., 10 Oct. 1694.

Albemarle ss. Thomas Towers, 350 a., for transportation of 7 persons, 11 July 1694.
The persons viz. Thomas Towers and his Wife Each twice transported Mary Towers Margrett Burley and Charles Thomas
Survey and return for Thomas Towers, 160 a., 31 Oct. 1694.

Albemarle ss. Isaac De LaMare, 150 a., for transportation of names underwritten, 11 July 1694.
The persons viz. Isaac Delamare Francis Delamare and Ephraim Coates Survey and return for Isaac and Francis DeLamare, 125 a., 18 Oct. 1694.

p. 94 (reverse): Warrants and Returnes.
Albemarle ss. John Harris, 150 a., for transportation of 3 persons, 13 Mar. 1693.

The persons viz. Susanah Harris Jno. Deadman and Lewis dennis
Assignment by Susan Harris to Albert Albertson, 10 July 1694.

Albemarle ss. Albertson junior, 100 a., for transportation of names
underwritten, 15 Mar. 1693.
The persons are Albert Albertson and his Wife
Survey and return for Albert Albertson junior, 300 a., 100 a. by this
warrant, 50 a. by a Right viz. Elizabeth Rucks assigned him by Rich.
Rucks out of his Warrant for two hundred Acres dated 10 Mar.
1693, 150 a. by warrant assigned by Susanah Harris dated 13 Mar.
1693, 13 July 1694.

p. 95
Albemarle ss. Stephen Scott, 300 a., for transportation of 6 persons,
11 July 1694.
The persons viz. by an old Warrant Stephen Scott Sarah his Wife
Stephen Scott junior and Ellinor Scott by a certificate from
Pasquotank Precinct two persons namely Stephen Scott and
Elizabeth Scott freedom right. Survey and return for Stephen Scott,
300 a., 23 Oct. 1694.

Albemarle ss. Jno. Burnsby junior, 200 a., for transportation of 4
persons, 20 Oct. 1694.
The persons viz. James Gad Ellinor Scott Elizabeth Wells Edw.
Wells all assigned by James Gad
Survey and return for Jno. Burnsby junior, 200 a., 26 Oct. 1694.

p. 95 (reverse): Warrants and Returnes
Albemarle ss. Peter foree, 200 a., for transportation of 4 persons, 11
July 1694.
The persons viz. Peter foree Katherin Foree Mary Foree Margrett
Foree
Survey and return for Peter Fore, 194 a., 22 Oct. 1694.

Albemarle ss. Cornelius Leery, 300 a., for transportation of 6 persons,
18 Sept. 1694.
Jno. Wright Eliz. Wright Austin Wright Mary Write Cornelius Lerry
Mary Lerry
Survey and return for Cornelius Lerry, 150 a., 20 Sept. 1694.

Albemarle ss. Jonathan Bateman, 1000 a., for transportation of 20
  persons, 13 Mar. 1693.
  Jonathan Bateman, Margrett his Wife, Jonathan Bateman, Jno.
  Bateman, Robt. Davis, Rich Williams, Eliz. Williams, Saml. Pool,
  Henry Butler, Robert Robins, Johanah Robins, Negro Besse,
  Negro Sarah, Lawrence ArNold, Ann Collier, Eliz. Arnold,
  Rebecca Arnold, Jno. Arnold, Jno. Williams, Eliz. Williams.

p. 96
Albemarle ss. Jerimiah Sprouse, 500 a., for transportation of 10
  persons, 20 Oct. 1694.
  The persons viz. Patience Sprouse, Jerimiah Sprouse, Geo.
  Nicholls, Mary Nichols, Lambert Senior, Lambert Junior, Jane
  Lambert, Judith Spray, Eliz. Sprouse, Mingo a Negro.
  Assignment by Jerimi. Sprouse to John Lumbrozier, 26 Oct. 1694.

Albemarle ss. John Lumbrosier, 300 a., for transportation of 6
  persons, 11 July 1694.
  The persons viz. John Robison Elizabeth his Wife John Lumbrozer
  Jno. Robison junior Jobe Robison Elizabeth Robison
  Survey and return for John Lumbrizier, 300 a., and 100 a. assigned
  him by Jerimiah Sprouse's warrant dated 20 Oct. 1694, 26 Oct.
  1694.

p. 96 (reverse): Warrants and Returnes
Albemarle ss. Mr. [*sic*] Anne Durant, 400 a., for transportation of 8
  persons, 30 Aug. 1694.
  John Stinton, Dick, Abraham, Maria, Peter, Grace, Maria junior,
  and Harry
  Assignment by Ann Durant of 7 rights to Ann and Elizabeth
  Waller, 1 Oct. 1694.
  Survey and return for Ann and Elizabeth Waller, 350 a., 4 Oct. 1694.

Albemarle ss. Richard Stamp, 200 a., for transportation of 4 persons,
  11 July 1694.
  The persons viz. Jno. Stamp Rich. Stamp and Thomas Stamp, and
  one right assigned by Jno. Lumbrozier viz. Jno. Relfe
  Survey and return for Richard Stamp, 200 a., 15 Oct. 1694.

p. 97
Albemarle ss. Mr. Thomas Miller, 640 a., for transportation of 13
  persons, 23 Oct. 1694.

Thomas Miller, Senior Thomas Miller junior 3 times transported, Tho. Elliot, and his Wife, Saml. More, and his Wife, Saml. London, Jno. Putman, Elizabeth Larkin Lewis a french man, and Tho. Smith

Albemarle ss. Benjamin West, 400 a., for transportation of 8 persons, 20 Aug. 1694.
Saml. Blackwell, Mercy Jones, Thomas Jones, Mercy Relfe, by assignment from John Morgan and John Morgan and, Elizabeth Morgan, by assignment from the said Morgan Benj. West, and francis West Survey and return for Benjamin West, 400 a., 20 Oct. 1694.

p. 97 (reverse): Warrants and Returnes
Albemarle ss. Anthony Markam, 350 a., for transportation of 7 persons, 6 Mar. 1693.
The persons viz. Charles Sprouse, Dorathy Sprouse, Henry Sprouse, An Sprouse, Unity Sprouse, Mary Miller, Alice Sprouse, all assigned by Jerimiah Sprouse
Survey and return for Anthony Markam, 190 a., 19 Oct. 1694.

Albemarle ss. Anthony Markam, 400 a., for transportation of 8 persons, 15 Aug. 1694.
Anthony Markam, Joy Markam, her freedom right Joseph Hunt, Walter darby, Danl. Mckeele, 2 Negros Peter fur

Albemarle ss. Isaac Rowden, 250 a., for transportation of 5 persons, 15 Jan. 1693.
The persons viz. Elizabeth Plumb Robert Dally Jno. Tosh Isaac Rowden a Negroe man
Survey and return for Isaac Rowden, 230 a., 30 Oct. 1694.

p. 98
Albemarle ss. John West, 600 a., for transportation of 12 persons, 13 Mar. 1693.
The persons names are Winifrid West, Jno. Wades, Peter, Quon, Ceesar Negros, Henry Slate and Wm. Loverige, assigned out of Geo. Harris Warrant Eliz. Boult, and Geo. Kemp, assigned out of Charles boults Warrant and Jno. Browne
Survey and return for Mr. Jno. West, 600 a., 13 Oct. 1694.

Albemarle ss. Jno. belman, 650 a., for transportation of 13 persons, 12 Apr. 1694.
Jno. Crew and his Wife, Elizabeth Crew, his daughter one Negro man, two servant women one named Eliz. tod and Henderson Walker Robert Evins Francis Midleton Rich. Pryor one Negro woman and Hanah Hail Nicholas Daw by order of Capt. Walker on record in the Concell Journal
Survey and return for Jno. Belman, 280 a., 16 Oct. 1694.

p. 98 (reverse): Warrants and Returnes
Albemarle ss. Stephen Manwaring, 450 a., for transportation of 9 persons, 13 Mar. 1693.
The Persons viz. Ed. Berry Andrew Kinsey John Deadman Robert Brightwell Alice Brightwell Rich. Parker Jno. Casleton Step. Manwaring Robert Brightwell junior
Survey for Stephen Manwaring, 640 a., 40 a. by this warrant and 600 a. by warrant dated 16 Mar. 1693, 4 Oct. 1694.

Albemarle ss. Stephen Manwaring, 600 a., for transportation of 12 persons, 16 Mar. 1693.
Roger Pointon Edw. Davis Charles Marram Geo. Loveday Mary Mancell Ellex. Speed Alice Plater Ja. Smith Francis Salem Tho. Evins Senior Tho. Evins junior John Dunston
Survey for Stephen Manwaring 640 a., 600 a. by this warrant and 40 a. by warrant dated 13 Mar. 1693, 4 Oct. 1694.

p. 99
Albemarle ss. Francis Tomes, 640 a., for transportation of 13 persons, 5 Jan. 1693.
George Kendrick and Wife and one daughter and a maid Servant Francis Tomes his Wife Priscilla and one Servant Geo. one Maid servant Elizabeth Four Negroes Pottimer a Negroe
Survey and return of 240 a., 6 May 1694.

Albemarle ss. Jno. Wilson, 350 a., 11 July 1694.
Persons Jno. Wilson 2 transportation James Kinsello, Danl. Camwell Mathew Witlerit, Rich. Flower Francis Merrit
Assignment by Jno. Wilson, cooper, to Wm. Duckenfeild Esqr., 26 Jan. 1694.
14 Mar. 1692/3. Jno. Wilson entered 300 a. and assigned it to Wm. Duckenfeild Esqr., 26 Jan. 1694.

p. 99 (reverse)
Albemarle ss. Jno. Hare, 250 a., 11 Jan. 1695.
    Persons Jno. Hare, Lidia Hare, Jno. Bentley, Wm. Orendall, Ed.
    Orendall
    Survey for Jno. Hare, 100 a., 3 Feb. 1695/6.

Albemarle ss. Jno. Hare, 100 a., Perquimans Precinct, 17 Feb. 1696.
    For the transportation of Jno. Hare and Lydia Hare

Albemarle ss. Edw. Wilson, 300 a., 28 Mar. 1694.
    persons Ed. Wilson, Wm. Vincent, Mary vincent, An, Willim.
    junior, and Jno. vincent
    Survey for Edw. Wilson, 250 a., 30 Jan. 1695/6.

p. 100
Albemarle ss. Edw. Wilson, 250 a., Perquimans Precinct, 17 Feb. 1696.
    For the transportation of Edw. Wilson Wm. Mary An and Jno.
    Vincent

Albemarle ss. Fra. Wells, 200 a., 12 June etc.
    The persons Tho. Cullett Alexander Cullett Katherine Cullett,
    Arthure Carleton by assignment from said Carleton.
    Survey for Francis Wells, 200 a., 30 Jan. 1695/6.

Albemarle ss. Tho. Pollock Esqr., 450 a., 19 Mar. 1693.
    Persons Wm. Bred Lidia Bred Eliz. Palmer Tho. Palmer Timothy
    Callohan Jno. Hoolbeach Marea a Negro Archibald Grerey Robert
    Stanford
    Survey for Robert West Tho. West and Jno. West
    Assignment by Tho. Pollock Esqr. 2 tracts, 200 a. and 250 a., 15
    Oct. 1694.

p. 100 (reverse)
Albemarle Sc. Survey for Henderson Walker Esqr., 400 a., 10 Oct.
    1696
    Henderson Walker Esqr., 400 a., Perquimans Precinct, for
    transportation of 1 person for every 50 a., 9 Feb. 1696.
    Persons Imported Viz. Walter Green Eliz. Green Mary Green Tho.
    Hassold Timothy Clare francis an Inglish Boy Sarah James John
    James

p. 103 (reverse)

Albemarle ss. Mr. John West, 600 a., Pasquotank Precinct, for transportation of 1 person for every 50 a., 1 Jan. 1694. The persons Imported are Winifrid West, Jno. Wade, Peter, Quon, Ceesar negros, Henry Slate, Wm. Loverige, Elizabeth Bolt, Geo. Kemp, Jno. Browne

p. 104
Albemarle ss. Thomas Towers, planter, 160 a., Pasquotank Precinct, for transportation of 1 person for every 50 a., 1 Jan. 1694. The persons Imported are Thomas towers and his Wife Each two transportations.

p. 104 (reverse)
Albemarle ss. Isaac de Lamare and Francis De LaMare, planters, 125 a., Pasquotank Precinct, for transportation of 1 person for every 50 a., 1 Jan. 1694.
The persons Imported are Isaac De Lamare Francis De Lamare and twenty five acres upon Eprahim Coates

p. 105
Albemarle ss. John Belman, planter, 280 a., Pasquotank Precinct, for transportation of 1 person for every 50 a., 1 Jan. 1694. The persons Imported are John Crew and his Wife, Elizabeth Crew one Negroe one Woman Servant, and 30 acres for another [*torn*]

p. 105 (reverse): [Patents for] Land
Albemarle ss. George Fordyce, planter, 244 a., Chowan Precinct, for transportation of 1 person for every 50 a., 1 Jan. 1694. The persons Imported are George Fordyce, Geo. Fordice junior Mary Fordyce Sarah Fordyce Hanah Fordyce

p. 106
Albemarle ss. Albert Albertson junior, planter, 300 a., Perquimans Precinct, for transportation of 1 person for every 50 a., 1. Jan. 1694. The persons Imported are Susan Harris Jno. Deadman Lewis Dennis Eliz. Rookes Albert Albertson and his Wife

p. 106 (reverse): Patents for Land
Albemarle ss. Stephen Scott, planter, 300 a., Pasquotank Precinct, for transportation of 1 person for every 50 a., 1 Jan. 1694. The persons Imported are Stephen Scott Sarah his Wife Stephen Scott junior Elinor Scott Stephen Scott and Elizabeth his Wife Freedom rights.

p. 108

Albemarle ss. Jno. Burnsby junior, planter, 200 a., Pasquotank Precinct, for transportation of 1 person for every 50 a., 1 Jan. 1694. The persons Imported are James Gad Ellinor Scott Edw. Wallis Elizabeth Wallis.

p. 108 (reverse): Patents for Land

Albemarle ss. Peter Foree, planter, 194 a., Pasquotank Precinct, for transportation of 1 person for every 50 a., 1 Jan. 1694. The persons Imported are Peter Foree Katherine Fore Mary Foree Margret Foree

p. 109

Albemarle ss. Cornelius Lerry, planter, 150 a., Perquimans Precinct, for transportation of 1 person for every 50 a., 1 Jan. 1694. The persons Imported are John Wright Elizabeth Wright Austin Wright

p. 109 (reverse): Patents for Land.

Albemarle ss. John Arnold, planter, 150 a., Perquimans Precinct, for transportation of 1 person for every 50 a., 1 Jan. 1694. The persons Imported are John Arnold John Williams Eliz. Williams by assignement from Jonathan Bateman

p. 110

Albemarle ss. John Lumbrozier, planter, 400 a., Pasquotank Precinct for transportation of 1 person for every 50 a., 1 Jan. 1694.
The persons Imported are Patience Sprouse, Jerimiah Sprouse, John Robison Senior, Eliza. his Wife, Jno. Lumbrozier John Robison junior, Jobe Robison, Elizabeth Robison

p. 110 (reverse): Patents for Land.

Albemarle ss. Ann Waller and Elizabeth Waller, 350 a., Perquimans Precinct, for transportation of 1 person for every 50 a., 1 Jan. 1694.
The persons Imported are Dick, Abram. Maria Peter Grace Maria junior and Harry Negros.

p. 111

Albemarle ss. Richard Stamp, planter, 200 a., Pasquotank Precinct, for transportation of 1 person for every 50 a., 1 Jan. 1694.
The persons Imported are Jno. Stamp Rich. Stamp Thomas Stamp and Thomas Relfe

p. 111 (reverse): Patents for Land
Albemarle ss. Thomas Miller, planter, 640 a., Pasquotank Precinct,
for transportation of 1 person for every 50 a., 1 Jan. 1694.
The persons Imported are Thomas Miller Senior Thomas Miller
junior 3 times transported Tho. Eliot and his Wife Saml. More and
his Wife Saml. London Jno. Putman Elizabeth Larkin Lewis a
French man and Henry Smith.

p. 112
Albemarle ss. Benjamin West, planter, 400 a., Pasquotank Precinct,
for transportation of 1 person for every 50 a., 1 Jan. 1694.
The persons Imported are Saml. Blackwell, Mercy Jones, Tho.
Jones, Mercy Relfe, Jno. Morgan, Eliz. Morgan, Benj. West, francis
West

p. 112 (reverse): Patents for Land
Albemarle ss. Anthony Markam, planter, 190 a., Pasquotank Precinct,
for transportation of 1 person for every 50 a., 1 Jan. 1694.
The persons Imported are Charles Sprouse Dorathy Sprouse
Henry Sprouse and 40 acres for Ann Sprouse.

p. 113
Albemarle ss. Anthony Markam, planter, 560 a., Pasquotank Precinct,
for transportation of 1 person for every 50 a., 1 Jan. 1694. The
persons Imported are ten Acres upon Ann Sprouse Unity
Sprouse, Mary Miller, Alice Sprouse, Anthony Markam, Joy
Markam, Joseph Hunt, Walter darby, Danl. Mackeel 2 Negros and
Peter Fur

p. 113 (reverse): Patents for Land
Albemarle ss. Isaac Rowden, planter, 230 a., Pasquotank Precinct, for
transportation of 1 person for every 50 a., 1 Jan. 1694. The
persons Imported are Ebenezer Plumb Robert Dally Jno. Tosh
Isaack Rowden and a Negro Man

p. 114
Albemarle ss. Jno. Belman, planter, 314 a., Pasquotank Precinct, for
transportation of 1 person for every 50 a., 1 Jan. 1694. The
persons Imported are one Woman Servant for fourteen acres
Henderson Walker, Robert Evans, Francis Middleton, Rich.
Pryer, one Negro Woman, Hanah Hail

p. 115 (reverse): Patents for Land

Albemarle ss. John Cooke, planter, 300 a., Perquimans Precinct, for transportation of 1 person for every 50 a., 1 May 1695. The Persons Imported viz. Lawrence Gonsalvo Dorathy and Sarah his Wifes Tho. Gonsalvo James Freeman Christopher Norton

p. 116

Albemarle ss. Stephen Manwaring, planter, 640 a., on Perquimans River, for transportation of 1 person for every 50 a., 1 May 1695. The persons viz. Roger Pointon Edw. Davis Charles Marram Geo. Loveday, Mary Mancel, Alex. Speed Alice Plater James Smith Francis Salem Tho. Evins Senior Tho. Evins junior John dunston Edw. Berry

p. 116 (reverse): Patents for Land.

Albemarle ss. Francis Tomes Esqr., 640 a., Perquimans Precinct, 140 a. by purchase from Wm. Charles, 260 a. by purchase from Charles Sprows and the rest for transportation of 1 person for every 50 a., 1 May 1695.
The persons Imported Francis Tomes's Wife Precilla Geo. Kendrick and his Wife and one Daughter and a Maid servant.

p. 118

Albemarle County ss. Rob. West Tho. West and Jno. West, 250 a., Pasquotank Precinct, 17 Feb. 1696.
For the Transportation of Wm. Bread Lidia Bread Eliz. Palmer Tho. Palmer.

p. 118 (reverse)

Albemarle County ss. Francis Wells, 200 a., Chowan Precinct, for transportation of 1 person for every 50 a., 25 Feb. 1696. For transportation of Tho. Alexander Katherine Gullet Arthure Carleton

Albemarle ss. Wm. Charleton, 250 a., 11 July 1694.
persons Lawrence Bethinia Luke Ellinor Meazell Wm. Charleton and 4 first assigned by Law. Meazell
13 June 1695 Survey for Wm. Charleton 250 a.

p. 119

Albemarle County. Wm. Charleton, 240 a., Chowan Precinct, 25 Feb. 1696. For the transportation of Lawrence, Luke, and Bethinia Meazell Ellinor Meazell and Wm. Charleton

Albemarle ss. Robert West Tho. West and Jno. West "in Comon," 200 a., Pasquotank Precinct, 17 Feb. 1696.
For the transportation of Timothy Callohan Jno. Hoolbeach Marea a Negro Archibald Grery and Robert Stanford.

p. 119 (reverse): Patents.
Albemarle ss. Danl. Snooke, 200 a., for transportation of 1 person for every 50 a., 21 July 1694.
Tho. Wallingford Danl. Snooke Margrett Snooke Roger Pointon. Survey and return for Danl. Snooke, 450 a., 200 a. by this warrant and 200 a. by 4 rights assigned by Jno. Lilly, and 50 a. by 1 right assigned out of Charles Macdanll.'s warrant, 30 Jan. 1695/6.

Albemarle ss. Jno. Lilly, 400 a., 21 July 1694.
Jno. Lilly Senior Eliz. Lilly Jane Lilly Eliz. Johnson Jno. Lilly Junior 3 transport Hanah Lilly.
Assignment by Jno. Lilly of 4 of the first rights to James Thigpen and the remainder to Danll. Snooke, 6 Aug. 1694.

Albemarle ss. Edw. Holmes, assignee of Danl. Snooke, 450 a., Perquimans Precinct, (continued on reverse of p. 121)

p. 120
Albemarle ss. Henry Palin junior, 139 a., Pasquotank Precinct, 25 Feb. 1696.
For the transportation of Jno. Bornsby Senior Charles Bolt Tony a Negro

Albemarle ss. Danll. Philips, 400 a., 11 July 1694. persons viz. Michael Mackdanl. Joan his wife, Mary McDanll., Francis McDanl., Rich Kemp, Rich. Foster, and by assignment Tho. Wallis and Eliz. Wallis. Survey for Tho. Barcock, assignee of Danl. Philips, 400 a., 200 a. by this warrant and 200 a. by warrant dated 29 Oct. 1695, 11 July 1696.

Tho. Barcock [*torn*] (continued top of p. 122)

p. 120 (reverse)
Albemarle ss. Henry Palin junior, 750 a., 11 July 1694.

The persons viz. Henry Palin, and his wife, Dick a Negro, Jno. Bornsby senior, Sarah his wife, Wm. Croney, Jno. Bornsby junior, Charles Boult, Tony, Boatswan Negros Ellinor White Servant, Sarah Hammond, Wm. Bornsby, and Henleys Wife and his Mother, 15.

Survey for Henry Palin junior, 234 a., 5 Sept. 1695.

Survey for Henry Palin junior, 139 a., 6 Sept. 1695.

Albemarle ss. Henry Palin junior, 334 a., Pasquotank Precinct, for transportation of 1 person for every 50 a., 25 Feb. 1696. for the Importation of Henry Palin and, his wife, Dick a Negro, Jno. Bornsby Senior, Sarah his wife, Wm. Croney

p. 121

Albemarle ss. Rich. Pope, 650 a., 19 Mar. 1693.

[*torn*] persons Imported viz. Rich. Pope [*torn*] McMorin 2 Negros Wm. Indicott Negro 4 Negros Wm. Jones Stephen [R]ichison a Woman Servant, 13

Survey for Mr. Rich. Pope, 314 a., 30 Jan. 1695/6.

Albemarle ss. Rich. Pope, 314 a., Pasquotank Precinct, 25 Feb. 1696. For the Importation of Rich. Pope Jno. McMorin Wm. Indicot and 4 Negros.

p. 121: (reverse): (continued from reverse of p. 1.19)

for transportation of 1 person for every 50 a., 25 Feb. 1696.

The persons names Tho. Wallingford Danl. Snooke Margrett Snooke Roger Pointon Jno. Lilly junior 3 transportations Hanah Lilly Saml. Powell.

p. 122: (continued from p. 120)

29 Oct. 1695.

persons viz. Tho. Barcock Margrt. his wife a Servant named Willm. Tho. James by old warrant 2 Negros and 2 transportation of Rich. Car.

Survey for Tho. Barcock, 200 a., 12 June 1696.

Survey for Tho. Barcock, 400 a., 200 a. by assignment of Danl. Philips and by survey, 12 J[une 1696]

Albemarle ss. Tho. Barcock, 400 a., s.w. side Pasquotank River, 25 Feb. 1696

For the transportation of Michael MacDanll. Jone his wife Mary McDaniell Francis McDanl. Tho. Barcock and his wife a servant named William Tho. James.

p. 122 (reverse)
Tho. Barcock, 200 a., n.e. side Pasquotank River, 25 Feb. 1696 [*torn*] the transportation of [*torn*] Negros and 2 transportations of Rich. Car.

Albemarle. Patrick Henley, 1100 a., 3 Mar. 1693.
the persons viz. Jno. Culpeper, Jno. Robison, Jacko, Grace, 2 Negros Valentine Bird, betty, bes, Mingo, and Tom Negros, Andrew, Jumpo, Maria, Jane, An Farmer, Pa. Henley, Eliz. Duff, betty negro, Sarah Henley Margrett Byrd Sarah Byrd, 22 Survey for Stephen Scott, assignee of Patrick Henley, 247 a., 12 June 1696.

Albemarle ss. Stephen Scott, 274 a., s.w. side Pasquotank River, 25 Feb. 1696.
For the transportation of Jno. Culpeper Jno. Robison Valentine Byrd Jaco. Grace and Betty Negros.

p. 123
Albemarle ss. Rich. Madren, 150 a., 11 July 1694.
persons Rich. Madren Eliz. his wife Ann Baldrige, 3 Survey for Rich. Madren, 150 a., 12 June 1696.

Albermale C. Richard Madren, 150 a., s.w. side Pasquotank River, 25 Feb. 1696.
For the transportation of Rich. Madren Eliz. his wife An Daldrige

p. 123 (reverse)
Albemarle ss. Jno. Hawkins, 250 a., 3 Mar. 1693.
persons viz. Jno. Hawkins Sarah his wife 2 Negroes Jno. Cabbage, 5 Survey for Mr. Jno. Hawkins, 252 a., 250 a. by this warrant and 2 a. by assignment, 12 June 1696.

Albemarle. Jno. Hawkins, 252 a., n.e. side Pasquotank River, 25 Feb. 1696.
For the Importation of Jno. Hawkins Sarah his wife 2 Negroes Jno. Cabbage

Albemarle ss. Jno. Jenings, 1100 a., 9 Mar. 1693

[*torn*] persons viz. Tho. Robison, Betty, dick, Jack, Negroes Wm. Jenings, Martha his wife, Jno. Jening, Annis Jennings, Ralph Garnet, Margret Garnet, Nat. Nicols, Ann [G]rant, Wm. Garner, a servant boy named Robert, Tho. Relfe 2 Rts. Dorathy his wife, Tho. Relfe junior, [*torn*] More, Wm. Gardner, Jno. Jenings, Wm. Relfe, 22.

Survey for Wm. Jenings junior, assignee of Jno. Jenings, 450 a., 12 June 1696.

Survey for Tho. Sawyer, assignee of Jno. Jenings, 450 a., 12 June 1696.

Survey for Tho. Sawyer, assignee of Jno. Jenings, 200 a., 12 June 1696.

p. 124

Albemarle ss. Wm. Jenings, 450 a., n.e. side Pasquotank River, 25 Feb. 1696.
For the transportation of Tho. Robison, Bett, Dick, Jack, Negroes, Wm. Jenings, Martha his Wife, Tho. Jenings, Annis Jenings, Ralphe Garnett

Albemarle. Tho. Sawyer, 450 a., n.e. side Pasquotank River, 25 Feb. 1696.
For the transportation of Margrett Garnet, Nath. Nicols, Ann Grant, Wm. Garner, a servant boy named Robert, Tho. Relfe 2 Rts. Dorathy his wife Tho. Relfe junior

p. 124 (reverse)

Albemarle. Tho. Sawyer, 200 a., n.e. side Pasquotank River, 25 Feb. 1696. For the Importation of Jno. More Wm. Gardner Jno. Jenings Wm. Relfe.

Albemarle ss. Danl. Johnson Senior, 250 a., 24 Sept. 1695.
persons Rich. Roads, Jno. Taylor, Rich. Fowler, assigned by Henry White Jno. Hatten, Eliz. Hatton, assigned by Jno. Hatton Survey for Mr. Danll. Johnson, 240 a., 31 Jan. 1695/6.

p. 125

Albemarle. Danl. Johnson, 240 a., Pasquotank Precinct, 25 Feb. 1696.
For the Importation of Rich. Roads, Jno. Taylor, Rich. Fowler, Jno. Hatton, Eliz. Hatton

Albemarle ss. Rich. Woolerd, 300 a., Perquimans Precinct, 25 Feb. 1696. For the Importation of Rich. Woolerd Ann Woolerd Ed. Sap Mary his wife Mary and Elizabeth his daughters.

Albemarle ss. Rich Woolerd, 350 a., 17 Sept. 1694.
persons Rich. Woolerd An Woolerd Edw. Sap Mary his Wife Mary and Eliz. his daughters Edw. Saps 2d transportation
Survey for Rich. Woolerd, 300 a., 7 June 1695.

p. 125 (reverse)
Albemarle ss. Laurence Hunt, 200 a., 15 Oct. 1694. Persons Lawrence Hunt, Eliz. his Wife, Rich. Berry 2 transportations, 4
Survey, 200 a., 31 Oct.

Albemarle ss. Lawrence Hunt, 200 a., Perquimans Precinct, 25 Feb. 1696. For the transportation of Laurence Hunt Eliz. his Wife Rich. Berry 2 transportations

Albemarle. Jno. Willoughby, 200 a., 13 Mar. 1693.
persons Jno. Willoughby Deborah his Wife and 2 Children, 4
Survey for Jno. Willoughby, 192 a., 20 Sept. 1695

Albemarle ss. Jno. Willoughby, 192 a., on Perquimans River, 25 Feb. 1696
for the Importation of Jno. Willoughby Deborah his Wife and 2 Children

p. 126
Albemarle ss. James Gad, 200 a., 11 July 1694.
persons James Gad 2d transportations Isabel and Elizabeth 2 women servants, Tho. Poore, 4
Survey for James Gad 200 a., 22 Oct. 1694.

Albemarle ss. Ja. Gad, 200 a., Pasquotank Precinct, 25 Feb. 1696 For the Importation of James Gad Isabell and Eliz. 2 Woman Servants Tho. Poore
Wm. Windbery, 250 a., 27 Apr. 1696.
Persons Wm. Windbery and by assignment of W. Jones, Wm. Jones Senior Wm. jones junior 3 times transported 27 Apr. 1696 Survey for Wm. Windbery 250 a.

p. 126 (reverse)
Albemarle ss. Wm. Windbery, 250 a., Pasquotank Precinct, 25 Feb.
1696.
For the Importation of Wm. Windbery Wm. Jones Senior Wm.
Jones junior 3 times transported.

Albemarle ss. Henry Sawyer, 300 a., 2 June 1695.
persons Susan Jones Jane Sawyer Alexander Davis 3
transportations Sarah Sawyer
Survey for Henry Sawyer, 190 a., 2 Apr. 1696.

Albemarle ss. Henry Sawyer, 190 a., Pasquotank Precinct, 25 Feb.
1696. For the Importation of Susan Jones and 3 Importations of
Alexander Davis

p. 127
Albemarle ss. Thomas Cartwrite, 650 a., 11 July 1694.
persons Tho. Carteret, Mary, his Wife, Jno. Carterett, Wm.
Carterett, Ed Foster, Jno. Callono, James Perishaw, Peter
Dardinoe, Wm. Bentley, Charles Haly, Grace Carteret, Griffen
Lawrence, Mary his wife
Survey for Tho. Cartwrite, 640 a., 14 Oct. 1695.

Albemarle ss. Tho. Cartwright, 640 a., Pasquotank Precinct, 25 Feb.
1696.
For the transportation of Tho. Cartwright, Mary his Wife, Jno. and
Wm. Cartwrt., Ed. Foster, Jno. Callanore, Ja. Perishaw, Peter
Dardinoe, W. Bentley, Cha. Haley, Grace Cartwrt., Griffen
Lawrence, Mary his wife.
Philip Evins, 200 a., 28 Mar. 1696
Persons Philip Evins 2 transportations Wm. Walbeton and Wm.
Philips assigned by Geo. Harris
Survey for Philip Evins, 127 a., 28 Mar. 1696

Albemarle ss. Philip Evins, 127 a., Pasquotank Precinct, 25 Feb. 1696
For the Importation of Philip Evins 2 transportation Wm.
Walbeton

p. 127 (reverse)
Albemarle ss. Tho. Stanton, 350 a., 17 Oct. 1694.

persons etc. Tho. Stanton Rich Miller, Tho. Righorne, Tho. Burnsby, Wm. Bournsby, Jno. Newman, assigned out of Jno. Bournsby Warrant and Miles Boursby

Survey for Tho. Stanton, 424 a., 350 a. by this warrant and 74 a. by 2 rights assigned out of Jn. Bournsby's warrant dated 11 July 1694, viz. Jno. Camell and Jno. Morgan, 2 Sept. 1695.

Albemarle ss. Tho. Stanton, 424 a., Pasquotank Precinct, 25 Feb. 1696.
For the Importation of Tho. Stanton Rich Miller Tho. Righorne Tho. Bournsby Wm. Bournsby Miles Bournsby Jno. Newman

p. 128
Albemarle ss. Wm. Glover, 550 a., 16 Nov. 1695.
Persons Zachary Nixon Law. Keeton Edw. London Jno. King Wm. Bread Joseph a servant Jno. Davis Griffen Wallis Ellinor a servant Jno. Nixons Wife Robert Griffen by assignment from Ed. Mayo
Assignment by W. Glover of 7 rights to Capt. Wm. Speight Survey for Capt. Wm. Speight, 320 a., 30 Jan. 1695/6.

Albemarle ss. Thomas Speight, son and heir of Capt. Wm. Speight, 320 a., Perquimans Precinct, 9 Feb. 1696.
for the transportation of Zachary Nixon Law. Keeton Ed. London Jno. King Wm. Bread Joseph a servant Jno. Davis

Albemarle ss. Mr. Tho. Speight, 500 a., 2 Feb. 1696/7.
Persons Tho. Speight Rich Malbone Nich. Peirce Jno. Morris Eliz. Morris Jno. Morris junior W. Morris Mary Morris Nathanl. Raven Tony a Negro
Survey for Mr. Tho. Speight, 210 a., 2 Mar. 1696/7.

Albemarle ss. Mr. Tho. Speight, 210 a., Chowan Precinct, 25 Feb. 1696.
For the transportation of Tho. Speight Rich. Malbone Nich. Peirce Jno. Morris Eliz. Morris

Albemarle ss. Jno. Jones, 450 a., 11 July 1694.
Persons Jno., Eliz., and Susan Jones, Sarah Davis, by assignment Danl. Philips, Wm. Johnson, Mary Sawyer, Jno. Smith, An Smith, 9.
Assignment by Jno. Jones of 2 rights and 32 a. to Tho. French
Survey for Jno. Jones, 318 a., 1 Apr. 1696.

p. 129
Albemarle ss. Jno. Jones, 318 a., n.e. side Pasquotank River, 25 Feb.
1696.
For the transportation of Jno., Eliz., and Susan Jones, Sarah Davis,
Danl. Philips, Wm. Johnson, Mary Sawyer
Survey for Tho. French, 85 a., 23 Apr. 1696.
Assignment by Tho. French of 47 a. out of An Smith's right
assigned by Jno. Jones to Robert Taylor.

p. 129 (reverse)
Albemarle ss. Tho. French, 85 a., n.e. side Pasquotank River, 25
Feb. 1696.
For the transportation of Jno. Swith and An Smith by assignment
out of Jno. Jones Warrant

Albemarle. Robert Taylor, 650 a., 9 Mar. 1693.
Persons Robert Taylor 2 Rightes, and his Wife, Betty, Willaby
Negros Tho. Barat, Negro Manuel, Jno. Mathews, An Taylor, and
by assignment of Mary Lawrence Danl. Frizell, Margrt. his wife,
Alex Jordan, David Wilson, 13.
Survey for Robert Taylor, 640 a., 24 Apr. 1696.

Albemarle ss. Robert Taylor, 640 a., n.e. side Pasquotank River, 25
Feb. 1696.
For the transportation of Robert Taylor a transport and his Wife 3
Negros Tho. Barrat, Jno. Mathews An Taylor, Danl. Frizell, Margrt.
his Wife, Alex Jordan, David Wilson

p. 130
Albemarle ss. Rowland Buckley, 400 a., 11 July 1694.
Persons Rowland Buckley 2 transportations Ellinor his wife,
Rowland Buckley junior, W. Windbery, Mathew Strickley, Mary
Buckley, Henry Buckley, 8.
Assignment by Rowland Buckley to Tho. Relfe of Henry Buckley's
right.
Survey for Rowland Buckley, 350 a., 27 Apr. 1696.

Albemarle ss. Rowland Buckley, 350 a., s.w. side Pasquotank River, 25
Feb. 1696.

For the transportation of Rowland Buckley 2 transportations Ellinor his Wife Rowland Buckley junior Wm. Windbery Mathew Strickley Mary Buckley

Albemarle ss. Francis Hendrick, 550 a., 15 Oct. 1694.
persons Francis Henrick, James Moris, Jno. Hutchins, Ed. Woodle, Abraham Wottle, and W. Johnson, Eliz. Johnson, Ed. Chambers 2 transported, 11.
Survey for Francis Henrick, 206 a., 24 Oct. 1695.

p. 130 (reverse)
Francis Henrick, 206 a., s.w. side Pasquotank River, 25 Feb. 1696. for the transportation of Francis Henrick James Morris Jno. Hutchins Edw. Woodle Abra. Wottle

North Carolina ss. Jno. Upton, 400 a., 10 Oct. 1695.
Persons Jno. Upton 2 transportations his wife Simon Peirson, Johanah Peirson, Mary Peirson, John Byrd, Judah Byrd, 8. Survey for Jno. Upton, 191 a., 30 Oct. 1695.

Albemarle ss. John Upton, 191 a., n.e. side Pasquotank River, 25 Feb. 1696.
For the transportation of Jno. Upton 2 transportations his wife and Simon Peirson

Albemarle ss. Jno. Mason, 250 a., 3 Mar. 1693.
Persons Morgan Tho. his wife and 2 Children and one servant.
Survey for Jno. Mason, 176 a., 11 Sept. 1695.

p. 131
Albemarle ss. Jno. Mason, 176 a., s.w. side Pasquotank River, 25 Feb. 1696.
For the transport of Morgan Tho. his wife and 2 Children

Albemarle. Cornelius Jones, 450 a., 11 July 1694.
Persons Jno. and Mary Scarbrough and 2 Children Cornel., and Eliz. Jones Abra. Watkins and Simond Rice 2 transportations, 9.
Survey for Cornelius Jones, 300 a., 20 Sept. 1695.

Albemarle ss. Cornelius Jones, 300 a., n.e. side Pasquotank River, 25 Feb. 1696.

For the transportation of Jno. and Mary Scarbrough and 2 Children and Cornelius and Eliz. Jones.

p. 131 (reverse)
North Carolina ss. Wm. Ramur, 550 a., 9 May 1696.
  Persons Wm. Raymor and his wife Edw. Ramor Andrew a Negro Walter McLamel, And assigned by Edw. Mayo 4 Indians, Jno. Williamson, and Jno. Luken, 11.
  Survey for Wm. Ramor, 450 a., 9 May 1696.

Albemarle ss. Willm. Ramor, 450 a., n.e. side Pasquotank River, 25 Feb. 1696.
  For the transportation of Wm. Ramor and his Wife Edw. Ramor Andrew a Negro Walter McLamell 4 Indians

North Carolina ss. Jno. Sawyer, 500 a., 30 Oct. 1695.
  Persons Robert and Mary Sawyer 2 transportations Mary McDanl. and, Fra. Sawyer, and by assignment of Tho. French, Tho. French, Hanah Wingfeild, Geo. Fleming, Rebecca Nicolls, 10.
  Survey for Jno. Sawyer and Robert Sawyer, 400 a., 30 Oct. 1695.

Albemarle ss. Jno. Sawyer and Robert Sawyer "in Comon," 400 a., s.w. side Pasquotank River, 25 Feb. 1696.
  For the transportation of Robert and Mary Sawyer 2 transportations Mary MacDanll. Francis Sawyer Tho. French hanah Wingfeild

p. 132
North Carolina ss. Wm. Bray, 500 a., 21 Sept. 1695.
  Persons Edw. Bentall, Mary Bentall, Rebecca Bentall, Wm. Bentall, Jno. Pottinger, Saml. Lister, Eliz. Johnson, Mary Johnson, assigned by Edw. Bentall Wm. Bray, Martha his wife, 10.
  Survey for Willm. Bray, 350 a., 21 Sept. 1695.

Albemarle ss. Willm. Bray, 350 a., n.e. Pasquotank River, 25 Feb. 1696.
  For the transportation of Edw., Mary, Rebecca, and Wm. Bentalls, Jno. Porringer, Saml. Lister, Eliz. Johnson

Albemarle ss. Geo. Harris, 1100 a., 11 July 1694.
  Persons Henry Slade, Wm. Loverige, temperance his Wife Wm. and hanah Loverige, Jacob Carver Phillis Williamson, Christo. and

Ja. Williamson, Tho. Page his wife and 3 Children Eliz. Powell, Mary Empson Geo. Harris and his wife Wm. Steward Jno. Hall Tho. Empson An Grandee Diana Williamson, 23. Off which Henry Slade and W. Loverige assigned to [*blank*] Jacob Carver and Phillis Williamson to Tho James An Grandee Diana Williamson Christopher and James Williamson Tho. [Page] to David Prichard Senior

Tho. Page's Wife and 3 Children to David Prichard junior

24 more to Jno. Belman

Survey for David Prichard, 640 a., 12 June 1696.

Survey for Jno. Belman, 198 a., 12 June 1696.

Survey for Geo. Harris, 624 a., 252 a. by this warrant, 12 June 1696.

Survey for David Prichard junior, 155 a., 5 a. by this warrant, 12 July 1696.

p. 132 (reverse)

Albemarle ss. John Belman, 198 a., Pasquotank Precinct, 25 Feb. 1696.
    For the transportation of Temperance Wm. and Hanah Loverige and Philis Williamson

Albemarle ss. David Prichard, 400 a., 11 July 1694.
    Persons David, Sarah, David, Hugh, Prichard Jno. Moteley, Eliz., and An Madren, Thomas Prichard, 8.
    Survey for David Prichard, 640 a., 400 a. by this warrant and 340 a. by Geo. Harris's warrant, 12 June 1696.

Albemarle ss. David Prichard, 640 a., Pasquotank Precinct, 25 Feb. 1696. for the transportation of An Grand, Diana, Christopher, and James Williamson, Tho. Page, David, Sarah, David, Hugh, Tho. Prichard, Jno. Motely, Eliz. and An Madren

p. 133

North Carolina ss. George Harris, 300 a., 24 Oct. 1695.
    Persons Christopher, Ruhamah, Christopher, Willm., Jno., Granger, Tho. Brown, assigned by Christopher Granger, 6.
    Survey for Geo. Harris, 624 a., 252 a. by this warrant and 372 a. by warrant dated 11 July 1694, 12 June 1696.

Albemarle. George Harris, 624 a., Pasquotank Precinct, 25 Feb. 1696.
    For the transportation of Christopher Ruhama, Christopher, Wm., Jno. Granger, Thomas Brown, Eliz. Powell Mary Empson, Geo. Harris, his wife, Wm. Stuart, Jno. Hall Tho. Empson.

Albemarle ss. Ralfe Garnett, 400 a., 11 July 1694.
Persons Ralfe Garnett, Giles Dowlear, Henry Gilliard, Sarah Hatton, Edmond Roe, Eliz. Roe, Ralfe Garnet, Joana Garnett, 8.
Survey for Ralfe Garnett, 250 a., 12 June 1696.

p. 133 (reverse)
Survey for David Prichard junior, 155 a., 150 a. by this warrant and 5 a. by Geo. Harris' warrant dated 11 July 1694, 12 June 1696.

Albemarle ss. Ralfe Garnett, 250 a., Pasquotank Precinct, 25 Feb. 1696.
For the transportation of Ralfe Garnett Giles Dowlere Hen. Gilliard Sarah Hatton Edmond Roe

Albemarle ss. David Prichard junior, 155 a., Pasquotank Precinct, 25 Feb. 1696.
For the transportation of Eliz. Roe Ralfe Garnet Joana Garnett Tho. Page The four first as Marying the Relict of Garnett.

p. 134
Albemarle ss. Tho. Pollock Esqr., 65 a., 19 Mar. 1693.
Persons Sam. Stephens, Ed. Telwell, Robert Boon, Jno. Michaell, Lawrence Gonsolvo, Peter Ashle, Aaron Loverige, Stephen Lewis, Mary a Woman, Ashline a More, Antho. a Negro, Peter Rice, W. Strange, 13.
Survey for Tho. Pollock esqr., 640 a., 14 Apr. 1697.

Collonel Tho. Pollock, 640 a., Chowan Precinct, 20 Apr. 1697.
for the transportation of Saml. Stephens Ed. Tellwell Robert Boon Jno. Michaell Lawrence Gonsolvo Peter Ashle Aaron Loverige Stephen Lewis Mary a woman Ashn. a More Antho. Negro Peter Rice W. Strange

Albemarle. Tho. Pollock Esqr., 650 a., 19 Mar. 1693.
Persons Jno. Robison Tho. Pollock James Pollock Martha Pollock Peter Cornelius and 8 Negros.
Survey for Collonel Pollock, 640 a., 13 Apr. 1697.

Albemarle ss. Collonel Tho. Pollock, 640 a., Chowan Precinct, 20 Apr. 1697.
For the transportation of Jno. Robison Tho. James Martha Pollock Peter Cornelius and 8 Negroes.

p. 134 (reverse)
North Carolina ss. Wm. James, 200 a., 20 Mar. 1695/6.
 Persons Tho. James Eliz. his wife Jacob Carver and Philip
 Williamson the two last by assignment of Geo. Harris.
 Survey for Tho. James, 200 a., 12 June 1696.

Albemarle ss. Tho. James, 200 a., Pasquotank Precinct, 25 Feb. 1696.
 For the transportation of Tho. James Eliz. his wife Jacob Carver
 Philip Williamson

Albemarle ss. Jno. Hopkins, 600 a., 17 July 1694.
 Persons Sarah Hopkins, Johanah Kinkard, Sarah Kinkard, each 2
 transportations John Hopkins, Valentine Barton, Rich. Arnold
 junior, Rich. Arnold Senior, Jane his daughter, Abigael his Wife, 12.
 Survey for Jno. Hopkins, 300 a., 30 Jan. 1695/6.
 Survey for Jno. Hopkins, 300 a., 30 Jan. 1695/6.

Albemarle ss. Jno. Hopkins, 300 a., on Yawpim River, 17 Feb. 1696.
 For 2 transportations of Sarah Hopkins Johanah and Sarah Kinkard.

p. 135
Albemarle ss. John Hopkins, 300 a., Perquimans Precinct, 17 Feb.
 1696.
 For the transportation of John Hopkins Valentine Barton Rich.
 Arnold Senior Abigaele his wife Rich. and Jane his daughter and
 son.

Albemarle ss. Jno. Porter, 900 a., 8 Mar. 1693.
 Persons Jno. Porter Senior Jno. Porter junior Mary his wife Jno.
 Edmund Sarah his Children and 12 negros.
 Survey for Mr. Jno. Porter Junior, 470 a., 30 Jan. 1695/6.
 Survey for Mr. Jno. Porter junior, 298 a., 30 Jan. 16[95/6].

p. 135 (reverse)
Albemarle ss. Mr. Jno. Porter, 298 a., Chowan Precinct, 17 Feb. 1696.
 For the transportation of Jno. Porter Senior Jno. Porter junior
 Mary his wife Jno. Edm. and Sarah his Children.

Albemarle ss. John Mason, 200 a., 11 July 1694.
 Persons Morgan Rice Jno. Morgan Tho. Cob Sarah Mason, 4
 Assignment by Jno. Mason to Patrik Baly, "the last of" Feb.
 1694/5.

Survey for Patrick Baly, 329 a., 200 a. by this warrant and 129 a. by former warrant, 3 Feb. 1695/6.

Albemarle ss. Patrick Bayley 329 a., Pasquotank Precinct, 17 Feb. 1696. for the transportation of Tho. Evins Jno. Dear Tho. Jones An Jones and 20 acres on Cutbert Phelps and 30 acres upon An Smith in Speights warrant.

p. 136
Albemarle ss. Mr. Henry White, 450 a., 11 July 1694.
Persons Henry White, Senior An White, Rich. Rodes, Jno. Taylor, Rich. Fowler, Henr. White junior, Mary White, herbert apwen, Toby a Negroe, 9.

Albemarle ss. Mr. Henry White, 100 a., Pasquotank Precinct, 17 Feb. 1696. for the transportation of Henry White Senior An White, 2.

p. 136 (reverse)
(fragment) 17 Feb. 1696.
For the transportation of Morgan Rice Jno. Morgan Tho. Cob Sarah Mason, Margrett Hambleton 2 transportations Robert Hudson

Albemarle ss. Robert White, 450 a., 20 Aug. 1694.
Persons Rob, Mary, Vincent, Rob. White, Cutbert Phelps Tho. Evins, Jno. Dear, Tho. Jones, An Jones, 9.
Assignment by Robert White of 5 rights to Tho. Jones, 19 Sept. 1694.
Assignment by Robert White of "the whole remain" to Eliz. Sherwood, 19 Sept. 1695.
Survey for Thomas Jones, 230 a., 30 Jan. 16[*torn*].
Survey for Sarah Sherwood, 250 a., 220 a. by this warrant and 30 a. assigned out of Capt. Wm. Speights Warrant, 13 Jan. 1695/6.

Albemarle ss. [Tho.] Jones, 230 a., Pasquotank Precinct, 17 Feb. 1696.
For the transportation of Robert, Mary, vincent Robert White, Cutbert Phelps, 5.

p. 137
Albemarle ss. James Thigpen, 350 a., 24 Sept. 1694.
Persons Jno. Lilly Senior, Jno. Lilly Junior, Eliz. Lilly, Jane Lilly, assigned by Jno. Lilly, Eliz. Hunt, Eliz. Shelton, and Jane a Negro, assigned by Major Saml. Swann, 7.

August 10 1695. Survey for James Thigpen, 330 a., 3 Feb. 1695/6.

Albemarle ss. James Thigpen, 330 a., Perquimans Precinct, 17 Feb. 1696.
For the transportation of Jno. Lilly Senior Jno. Lilly junior Eliz. Lilly Jane Lilly assigned by Jno. Lilly Eliz. Hunt Eliz. Shelton and Jane a Negro assigned by Major Swann.

Albemarle ss. Wm. Jackson Senior, 116 a., 8 Oct. 1694.
Persons Robert Bowman Isaac Skinner and 16 acres due by a former Warrant and patent Fol. 55.
Survey for Wm. Jackson, 116 a., 28 Aug. 1695.

Albemarle ss. Wm. Jacson the Elder, 116 a., Pasquotank Precinct, 17 Feb. 1696.
for the transportation of the persons in the above Warrant.

p. 138
Albemarle ss. Wm. Walters, 150 a., 11 July 1694.
Persons viz. Jno. Cannon Senior Jno. Cannon junior Alice Canon, 3.
By Wm. Walters assigned to Wm. Charleton.
By Wm. Charleton assigned to Philip Ward.
By Philip Ward assigned to Geo. Dear.
Survey for Geo. Dear, 27 a., 18 Oct. 1695.

Albemarle ss. Geo. Dear, 27 a., a small island called Batt's Grave lying in Albemarle Sound, 17 Feb. 1696.
For the transportation of Jno. Canon Senior.

Albemarle ss. Geo. Mathews, 1200 a., 31 Jan. 1695.
Persons Pa. Raverty, Moris Conovon, Alex Jordan, Wm. Naseby, Charles Wyer, Eliz. Stanley, Eliz. Ax, Rob. Bugles, Wm. Dennis, Johanan Dennis, Humphrew Willis, Eliz. his wife, Mary Willis, Ellex. More, Isaac Mello, Alex Oliver, Cha. Hues, Cater MacDaniell, Tho. Evins, Wm. Dennis, and one more and Geo. Mathews Jane Mathews An Mathews, 24.

Nov. 13 1695. Survey for Geo. Mathews, 200 a., 3 Feb. 16[*torn*]
Geo. Mathews, 200 a., Perquimans Precinct, 17 Feb. 1696.
For the transportation of Patrick Reverty Morris Conovon Alex Jordan Wm. Naseby

p. 139
Albemarle ss. Wm. Rawlison, 200 a., 11 July 1694.
Persons Wm. Rawlison Eliz. Rawlison Wm. Rawlison junior Eliz. Dauston, 4.
By Rawlison assigned to Jno. Tomlingson
Sept. 12 1695. Survey for Jno. Tomlingson, 534 a., 184 a. by this warrant and 350 a. by his warrant of the same Date.

Albemarle ss. Jno. Tomlingson, 350 a., 11 July 1694.
Persons John Tomlingson 2 transportations Barbery Middleton Danl. Ophee, James a Negro George Maschamp 2 transportations, 7.
Sept. 12 1695. Jno. Tomlinson, 530 a., 350 a. by this warrant and 184 a. by Ralisons Warrant.

Albemarle ss. John Tomlingson, 534 a., Pasquotank Precinct, 17 Feb. 1696.
For the transportation of the persons in the two above Warrants.

Albemarle ss. James Fisher, 400 a., 13 July 1694.
Persons James Fisher, Anne Fisher, Mary Graves, James Fisher, Wm. Bentley, Eliz. Block, Mary Block, Eliz. Block junior, 8.

June 6 1695. Survey for James Fisher, 225 a., 7 June 1695.

Albemarle ss. James Fisher, 225 a., in Yawpim Creek, 9 Feb. 1696.
For the transportation of James Fisher Ane Fisher Mary Greaves James Fisher Wm. Bentley

p. 140
Albemarle ss. Jno. Stepny, 300 a., [no date]
Persons Jno. Stepny Mercy Stepny Wm. Baly Grace Baly Jno. Baly Wm. Baly junior, 6.

June 4 1695. Survey and return for Mr. Jno. Stepny, 293 a., 7 June 1695.

Albemarle ss. Capt. Jno. Stepny, 293 a., Perquimans Precinct, 13 Feb. 1696.
For the transportation of Jno. Stepny Mercy Stepny, Wm., Grace, Jno. Bayly Wm. Bayly Junior

Albemarle ss. Tho. Harvey Esqr., 400 a., 5 Jan. 1693/4.

Persons Jno. Jenkins Johana Harvey Jno. Thomas Elinor Thomas Jno. Rankin Grace Seamor Sara Harvey Jack a Negroe, 8.

July 17 1695. Survey and return for Tho. Harvey Esqr., 30 Jan. 1695/6.

Albemarle ss. Tho. Harvey Esqr., 300 a., Perquimans Precinct, 9 Feb. 1696.
For the transportation of Jno. Jenkins Johanah Harvey Jno. Tho. Elinor Thomas Jno. Rankin Grace Seamor

p. 140 (reverse)
Albemarle ss. Mr. Charles Oneal, 800 a., 20 Oct. 1694.
Hugh Oneal, Mary his wife, Charles, and Danl., his sons, Joice, Winifred, and Frances, Jno. Coman, Jno. Martin, Eliz. Woodall, Gilbert Woodall, Hanah Welcom, Rachell Cooke, Anthony Markham, and 2 negroes,
Due to him by his Father Hugh Oneal's Warrant Dated 29 of March 1680, 16.
Oct. 24 1694. Survey and return for Mr. Charles Oneale, 500 a., 25 Oct. 1694.
Survey and return for Charles Oneal, 100 a., 6 May 1697.

Albemarle ss. Charles Oneal, 500 a., Pasquotank Precinct, 25 Feb. 1696.
For the transportation Hugh Oneal, Mary his wife, Charles, Danl. His sons, Joice, Winifred, Frances, Jno. Comon, Jno. Martin, Eliz. Woodall.

p. 141
Albemarle ss. Tho. Luten, 400 a., 3 Apr. 1694.
Persons James Nokes Margret his wife Tho. Stamp Jno. Stamp Wm. Preston Dunken Campbell Israel Shephard and Elinor Wardell
Due to Tho. Luten as Marying relect of Jno. Currier, 8.
Mar. 31 1697. Survey and return for Capt. Tho. Luten, 226 a., 31 Mar. 1697.

Albemarle ss. Capt. Thomas Luten, 226 a., Chowan Precinct, 17 Apr. 1697.
For the transportation of James Nokes Margrett his wife, Tho. Stamp Jno. Stames Wm. Preston

Albemarle ss. Tho. Gillum, 650 a., 12 June 1695.

Tho. Gillam, Joseph Pitts, John Overton, Jno. Pink, and his Wife, assigned by James Mills, Ed. Halloway, Katherine his wife, Wm. Woolerd, Sarah Wollerd, Tho. Leonard, Henry Thigpen Senior Henry Thigpen junior Mary Thigpen, 13.

Apr. 3 1697. Survey and return for Tho. Gillam, 560 a., 3 Apr. 1697.

Albemarle ss. Tho. Gillam, 560 a., Chowan Precinct, 17 Apr. 1697.
   For the transportation of Tho. Gillam Joseph Pitts Jno. Overton Jno. Pinke and his wife Edw. Holloway Katherine his wife Wm. Wollerd Sarah Woolerd Tho. Leonard Henry Thigpen Henry Thigpen junior.

p. 142
Albemarle ss. Edward Smithwike, 400 a., 9 Mar. 1693.
   Persons Jno. Phenee, Katherine Haskins, Margrett Coleman, An Gregory, Saml. Bottomley, Nico. Gent, Mary Philips, Andrew Kensey, 8.
   Mar. 30 1697. Survey and return for Edward Smithwike, 270 a., 30 Mar. 1697

Albemarle ss. Edward Smithwike, 270 a., Chowan Precinct, 17 Apr. 1697. For the transport of Jno. Pheine Katherine Haskins Margret Coleman An Gregory Sam Botomley Nicholas Gent

Albemarle ss. Wm. Walston, 300 a., 11 May 1695.
   Persons Wm. Walston, Hester Walston, Philip Waston, Wm. Walston junior, Wm. Jessop Rich. Bayley
   Survey and return for Wm. Walston, 223 a., 1 Apr. 1697.

Albemarle ss. Wm. Walston, 223 a., Chowan Precinct, 17 Apr. 1697.
   For the transportation of Wm. Walston Hester Walston Philip Walston Wm. Walston junior Wm. Jessop.

p. 143
North Carolina ss. Mr. Cotton Robison, 1400 a., 10 Jan. 1696.
   persons Geo. Miles, Margret Miles, Danl. Cox, Anthony Walters, Rebecca Walters, Wm. Walters, Kat. Walters, Jno. Jackson, Elia. Jackson, Rebecca Jackson, Sarah Jackson, Jo. Danl., Alice Danl., Kat Danll., Tho. Sharp, Rob. Jones, Eliz. Jones, Jorganon Jones, Roger ODains(?), Jno. Bottle, Jno. Bottle junior, Philip Bottle, Sam

Newhooke, Jno. Witts, Margrett Harwood, Cotton Robison, Jane Bottle, Jane Newhooke, 28.
Survey and return for Mr. Cotton Robison, 300 a., 6 Apr. 1697.
Survey and return for Mr. Cotton Robison, 500 a., 8 May 1697.

Albemarle ss. Mr. Cotton Robison, 300 a., Chowan Precinct, 17 Apr. 1697.
For the transportation of Geo. Miles Margrett Miles Danl. Cox Anthony Walters Rebecca Walters Wm. Walters

Albemarle ss. Mr. Cotton Robison, 500 a., Chowan Precinct, 15 May 1697.
For the transportation of Katherine Walters, Jno. Jacson, Eliz. Jacson, Rebecca Jacson, Sarah Jacson, Jno. Daniel, Alice Danl., Kat. Danill, Tho. Sharp, Robert Jones

p. 144
North Carolina ss. Jno. King, 250 a., 10 Jan. 1696.
Persons Jno. Wilford, Jane Wilford, Sara Wilford, Jane and Jno. Wilford junior, 5.
Survey and return for Jno. King, 150 a., 22 Apr. 1697.
Survey and return for Jno. King, 324 a., 74 a. by this warrant and 250 a. per warrant dated 22 Nov. 1696, 22 Apr. 1697.

North Carolina ss. Jno. King, 250 a., 22 Nov. 1696.
Fra. Seagrave and Lucy his wife Tho. Seagrave Fra. Seagrave junior Wm. Powell.

Survey for Jno. King, 324 a., 250 a. by this warrant and 74 a. by warrant dated 10 Jan. 1696.

Albemarle ss. John King, 324 a., Chowan Precinct, 15 May 1697.
For the transport of Jno. Wilford Jane Wilford Sarah Wilford Fra. Seagrave Lucy Seagrave, Tho. Seagrave, Fra. Seagrave junior.

Albemarle ss. Mr. Jno. King, 150 a., Chowan Precinct, 15 May 1697.
For the transportation of Wm. Powell Jane and Jno. Wilford junior.

p. 145
Albemarle ss. Elizabeth Dunston, 600 a., 11 July 1694.

persons viz. Peleg Dunston, Mathew Scott, Sarah Scott, Eliz. Scot, Eliz. Dunston, Aaron Loverige, Nath. Edgecame, W. Hickman, Ellinor Tobbet Tho. Anderson, Eliz. Dean, Jno. Dean, 12.

Assignment by Eliz. Dunston to Alexander McFarlin, 19 Apr. 1695.

Assignment by McFarlin to Nath. Chevin and by him assigned to Tho. Garret, 6 Apr. 1697.

Survey and return for Tho. Garret, 500 a., 26 Apr. 1697.

Albemarle ss. Tho. Garret, 500 a., Chowan Precinct, 15 May 1697.
For the transport of Peleg Dunston, Mathew Scott, Sarah Scott, Eliz. Scott, Eliz. Dunston, Aaron Loverige, Nath. Edgecome, W. Hickman, Ellinor Tobbet, Tho. Anderson

Albemarle ss. James Blount, 200 a., 5 Dec. 1694.
the Person viz. Geo. Dear Eliz. Dear Rich Dear James Blount, 4.
Survey and return for James Blount, 200 a., 6 Apr. 1697.

Albemarle ss. James Blount, 200 a., Chowan Precinct, 15 May 1697.
For the transportation of Geo. Dear Eliz. Dear Rich Dear James Blount

p. 146
Albemarle ss. Julianay Taylor, 500 a., 14 Mar. 1694.
Persons Henry, Mary, Julianah, Hudson, Jno. Taylor, An Taylor, Ja. Watson, Jno. Blith, Sarah a Negro, Sanders Indian, Julianah Taylor her freedom Right, 10.
Four of these assigned to Johanah Taylor And two viz. Sanders Indian and Sarah Negro assigned to Jane Byard.
Survey and return for Johanah Taylor, 164 a., 23 Mar. 1696/7.
Survey and return for Mr. Benj. Lakar, 187 a., 125 a. per this warrant, 62 a. per warrant dated 17 Jan. 1693/4., 23 Apr. 1697.

Albemarle ss. Johanah Taylor, 164 a., Perquimans Precinct, 15 May 1697. For the transportation of Henry Mary and Julianah Hudson and Jno. Taylor.

Albemarle ss. Mr. Benj. Lakar, 187 a., Perquimans Precinct, 15 May 1697.
For the transportation of An Taylor James Watson Jno. Blith Jane Lakar Marea Negroe.

p. 147
Albemarle ss. Wm. Wilkison Esqr., 900 a., 26 Mar. 1694.
Persons Charles Jones, Wm. Elfeck, Hester Pope, Jno. Ingram, Bes, Will, Dick, Jack, Debora, Franck, Mingo, Robin, Kent, Sambo, Coffe, Jack, Cotto, Betty, Negros, 18.
Due upon this Warrant 488 a. rest made use of in former Patents.
Survey and return for Col. Wm. Wilkison, 168 a., 25 Mar. 1697.

p. 148
Albemarle ss. Wm. Mowbery, 200 a., 14 July 1694.
Persons Wm. Mowbery and Hanah his Wife Will. an Indian Jno. Howell.
Survey and return for Wm. Mowbery, 200 a., 30 Oct. 1694.

Albemarle ss. Wm. Mowbery, 200 a., Pasquotank Precinct, 10 Nov. 1694.
For the transportation of Wm. Mowbery Hanah his wife Will Indian J. Howell.

Albemarle ss. Jane Harbut, 350 a., 13 July 1694.
Persons Jane Harbut, Wm. Harbut, Mary Harbut, Eliz. Benit Robert Stacy, Edw. Boughoo, Wm. Harbut junior, 7.
Survey for Ellen Hibbins assignee of Jane Harbut Daughter and Heires of [*blank*] Benitt 284 a., 7 June 1695.

Albemarle ss. James Hibbins and Ellinor his wife, 284 a., in Yawpim River, 10 June 1694.
For the transport of Jane harbut Wm. Harbut Mary Harbut W. Harbut junior Eliz. Benitt Rob. Stacy.

p. 149
Albemarle. John Odum, 350 a., 7 Jan. 1696.
Persons John, An, An, Jane, Mary, Rachell Odom, Ed. Williams assigned by Abra. Williams
Survey for John Odam, 350 a., Chowan Precinct, 17 Apr. 1699.
For the transportation of John An An Jane Mary Rachell Odum, Ed. Williams

Albemarle ss. Capt. Henderson Walker, 1120 a., 3 Mar. 1693.
persons Timothy turton, Leah, Thomas, Jno., William, Leonard turton, two Negros Jno. Hawkins, Alice his mother, Jno. Hussy,

Jno. Morgan, Margr. Drake, Tho., Eliz., Sarah Hawkins, Rich. Mitchell, Rich. Thompson, Wm. Camell, Peter, An, Mary, Adam Bassett
Mar. 26, 1697 Survey for Capt. Henderson Walker, 428 a.

Albemarle ss. Capt. Henderson Walker, 428 a., Chowan Precinct, 15 Apr. 1697.
For the transportation of Timothy, Leah, Tho., Jno., Wm., Leonard Turton, two Negros and Jno. Hawkins

p. 150
Albemarle ss. Lewis Williams, 150 a., 10 Jan. 1696.
persons Lewis Williams, Senior Lewis Williams junior Eliz. Williams 2 transportations An, Anthony, Johana, Catherine Williams, Wm. Redman, Tho. Stanbrige, Mary his wife and Mary his daughter David Blake Alice Benit Jno. Butler Mary his wife Jno. Norris Tho. Norris Edw. Mary Eliz. Jno. Mary Base, 25.
Survey for Lewis Williams, 640 a., 13 Apr. 1697.
Survey for Lewis Williams, 400 a., 15 Apr. 1697.

Albemarle ss. Lewis Williams, 640 a., Chowan Precinct, 15 May 1697.
For the transportation of Lewis Williams Senior Lewis Williams junior Eliz. Williams each 2 transportations An, Anthony, Johana, Katherine Williams, Wm. Redman, Tho. Stanbrige, Mary his wife Granted to Tho. Parker (by Relaps of L. W.) March 21 1711/12.

Albemarle ss. Lewis Williams, 400 a., Chowan Precinct, 15 May 1697.
For the transport of Mary Standbrige, David Blake, Alice Bennit, Jno. Butler, Mary his Wife, Jno. Norris, Tho. Norris, Edw. Base.

p. 152
North Carolina ss. Lawrence Keeton, 250 a., 10 Oct. 1695.
the persons Saml. Wilson Jno. Jones Eliz. Thomas by assignment of Mr. Edw. Mayo to Zachery Keeton and by him to the abovesaid And Wm. Morton 2 Importations by assignment of the Said Morton
Survey for Lawrence Keeton, 204 a., 19 Oct. 1695.
Laurence Keeton, 204 a., s.w. side Pasquotank River, 25 Feb. 1696.
for the transportation of Saml. Wilson Jno. Jones Eliz. Thomas Wm. Morton 2 transportations

Albemarle ss. Tho. Cox, 650 a., 10 Oct. 169[*torn*].

Tho. Cox, Ruth his Wife, Edw. and Eliz. Cox Jno. Buck, and 8 Negros
proved by Mr. Jos. Chase and assigned to Mr. Joseph Chew and by him to Tho. Cox, 13.
Survey for Thomas Cox, 640 a., 20 Oct. 1696.

Albemarle ss. Thomas Cox, 640 a., Currituck Precinct, 25 Feb. 1696.
For the Importation of Tho. Cox Ruth his Wife Edw. and Eliz. Cox Jno. Buck and 8 Negroes, 13.

p. 155 (reverse)
Walter Greene, 300 a., for transportation of 6 persons, 30 [*torn*]
Walter Greene Eliz. his wife Mary his daughter Tho. Hassold Timothy Clare and Francis an English boy
Survey at Yawpim Creek, 300 a.
Assignment by Alexandr. Lillington of "Rites mentioned in my warrant, the Ninth and Tenth by name Sarah and John James," to Mr. Walter Greene, 26 Sept. 1681.
Survey of 100 a. more [*torn*] 400 a. Sept. 26 1681.
Survey for Walter Greene at Yawpim Creek 4[00] a.

p. 156
Albemarle. John Bolton, 250 a., for transportation of 5 persons, 5 Feb. 1679.
John Bolton, Elizabeth his wife Tho. Pendleton, Henry Pendleton and Mathew Pendleton
June 11 1681, Survey for Jno. Bolton, 100 a.
June 11 1681, Jno. Bolton, 100 a., at Newbegun Creek

p. 224
John Bolton, 100 a., for transportation of 2 persons, 18 Nov. 1681.
John Bolton and Elizabeth his wife.

p. 166
Albemarle. Richard Cooke, 250 a., for transportation of 5 persons, 5 Feb. 1679.
Richard Cook, Hannah his wife Rich. Cook Junior
George Cooke and Hannah Cook Junior

Survey for Richard Cook, 210 a. at Craven River, 10 June 1681.
Richard Cook, 210 a. at Craven River, 10 June 1681.

p. 223

Richard Cook, 210 a., Carteret Precinct, for transportation of 5 persons, 18 Nov. 1681.

Rich. Cook Hannah his wife Rich. Cook Junior George Cook and Hannah Cook Junior

p. 167

Albemarle. John Dye, 350 a., for transportation of 7 persons, 5 Feb. 1679.

Jno. Dye and Jane his wife Hannah Dye Trustrum Brooks Jno. Browne, two Indians James and Will

Survey at Newbegun Creek, 100 a.

Survey at Carteret, 250 a.

John Dye, 100 a. at Newbegun Creek, 4 July 1681.

John Dye, 250 a., at Craven River, 6 July 1681.

p. 222

John Dye, 100 a., Carteret Precinct, for transportation of 2 persons, 18 Nov. 1681.

John Dye and Jane his wife

John Dye, 250 a., Carteret Precinct, for transportation of 5 persons, 18 Nov. 1681.

Hannah Dye Trustrum Brooks Jno. Browne two Indians James and Will

p. 221

Albemarle. Isaac Guildford, 100 a., for transportation of 2 persons, 5 Feb. 1679.

Isaac Guildford and Elizabeth his wife

p. 169

Survey at Carteret, 100 a.

Isaac Guildford, 100 a. at Craven River, 5 July 1[*torn*].

p. 169

Isaac Guildford, 100 a., Carteret Precinct, for transportation of 2 persons, 18 Nov. 1681.

Isaac Guildford and Eliz. his wife

p. 220

Albemarle. Stephen Scott, 200 a., for transportation of 4 persons, 29 Mar. 1680.
Stephen Scott Sarah his wife Stephen Scott Junior Elinor Scott
Survey at Newbegun Creek, 50 a.
Survey for Stephen Scott at Newbegun Creek, 50 a.

p. 170
Stephen Scott, 50 a., Carteret Precinct, for transportation of 1 person, 18 Nov. 1681.
Stephen Scott

p. 219
Albemarle. William Voss, 450 a., for transportation of 9 persons, 29 Mar. 1680/1.
By assignment of the attorney of Samuell Stevens Esqr. to Peter Carterett Esqr. and by assignment of Peter Carterett Esqr. attorney. Capt. William Craford Esqr. to Ralph Coates and from Ralph Coates assigned to William Voss 6 rights for land: Dick Negro, Grace Senior, Grace Junior, old Mary, young Mary Dorothy, all Negroes. By order of Berkeley prec. Court 1 right of Francis Tomes, Joseph Ashley, William Voss and John Harris "to bee Laid on the Land adjoining to his purchased Land."
This Warrant renewed 17 Nov. 1694.
Survey at Berkeley River, 250 a.
Aug. 9 1681, Survey for William Voss at Berkeley River, 250 a.

p. 171
William Voss, 250 a., Perquimans River, for 5 rights transported, [*blank*] 1681.
Dick Negroe Grace Senior Grace Junior old Mary and young Mary

p. 218
Albemarle. James Perishaw "orphants of this County," 100 a., for transportation of 2 persons, 30 Mar. 1680.
James and Hannah Perishaw

p. 171 (there are two p. 171's)
Survey for orphans of James Perishaw, 100 a.
Aug. 17 1681, Survey for orphans of James Perishaw, 100 a.

James and Elianor Perishaw, orphans of James Perishaw deceased, 100 a., Perquimans Precinct, for transportation of 2 persons, [*blank*] 1681.
James and Hannah Perishaw

p. 172
Albemarle. George Castleton, 150 a., for transportation of 3 persons, 30 Mar. 1680.
George Castleton Isaac Fevermull, George Whittaker
Survey for George Castleton, 150 a.
Aug. 17, 1681, Survey for George Castleton, 150 a.

p. 216
George Castleton, 150 a., Perquimans Precinct, for transportation of 3 persons, [*blank*] 1681.
George Castleton, Isaac Feavermull, and George Whiteaker

p. 173
Albemarle. Mr. James Long, 450 a., for transportation of 9 persons, 30 Mar. 1680.
James Long Senior Alice his wife James Long Junior his sone Thomas Giles William and Robert Long sones Elizabeth his Daughter Mary Burton
Survey at Yawpim, 450 a.
Sept. 12 1681, Survey at Yawpim for Mr. James Long, 450 a.

p. 215
James Long, 450 a., Berkeley Precinct, for transportation of 9 persons, [*blank*] 1681.
James Long Senior Alice his wife James Long Junior his sone Tho. Giles Will and Robert Long sones Eliz. his Daughter Mary Burton

p. 174
Albemarle. Alexander Lillington, 650 a., for transportation of 13 persons, 29 Mar. 1680.
Alexander Lillington and Sarah and Elizabeth his wives Jno. and Joseph James Eliz. Willis and Baccus Negroe Tho. James Jno. James and Joseph James Sonnes and Sarah James his Daughter Edward Wilson servant.

Survey at the mouth of Bentlyes Creek, 400 a.

p. 214
Sept. 14 1681, Survey for Mr. Alexander Lillington, 400 a. at Bentlyes Creek "fronting to the Sound"
Alexander Lillington, 400 a., Berkeley Precinct, for transportation of 8 persons, [*blank*] 1681.
Alexandr. Lillington and Sarah and Elizabeth his Wifes John and Joseph James Eliz. Willis and Baccus Negroe Thomas James

p. 213
Henry Eglentine, 300 a., for transportation of 6 persons, 29 Mar. 1680.
Lawrance Gonsalvo Dorothy his late wife Sarah his wife Tho. Gonsalvo James Freeman Christopher Norton Survey at Yawpim Creek, 300 a.
Sept. 23, 1681, Survey for henry Eglentine at Yawpim Creek, 300 a.

p. 176
Henry Eglentine, 300 a., Berkeley Precinct, for transportation of 6 persons, [*blank*] 1681.
Laurance Gonsalvo Dorothy his late Wife Sarah his Wife Tho. Gonsalvo James Freeman Christophr. Norton

p. 212
Albemarle. John Barrow, 300 a., for transportation of 6 persons, 30 Mar. 1680.
John Barrow Sarah his wife freedome Rites Assigned by Collonel Jenkins Allexandr. Lillington Caleb Callaway John Barrow Will Hall servants Rites
Survey for John Barrow, 300 a.
Sept. 24, 1681, Survey for John Barrow, 300 a., at Yawpim Creek

p. 178
Walter Greene, 400 a., Berkeley Precinct, for transportation of 6 persons and 2 rights more which Greene bought of Alexandr. Lillington by assignment, [*blank*] 1681.
Walter Greene Eliz. his Wife Mary his Daughter Tho. Hassold Timothy Clare and Francis an english boy Assigned by Mr. [Alexander] Lillington Sarah and Jno. James

p. 211
Albemarle. John Taylor, 100 a., for transportation of himselfe and wife, 27 Mar. 1680.

John Taylor Magdaline his wife
Sept. 29, 1681. Survey for John Taylor the "Orphant Sone of John
Taylor late deceased," 100 a.

p. 179
John Taylor, orphan of Jno. Taylor deceased, 100 a., Shaftesbury
Precinct, for transportation of 2 persons, [*blank*] 1681.
John Taylor and Magdalen his wife

p. 210
Albemarle. Richard Oliver, 350 a., for transportation of 7 persons, 29
Mar. 1680.
Richard Oliver Alice his wife, Sarah, Ann, Mary, Felix and
Margarett his Daughters

Albemarle. Assignment by Richard Oliver to Edward Smithwick, 4
Oct. 1681.
Survey for Edward Smithwick, 350 a.
Oct. 1, 1681. Survey for Edward Smithwick, 350 a., s. side of s.e.
branch Matchacomack Creek

p. 180
Edward Smithwick, 350 a., Shaftesbury Precinct, for transportation
of 7 persons, [*blank*] 1681.
Rich. Olliver Allice his wife, Sarah, Anne, Mary Felix and Margarett
his daughters

p. 209
Albemarle. John Varnham, 300 a., for transportation of 6 persons, 29
Mar. 168[0].
John Varnham Esqr. Rich. Stone Hellinr. Talbott two Negroe
women one Negroe Man
Shaftesbury Precinct ss. Assignment by John Davies, who married
the relict and administratrix of John Varnham Esqr. deceased, to
Jno. Cannon, 29 Sept. 1681.
Survey for John Cannon, 150 a. Oct. 3, 1681. Survey for John
Cannon, 150 a.

p. 181
John Cannon, 150 a., Shaftesbury Precinct, for 3 rights transported
which Cannon bought of Mr. Davies by assignment, [*blank*] 1681.

John Varnham Esqr. Rich. Stone Hellinr. Talbott

p. 208

Albemarle. Edward Smitheck, 200 a., for transportation of 4 persons, 29 Mar. 1680.
Edward Smitheck, Lydia his wife John Shearing and Lydia Shearing Survey for Edward Smitheck, 200 a.
Oct. 3, 1681. Survey for Edward Smitheck, 200 a.

p. 182

Edward Smitheck, 200 a., Shaftesbury Precinct, for transportation of 4 persons, [*blank*] 1681.
Edward Smithick Lidia his Wife John Sheareing and Lidia Sheareing

p. 207

Albemarle. John Varnham, 150 a., for transportation of 3 persons, 29 Mar. 1680.
Siberah Marwood, Giles Marwood and Frances Marwood
Assignment by John Varnham to William Waters, 16 Apr. 1680.
Assignment by William Waters to Roger Hall, 5 Oct. 1681.

Albemarle. Ann Hall, 200 a., for transportation of 4 persons, 29 Mar. 1680.
John Benfeild, Thomas Twaight Jno. Alexandr. and Thomas Hodgskins
Albemarle. Roger Hall, 100 a., for transportation of 2 persons, 29 Mar. 1680.
Roger Hall and Ann his wife
3 warrants surveyed for Roger Hall, 450 a.
Oct. 5, 1681, Survey for Roger Hall, 450 a.

p. 206

Roger Hall, 450 a., Shaftesbury Precinct, for transportation of 9 persons, 6 transported and 3 bought by assignment, [*blank*] 1681. Siberah Marwood, Giles Marwood and Francis Marwood, John Benfeild Thomas Twaight Jno. Alexandr., and Tho. Hodgkins, Roger Hall and Anne his wife

p. 164

Thos. Clark, 500 a., 10 May 1697.
Wm. Meazle Mary Meazle Geo. Jones Ann Mathews Patr. Raverly Moriss Conov[a]ne Alexandr. Jordan Wm. Nash Charles Wier

Assigner per Geo. Mathews

Albemarle ss. Thos. Clark, 200 a., 11 July 1694.
[Th]os. Harlo Mary Harlo Mary Harlo Jno. Harlo

North Carolina ss. Tho. Clark, 1400 a., 10 May 1697.
Tho. Standly his Wife and Daughter Robt. Duglace Fra. Williss Manuel Elbee Jos. Elliss his Wife Mary Elliss Laurence Creet his Wife and Daughter Jno. Willson Robt. Willson twice Jno. Gilbert Wm. Hambleton Peter Bassett his Wife and Child Agnus Willowby and her Child Tho. Clark his wife and Negro James Hask Jno. Mercy

p. 162
N. Carolina ss. Mr. Jno. Porter, 450 a., 3 July 1695.
Francis, Mary, Francis Penrise, Mary and Francis Cork assigned by Privett assignment of Penrise Edw. Davis Susan Davis 2 Negroes assigned by Edward Davis
Survey for Mr. Jno. Porter, 580 a., 132 a. by warrant dated 8 Mar. 1693 and 45 a. by this warrant 12 July 1695. And assigned by Jno. Porter to Collonel Wm. Wilkison.

Albemarle ss. Collonel Wm. Wilkison, assignee of Mr. Jno. Porter, 580 a., Chowan Precinct, 25 Feb. 1696.
for the Importation of 3 Negros, Francis Mary Fra. Penise, Mary and Francis Cork Edward Davis Susan Davis and 2 Negros.

North Carolina ss. Danl. Akehurst Esqr., 500 a., 2 Sept. 1695.
Mary, Dorathy, Wm., Henry, Mary Scott, assigned by Jos. Spernon assignment of Tho. Wallis Danl. Akehurst his daughter 2 Negroes and Wm. Guy.
Survey for Danl. Akehurst Esqr., 250 a., 10 Oct. 1695.
Albemarle ss. Danl. Akehurst Esqr., 250 a., Pasquotank Precinct, 25 Feb. 1696.
for the Importation of Mary, Dorathy, Wm., Henry, Mary Scott.

p. 161
N. Carolina ss. Rich. Burtenshall, 550 a., 18 Dec. 1694.
Rich. Burtenshall Pricilla his wife Rich. Susan their Children and by assignment of Mr. Chew assignee of Jos. Chase. These follow Jos. Sambrin Jno. Souther Jno. Smith Jno. Tully Tho. Jackson Ralph Madren Fra. Robison
Survey of this warrant, 21 Nov. 1695.

Assignment by Rich. Burtenshall to Richard Bright, 24 Feb. 1696.
Albemarle ss. Rich. Bright, assignee of Rich. Burtenshall, [no a.],
Currituck Precinct, 25 Feb. 1696.
Rich. Priscilla Burtenshall and 2 children Jos. Sambrin Jno. Souther
Jno. Smith John Tully Tho. Jacson Ralph Madren Fra. Robison.

Albemarle ss. Wm. Stafford, 650 a., 10 Oct. 1695.
Wm. Stafford, Mary his wife, Mary, Wm. John Jane Edw. Stafford,
Arthur Stephens Joa. his wife Antho. Wherry Mary Stephens Joan
Stephens junior Jacob Stephens assigned by Arthur Stephens
Survey of this warrant, 640 a., 15 Nov. 1695.

Albemarle ss. Wm. Stafford, 640 a., Currituck Precinct, 25 Feb. 1696.
For the importation of Wm. Stafford his wife and 5 children
Arthur Stephens and his wife and 3 Children and Antho. Wherry.

p. 160
Albemarle ss. Mary Clarke, 550 a., 11 July 1694.
Jno. Clarke Sarah Hatton Tho. White and 8 Negros, 11.
Survey for Mr. Arthur Workeman assignee of Mary Clarke, 375 a.,
17 Sept. 1695.
Albemarle ss. Mr. Arthure Workeman, 375 a., Pasquotank Precinct,
25 Feb. 1696.
For the Importation of Jno. Clarke Sarah Hatton Tho. White and 5
Negros

Albemarle. Rich. Harris, 350 a., 14 Mar. 1693.
Rich. Harris, Susan Harris, Richardson Harris Eliz. Harris, Mary
Harris, Barbary [H]odge, Cadusho Negro
Survey for Rich. Harris, 268 a., 7 May 1695.
Albemarle ss. Richard Harris, 268 a., Currituck Precinct, 25 Feb.
1696.
For the Importation of Rich., Susan, Richardson, Eliz., Mary
Harris, Barbary Hodge, 6.

p. 159
Albemarle ss. Denis Cashaul, 300 a., 10 Oct. 1694.
Tho. Bayly Jno. Thorowgood Denis Cassaul 2 transportations and
his wife W. Green
Survey by this warrant, 290 a.

Albemarle ss. Denis Cassaul, 290 a., Currituck Precinct, 25 Feb. 1696.
For the Importation of Tho. Bayley Jno. Thorogood Denis Cassaul 2 transportations his wife and Wm. Green

p. 158: (continued from bottom of p. 157) 25 Feb. 1696.
For the Importation of Samll. Jones Jno. Millington Giles Chandler Luke Neale, 4.

N. Carolina ss. Gabriel Nuby, 450 a., 10 Oct. 1695.
Geo. Branch and his wife Wm., Geo., Francis, Eliz., Phillis Branch, Margrett Thomas one Negroe, 9
Survey for Gabriell Nuby, 640 a., 450 a. by this warrant, 190 a. by warrant dated 10 June 1695, 9 Aug. 1696.
North Carolina ss. Survey for Gabriell Nuby, 450 a., 10 June 1696.
Gabriell, Mary, Wm., Edw., Joseph Nuby, Wm., Mary, Eliz. Harloe, assigned by Danl. Akehurst and one Negro Woman by W. Glover.
Survey for Gabriell Nuby, 640 a., 450 a. by warrant dated 10 Oct. 1695, 190 a. by within warrant, 9 Aug. 1696.
Albemarle ss. Gabriell Nuby, 640 a., Perquimans Precinct, 25 Feb. 1696.
For the Importation of Geo. Branch, and his wife, Wm., Geo., Francis, Eliz., Phillis, Branch, Margrett Thomas, one Negroe, Gabriell, Mary, Wm., Edw. Nuby.

Albemarle ss. Andrew Cashaul, 200 a., 10 Dec. 1695.
Jane Vandermulen Tho. [L]amb Andrew Cashall and W. Green
Survey for Andrew Cashaul, 50 a., 20 Dec. 1695.
Albemarle ss. Andrew Cashaul, 150 a., Currituck Precinct, 25 Feb. 1696.
For the Importation of Andrew Cashaul

p. 157
Albemarle. Edward Warren, 350 a., 10 Oct. 1694.
Edw. Warren Eliz. his Wife Mary Warren Mary Barton Jacob Mash and 2 by assignment of Rich. Richards and Eliz. his Wife out of an old Warrant.
Albemarle ss. Edw. Warren, 350 a., Currituck Precinct, 25 Feb. 1696.
For the Importation of Edw. Warren Eliz. his Wife Mary Warren Mary Barton Jacob Mash Richard Richards and Eliz. his Wife

Albemarle ss. Saml. Jones, 200 a., 22 Feb. 1694.
Saml. J ones John Millington Giles Chandler and Luke Neal, 4.
Survey, 200 a., 10 Oct. 1695.
Saml. Jones, 203 a., Currituck Precinct (continued p. 158)

p. 156
Albemarle ss. Dennis Graham, 230 a., Pasquotank Precinct, 25 Feb. 1696.
For the Importation of Denis Graham Black Charles Wm. Steel Lawrence Bras Roger Hambleton

Albemarle ss. Jno. Sanderson, 500 a., 10 Oct. 1693.
Jno. Sanderson, Ellinor his Wife, Walter Mcclenehan, Cristopher Cnapper, Eliz. Warren, 2 Indian Women, Jack Tony Negros Marte Baker
Survey, 300 a., 30 Sept. 1695.
Albemarle ss. Jno. Sanderson, 300 a., Currituck Precinct, 25 Feb. 1696.
For the transportation of Jno. Sanderson Ellinor his Wife Walter Mcclenahan Christopher Cnapper Eliz. Warren one Indian Woman

p. 155
North Carolina ss. Benjamin Reynaud, 300 a., 10 Oct. 1696.
Benj. Reynaud Mary his wife Morgan Olimpa Mary their Children One Negro.
Survey for Benj. Reynaud, 300 a., 11 Oct. 1696.
Albemarle ss. Benjamin Reynaud, 300 a., Currituck Precinct, 25 Feb. 1696.
For the Importation of Benj. Renaud Mary his Wif Olimpa Morgan Mary his Children One Negro, 6.

N. Carolina ss. Dennis Graham, 300 a., 10 Oct. 1695.
Denis Graham and by assignment of Tho. Simons Wm. Steel Black Charles Lawrence Bras, Roger Hambleton, 6
Survey for Denis Graham, 230 a.

p. 154
N. Carolina ss. Tho. Hollaway, 200 a., 10 Oct. 1695.
Tho. Halloway Senior Tho. Halloway Junior each 2 times, 4.
Survey for Tho. Holloway, 200 a., 14 July 1696.

Albemarle. Thomas Holloway, 200 a., Perquimans Precinct, 25 Feb. 1696.

for the Importation of Tho. Holloway Senior and Thomas Holloway junior each 2 transportations.

Beaufort County Deeds, 1695 to 1729, State Archives, Division of Archives and History, Raleigh. [CR.09.401.1].

p. 1

North Carolina St. Mr. Tho. Blunt, 266 a., for transportation, 5 Mar. 1697.

Wm. Hancork Eliz. his wife assigned by Nic. Crisp assignee of Wm. Hancork and one negroe assigned by David Halsey and one negroe and 66 acers due by a former warrant dated 1 June 1695.

p. 2

North Carolina St. William Glover, 550 a., for importation, 10 Feb. 1696. James Fewox, Rob. Fewox, An Fewox, Ed. Batchalor, John Willson, An. Willson, Will Bartlett, Jonr. Willson, Tho. Bartlett, Eliz. Bartlett.

p. 5

North Carolina St. John White, 1200 a., for transportation of 24 persons. [*blank*] White Senior Jon. White Junior [Sa]rah White, Geo. White Francis White, Mary White, [*blank*]ne White, Luck White, [A]bigall White, Media White, [*blank*]m Stephens, Charles Reed, Mary Reed, Rod. Gaylor, [*blank*]d. Nash Prudence Nash Sampson Starborough, [*blank*]r Goodwin, Jenikens Jones, Jenkins Dorman, [*blank*]ius Griffin Isaick Jermigan.

Assignment of Warrant and rites unto Mr. Edmond Peirt by Na. Chevin, 18 Oct. 1701. Warrant and 12 rites in possession of Edmond Peirt, 9 Feb. 1701 /2.

p. 6

No. Carolina st. Farnefould Green, 550 a., for transportation of 11 persons, 9 Sept. 1701.

Abraham Leeds, Eliz. Leeds, Eliz. Leeds Junior, Sarah Leeds, Martha Leeds, Nat. Hall, [*blank*]ary Garrett, Jane Leeds, Wm. Hosea, Jon. Grimes, [*blank*]utell Leeds

Mr. William Barrow, 900 a., for transportation of 18 persons, 1 May 1701.
 (viz.) by assignment James Damrill, Tho. Nueman, Elis. Nueman, Jane Nueman, Wm. Bush, Martha his wife, Martha his daughter Wm. Bush Jr. Sarah Bush Elloner Bush, Wm. Collins, Abraham Batson Elis. Batson, Rose Batson, John Hopkins, Mary Read Hannah Morrison Ricd. Morrison, Susanna Morrison.

p. 7
Carolina. St. Joseph Ming, 200 a., for transportation of 24 persons viz.
 Jo. Ming Abraham Bosur 2 Passages Samll. Stockes Tho. Ming Jon. Porter Jon. Porter Jr. Ed Porter Jos. Porter Andrew Tom Maria Sandy Tony Mingo Oliver Cupid Jack Dick Mally Hagar and William negroes.

p. 9
North Carolina St. Nath. Chevin, 300 a., for transportation of 6 persons, 3 Mar. 1701/2.
 Per the assinement of John Smith. viz. John Smith, Jane Smith, Eliz. Horning, Jane Pidgin, Geo. Huggin, James Allin
 Assigns warrant and rights to Farnefould Green 3 Mar. 1701/2.

Mr. Richard Smith laid to rights on his entry of land in Broad Creek, 20 Oct. 1701
 viz. William Willson Ann Willson Senior Ann Willson Junior Mary Willson James Willson Richard Willson

James Nevill records 4 rights, 27 Mar. 1702.
 viz. Nicholas Tylor Richard Nevill Frances Garganus James Nevill Junior

p. 10
13 Apr. 1702. Thomas Dearham, 11 rights, land entry 6 July 1701, called Wades ould Feild
 viz. Obediah Benjamine Gummelton, John Billinsley, John Topp, Job Hall, Thomas Lee, Wm. Nasebett William Hoodson, Petter Gellown, Thomas Webb, Honnery Clark, Phillip French.

p. 11: 11 Apr. 1702. Thomas Dearham, 12 rights, land entry 11 Apr. 1702
 viz. Francis Sprye, Benjamine Barrington, Eliz. Barrington, Mary Barrington, Robert Oneal, Margarett Oneal, Oliver Smith, Thomas

Dearham, Eliz. Dearham, Mary Dearham, Richard Dearham, Ann Dearham.

11 Apr. 1702. Thomas Dearham, 6 rights, land entry 23 Aug. 1701 viz. Joseph Dearham, Eliz. Dearham Junior, Francis Dearham, Stephen a negro, John Kindred, William Rowland.

11 Apr. 1702. Thomas Dearham, 6 rights, land entry 3 July 1701 viz. Thomas Dearham Junior, Stephen Swetman, Robert Brice, Susanna King, Eliz. Knight, William Cunningham.

13 Apr. 1702. Jeremiah Goodridg, 4 rights, land entry 31 Mar. 1702 viz. Jeremiah Goodridg, Walter Croduck, Jacob Littelwood, John Anesley.

p. 13: 1 May 1702. Samuell Boutwell, 6 rights, land entry 30 Apr. 1702 viz. Grace Willson, Peter Read, James Read, Ann Read, Joseph Ming, Tho. Purton.

Pamticoe 7 July 1702. John Barras, assignment of 4 rights to Henery Eborne viz. Francis, Mary, and John Linfield, and Edward Hogg

p. 14
3 Aug. 1702. Henry Eborne, 6 rights, land entry 29 July 1702 in Matchapongoo Creek containing an old Field and so running up the Creek
viz. Henry Eborn, Eliz. his wife, John Barras Senior, and John Barras Junior, Moses Barras, Precilla Barras

p. 15
North Carolina St. Capt. Nicholas Thomas Jones, 1900 a., for transportation of 38 persons
viz. Nicholas Thomas Jones, Cornelius Benington, Henry Lyle, Wm. A negro, Rch'd a boy, Rch'd Baley, Pompey a negro, Pompey a negro boy, Betty an Indian Woman, Ann A mustie, Sarah Miles, Betty Miles, Ellenor Scott, John Lucas, Rch'd a Sailor, Wm. Barker, Tho. Barnett, Jo. Ming, Rob't Quary, Edmund Thomas, his wife, James Shelton, Geo. Masey, Ben. Yeamons, Jo'n. Watson, Jo'n a negro, Peter an Indian, Dido a negro woman, Thomas a negro, Robt. Quary, Thomas Howes, Peter Bonaway, Davis Sailor, Wm. Huchison, Jane a woman Matthew a negro, Jo'n Falkoner, James Shalloun.

p. 16
William Grealy, 5 rights, land entry 4 Aug. 1702, warrant 1 Oct. 1701.
   viz. Henry Bradly, Catharine his wife, Catharine his Daughter,
   Robert Bradly, Joseph Bradly. 4 Aug. 1702.

4 Sept. 1702. William Price, 3 rights
   viz. William Price and Margaret his wife, and William Wise proved
   at Bath Co. Court 14 Apr. 1702.

p. 27
Robert Mallines, 6 rights, land entry by James Welsh 22 Nov. 1701
   beginning at Currituck old fields so containing the whole old Fields
   viz. John Barnett, Daniel Swillven, Eliz. Swillven, Richard Prince,
   Eliz. Freman, Jeremiah Potter. 20 Aug. 1702.

James Welsh, 6 rights, land entry 27 Aug. 1703.
   viz. John Barnett, Daniel Sullivant, Eliz. Sullivant, Richard Prince,
   Eliz. Froman, Jeremiah Potter.

Mr. Frederick Jones of James City Co., Virginia, records warrant and
   rights, land entry in Matchapongo River called the Queen Dowry
   2 Dec. 1703. Nath'll Chevin, 640 a., for transportation of 13
   persons, 9 Sept. 1701. viz. Edward Davis, Susanna Davis, Thomas
   a negro, Tho. a negro Junior, Wm. Hanley, John Brown, Tho.
   Edwards, Wm. Ellis, John Hardee, Wm. Brown Samuel Fulton,
   Tho. Early, Wm. Wiggins.
   Assignment by Peter Godfrey to Mr. Frederick Jones of James City
   Co., merchant, 24 Nov. 1703.

17 July 1702. Peter Godfrey, 6 rights, warrant 9 Sept. 1701, land entry
   23 Jan. 1701/2 at Core Point.
   viz. Tho. a negro, John Hardy, Wm. Brown, Samll. Ou[?]ton Tho.
   Ellerlee, Wm. Widgen.

p. 28
8 Oct. 1702. Henry Lockey, 5 rights, land entry 22 July 1702.
   viz. Henry Lockey, Ann Lockey, Fraser Lockey, Thomas Lockey,
   George Lockey.

p. 29
Thomas Worseley, 4 rights, land entry by George Mongomery 19
   Dec. 1701.

viz. Francis Martin, Eliz. Martin Junior Wm. Martin, Ann Martin.

p. 30

Thomas Lepper, 3 rights, land entry 28 Oct. 1702.
    viz. John Read 3 Passages.

p. 31

John Nellson Junior, 12 rights, land entry 28 Oct. 1702.
    viz. John Nelson Junior 4 Passages, John Nelson Senior, Judith Woodis, William Capps, John Nelson Senior 2 Passages, Joan Nelson, Eliz. Nelson, Mary Nelson.

Francis Linfield, 4 rights, land entry 29 Dec. 1702.
    viz. Levi Truewhitt, Oliver Smith, Daniel Mathews, William Webster.

Edward Gaucling, 3 rights, warrant 18 Oct. 1702, land entry 18 Feb. 1702.
    viz. William Butcher, Henry Spring, John Barnett.

Richard Jesper, 13 rights, land entry 12 Nov. 1701.
    Richard Jasper, Elias Elexr. Garganus, Ann Garganus, Robert Garganus, Mary Garganus, Catharine Garganus, Sarah Garganus, Heny Riding, Ann Mary Riding, Grace Milton, Jemima Gill, Margarett Gill.

p. 34

North Carolina ss. William Brice, 450 a., for transportation of 9 persons, 22 June 1702.
    viz. William Brice, Ann Brice, Robert Shreave, Eliz. Depee, David Depee, Francis Linfield, Mary Linfield, John Linfield.

p. 38

James Leig, 10 rights, land entry by Hannah Cockarum 7 Oct. 1701 and since sold unto me
    viz. James Leigh, James Leigh Junior, Sarah Leigh Senior, Sarah Leigh Junior, Mary Leigh, William Holeman Patience Leigh John Leigh Eliz. Leigh, Sarah Depee

p. 40

Isaac Jacob, 13 rights, land entry 25 Feb. 1702/3.

viz. Margaret Melton, Ellenor Melton, Mary Vann Senior Mary Vann Junior John Hancok, David Depee, William Winn Dorothy Winn, Eliz. Goreman, Grace Winn, William Winn Junior Edward Winn, Mary Winn, assigned by Richard Jasper.

Bertie County Court Minutes, Part I, 1724-1725; 1731-1743, State Archives, Division of Archives and History, Raleigh. [CR 10.301.1.].

reverse of p. 15
(Nov. 1724) [Davis proves his Rights] John Davis came into Court and proved the Importation of the following Persons Videlicet John Davis Senior John Davis Junior William Davis Watkins Davis Robert Davis Arthur Davis Sarah Davis Jane Davis Mary Davis Rebecca Davis and Anne Davis Ordered That Certificate Issue of the same to Mr. Secretary.

p. 177
(Nov. 1741) Antho. Web proved his Rights Videlicet Antho. Web Martha Webb Wm. Web Anne Web White persons. And Negros Tim Peg, and Cate. pd.

Wm. Willifard proved his Rights Viz. Wm. Willifard Mary Willifard Mary Willifard Tamer Williferd Easter Willifard Anne Willifard Saml. William Willifard White persons and Negro Jane.

Wm. Moor Proved his Rights Viz. Wm. Moor Mary Moor Edwd. Moor Mary Moor Wm. Moor Junior ozbern Hetchperth white persons and Negro Rose.

Thos. Bonner proved his Rights Viz. Thos. Bonner Tho. Bonner Jr. Eliz. Bonner Patience Bonner Moses Bonner.

Thos. Amerson proved his rights viz. Thos. Amerson Wm. Amerson Priscilla Amerson Mary Amerson Mary Amerson Anne Amerson and Henry Emerson.

Hugh Horton provs his rights Viz. Hugh Horton Sarah Horton Eliz. Horton.

Jno. Moor provs his rights John Moor Sarah Moor Mary Moor Wm. Moor Sarah Moor Lucrecia Moor White persons

reverse of p. 177
Benjn. Hill proves his rights Videlicet Benjn. Hill Sarah Hill Sarah Hill
the younger, Priscilla Hill Benjn. Hill jr. Henry Hill Whites and
Negros Robin york, Cork Jinney Sinicer ben primus Tom york,
Benboe Toney Will Primus Cato dick peter Sipia Jacob Jenney
Dinah Lucy Hannah Bett Dinah Tom Danl. Broomfield Sebinah
Andrew Flora.

Thos. Barker proves his rights Videlicet Thos. Barker Ferribe Barker,
Jno. Pugh Thos. Pugh Fras. Pugh Pheribe Pugh Peggy Pugh Mary
Pugh whites and a Negro Mark, Robin, Barns, Jacob, Ceasar
Lymus, Peter, Pimbrook Shipio Jimmey, Barns Peter Cromell Pat,
affra Sebina, Rachel Sarah Hannah, Rose Priss, Shuke.

Needham Bryant proves his rights Videlicet Needham Bryan Susanna
Bryan Wm. Bryan Sarah Wimberly Wm. Bryan whites Negroes
Toney Tom Judey Bess

reverse of p. 181
(May 1742) Godfrey Lee on Oath proved his Rights Viz. Godfrey Lee
Sarah Lee and Sarah Lee the Younger Samuel Lee White persons.
Mingo, London, [*torn*]ny, Hanah, Lucy, York, Judy Isaac, Casar
Jenn[y] Lib, Blacks. Dr. the Fees.

Daniel Vanpelt on Oath proved his Rights Viz. Daniel Vanpelt Anne
Vanpelt John Vanpelt White persons. Cate and York Blacks.

Theophilus Williams on Oath prov'd his Rights Videlicet Theophilus
Williams, Christian Williams Joseph Williams James Williams,
Esther Williams, Lewis Williams Ferribee Williams White
persons. Toney, Boston, Pompey, Rose, Phillis, Patt, Jenny,
Jupiter Silva, Chloe Pegg, Blacks.

Henry Maynar on Oath proved his Rights, Videlicet Henry Mayner
Sarah Maynar, Mary Maynar John Maynar Martha Maynar, Henry
Maynar Junior Solomon Maynar White persons

p. 182
James Jones on Oath prov'd his Rights Videlieet James Jones
Elizabeth Jones John Morris William Morris Whites.

John Cricket on Oath prov'd his Rights Videlicet John Cricket Mary Cricket Thomas Cricket John Cricket Junior Edward Newgent William Neugent White persons, Lucey a Black.

reverse of p. 182:
  Joseph Wymberley prov'd his Rights on Oath Videlicet Joseph Wymberley Judith Wymberley Isaac Wymberley Mary Wymberley Zachariah Wymberley Joseph Wymberley Junior Whites Toney Ceesar and Mingo Blacks.

p. 183
Thomas Yates on Oath prov'd his Rights to Wit Thomas Yates Thos. Yates Junior Margaret Yates, Mary Yates White persons.

reverse of p. 183:
  John Perry prov'd his Rights on Oath Videlicet John Perry Sarah Perry Nichs. Perry Jacob Perry Isaac Perry Benja. Perry Sarah Perry Grace Perry James Perry Anne Perry Josiah Perry Saml. Thomas Whites. Mingo Ceesar, Venus, Bridget Hager Phillis Blacks.

John Howell proved his Rights on Oath Videlicet John Howell Alse Howell Sarah Howell Mathew Howell Arthur Howell White persons Jack, Peter, Dick, Nann, Moll, Harry, Abraham, Taffey Blacks.

Simon Homes prov'd his Rights on Oath Videlicet Simon Homes Mary Homes James Homes George Homes Moses Homes Eliza. Homes Simon Homes Junior John Homes Sarah Homes Timothy Homes, Anne Homes White persons.

Edward Homes prov'd his Rights on Oath Videlicet Edward Homes Lydia Homes Mary Homes John Page James Jernegan Whites Ceesar, Blacks.

Luke Slaughter prov'd his Rights on Oath Videlicet Luke Slaughter Charity Slaughter Whites. Ceesar Black.

John Wells prov'd his Rights on Oath Videlicet John Wells, Eliz. Wells Mary Wells Sarah Wells, Isaac Spivey

p. 184
John Askue prov'd on Oath his Rights Viz. John Askue Margret Askue James Askue, Mary Askue Sarah Askue John Askue Junior Josiah Askue Whites, Ceesar, Nann Blacks.

Alexander Valentine prov'd his Rights on Oath Videlicet Alxr. Valentine Elizabeth Valentine David Valentine Elizabeth Valentine Junior Alexr. Valentine the Younger Anne Valentine Paul Valentine Whites.

Henry Averitt proved his Rights on Oath Videlicet Henry Averitt, Mary Averitt Sarah Averitt Charles Averitt Mary Averitt the younger Elisha Jones Whites and Peter a Negro.

p. 185
John Rasberry on Oath proved his Rights Videlicet John Rasberry Bridget Rasberry, Rebecca Rasberry, and Mary Nichols Rasberry Whites.

p. 190
(Aug. 1742) William Rasberry on Oath proved his Rights to Wit William Rasberry Anne Rasberry, William Rasberry Junior James Rasberry John Rasberry Benja. Rasberry Philip Rasberry Thomas Rasberry White persons

Joseph Thomas on Oath proved his Rights to Wit Joseph Thomas Anne Thomas and Michael Thomas and Mary Thomas White persons.

Daniel Oquin proved his Rights on Oath to Wit Daniel Oquin Elizabeth Oquin Judy Oquin Daniel Oquin and Fredrick Jones white Persons

Henry Day on Oath proved his Rights to Wit Henry Day, Mary Day, Peter Day, John Frazier, Robert Frazier, Elizt. Frazier, Mary Frazier, Simon Day, William Day, John Day, Jeremiah Frazier white Persons

p. 193
(Nov. 1742) Nicholas Sessums proved his rights (to wit) Nicholas Sessums, Elizabeth Sessums Samuel Sizemore, Elizabeth Sessums jr. Rachel Sessums, Luranna Sessums Nicholas Sessums Junior William Sessums Anna Sessums, Sarah Sessums, Grace Sessums white Persons.

Peter West Esq. proved his Rights to Wit Peter West, Priscilla West Peter West Junior Elizt. West, Sarah West, white, Arthur, Bob, Dave, Moll, black Mary, Hannah, Ruth, blacks.

William Gardener proved his Rights Videlicet Wm. Gardener, Mary
Gardener, Uselfa Gardiner, Nehomi Gardener Lewis Gardener
Mary Gardiner whites, Pegg, black.

Thomas Jones proved his Rights Videlicet Thomas Jones Ann Jones
Sarah Jones, Thomas Jones, Ann Jones, John Jones, Mary Jones
Patty Jones Catherina Jones, Elijah Jones Elisha Jones whites and
Tom and Mingo blacks.

Thomas Wimberley proved his rights Videlicet Thos. Wimberley
Mary Wimberley, Judy Wimberly Abraham Wimberly Jacok
Wimberley Jacob Wimberley, Susannah Wimberley, Malachy
Wimberley Silfey Wimberley Thomas Wimberley Junior whites
and Moll, Pomp, Ben Cate and Lucy blacks.

reverse of p. 193
Stephen Cater, proved his rights to wit Stephen Cater, Sarah Cater
Winnefrett Cater George Cater, Syrack Cater francis Cater and
Stephen Cater Junior white Persons.

Thomas Quick proved his rights Videlicet Thos. Quick Ruth Quick
Bethia Quick Anne Quick, Willis Quick and Rachel Quick

Anthony Herring proved his rights Videlicet Anthy. Herring, Bridget
Herring, Sarah Herring frederick Herring and Jesse Herring

Wm. Fleetwood proved his rights Videlicet Wm. Fleetwood,
Susannah fleetwood Henry fleetwood, Mary fleetwood Elizt.
fleetwood Susannah fleetwood Frances fleetwood Wm.
fleetwood Junior Ann Fleetwood and Mary Parrot whites and
Peter, Pompy, Cate, Hannah blacks.

Thos. Ryan proved his rights Videlicet Thos. Ryan, Martha Ryan
David Ryan Elizt. Ryan Mary Ryan, James Ryan whites and Jack,
James, Bess, Doll, Linkhorn, Casar, Jack, Simon Lucy and York
blacks.

John Sowell proved his rights videlicet Jno. Sowell, Ann Sowell, and
Sarah Reasons Jno. Sowell Junior James Sowell, Mary Sowell
Elizabeth Sowell whites

John Howell proved his rights Videlicet John Howell, Jean Howell Edmond Glohan James Glohon and Elizt. Glohon white Persons and Pat and Sharper blacks.

William Egerton proved his Rights Videlicet William Egerton, Alice Egerton, Mary Egerton, Sarah Egerton Elizabeth Egerton whites

reverse of p. 194

John Collins Senior proved his rights Videlicet Jno. Collins Martha Collins David Collins, Joseph Collins Michael Collins Damsey Collins, Jesse Collins Absolom Collins whites, Tony, Judith, Robin, Venus, Rose blacks.

Henry Gibbs proved his rights Videlicet Henry Gibbs Susannah Gibbs, Mary Gibbs, Susannah Gibbs John Gibbs Stafford Gibbs whites, Ned and Peter blacks.

William Collins proved his Rights (to wit) William Collins, Margarett Collins, John Collins whites and Durenda a black.

p. 195

Francis Brown proved his Rights to wit Francis Brown John Brown, Francis Brown Junior Mary Brown, William Brown, John Brown, Sarah Brown Jean Brown, Elizabeth Brown Benjamin Brown, James FairChild whites

Noah Pridham proved his Rights (to wit) Noah Pridham, Sarah Pridham Hester Williams, John Williams, and Rachel Williams whites

Thos. Yates proved his Rights Videlicet Thos. Yates, Margrett Yates, Mary Yates proved at May Court and now at November Court, Peter Yates John Yates and Willm. Yates whites.

Archibald Bell proved his Rights Videlicet Archd. Bell, Mary Bell, George Bell Archd. Bell, Sarah Bell whites and Jack a Negro.

reverse of p. 195

John Penney proved his Rights Videlicet John Penney Susannah Penney Jean Penny Mary Penney Ann Penney and John Penny Junior whites

John Wimberley prov'd his rights Videlicet John Wimberley, Elizabeth Wimberley, Rachel Wimberley, Ruth Wimberley Ezekiel Wimberley Benjn. Wimberley, Mary Wimberley, John Wimberley Junior Levy Wimberly Sarah Wimberley, Moses Wimberly, whites and Judah a Black.

John Basemore proved his Rights Videlicet, John Bazemore, Mary Basemore Elizabeth Edwards Mary Edwards Jesse Basemore Tamar Basemore John Basemore, Sarah Basemore

John Vickars proved his Right Videlicet John Vickars, Mary Vickars Abraham Vickars Martha Vickars Mary Vickars Isaac Vickars and Jacob Vickars

Henry Bonner proved his Rights to wit Henry Bonner, Mary Bonner, Elizt. Bonner, Mary Bonner, Henry Bonner junior Anne Bonner, Rachel Bonner, Sarah Bonner, Ester Bonner, whites

p. 200
(Feb. 1742) [*Issued*] Edward Roberts proved his Rights to wit Edward Roberts Mary Roberts Sarah Roberts Charles Roberts and John Taylor whites.

reverse of p. 200: [*Issued*] Epaphroditas Moor proved his Rights to wit Eps. Moor, Elizabeth John, Mary, Ann, Rachel, Christian, Grace, and Penelope Moor, whites and Jack, Mark, Rose and Dinah blacks.

Issued Richd. Hargrove proved his Rights (to wit) Richd. Hargrove and John Hargrove whites and Sue, Jamey Janey and Cate Blacks.

p. 201
<*Issued*> Elias Stallings proved his Rights Videlicet Elias Stallings, Susannah Stallings Elias Stallings, Moses Stallings Judah Stallings Jessee Stallings, Josiah Stallings, Margrett Stallings, Susannah Stallings whites and Sarah and Philis black.

<*Issued*> Robt. Smith proved his Rights Videlicet Robert Smith, Mary Smith, John Smith, Elizabeth Smith, James Smith, Anne Smith, and William Smith whites

<*Issued*> William Perrey proved his Rights videlicet Wm. Perrey, Sarah Perrey, Mary Perrey, Judith Perrey, Charity Perrey, Lewis Perrey and Thos. Perrey whites and Ezekiel a Black.

<*Issued*>Thomas Bird proved his Rights Videlicet Thomas Byrd, Elizt. Byrd, Ledia Byrd Jane Byrd, Isabell Byrd, Rachel Byrd and Gabriel Byrd whites.

<*Issued*> John Manning proved his Rights Videlicet John Maning, Sarah Maning, Charles Maning, Martha Maning, Jean Bently, Beesly Maning, Lucretia Bently and Lurannah Bently and Ameritta a Black. 81

p. 202
<*Issued*> Charles Cavinah proved his Rights Videlicet Charles Cavinah, Jane Cavinah, Memorial Cavinah Mary Cavinah, David Cavinah, Needham Cavinah, Aquilla Cavinah, Nicholas Cavinah, Charles Cavinah, Arthur Cavinah, Henry Cavinah whites

reverse of p. 202
<[*Issued*]> Cader Powell proved his Rights to wit Cader Powell, Elizt. Powell, Susannah Powell, Mary Powell, Ann Powell, Charity Powell, Rebekah Powell, Susannah Powell, Elizt. Powell whites and Jack, Sambo and Boo Black

<*Issued*> Alice Thomas proved her Rights Videlicet Alice Thomas, James Thomas Jacob Thomas Mary Thomas whites and York, Rose, Ned, Simon, Philis and Penny black

<*Issued*> William Holmes proved his Rights to wit Wm. Holmes Ann Holmes Jno. Francis and Ann Holmes Whites and Tarty a Negro.

p. 203
<*Issued*> Richard Williford proved his Rights to wit Richd. Williford, Abigail Williford Mary Williford, William Williford Richard Williford, John Williford, Benton Williford, Priscilla Williford whites

Carteret County Court Minutes, 1723-1747, Vol. VIII, State Archives, Division of Archives and History, Raleigh. [CR.19.301.1].

p. 55 [stamped in upper right corner]

(Mar. 1742) Thos. Brent Came in Open Court and made Oath that he hath himself onely.

p. 60
(Mar. 1743) Thomas Lewis in Open Court made Oath that he hath only himself

Minutes of the Chowan County Court of Pleas and Quarter Sessions, 1714-1719, State Archives, Division of Archives and History, Raleigh. [CR.24.301.1].

p. 328 [stamped in lower left corner],
(Jan. 1714/15) Jno. Waugh Proves Right for the Importation [of] [*torn*] [Priscilla] Jackson and Deborah and Culln. [Flynn]

reverse of p. 328
Samll. Merritt Proves Rights for the Importation of himself, Mary, Ann, Mary Elizabeth Merritt Wm. Yates and Phillip and Tenisell Brown.

reverse of p. 330
(Apr. 1715) Wm. Mixon Proves Rights for the Importation of himself, Wife and 3 Children into this Government

reverse of p. 331
Thos. Bale Proves 3 Rights for the Importation of himself Wife and one Child into this Government.

p. 332
Wm. Wade Proves 3 Rights for the Importation of Wm. and Elizabeth Wade and Ann Pertain.

reverse of p. 334
(July 1715) Patrk. Laughly proves Rights for the Importation of Jno. Welch Senior Jno. Welch Junior Eliz. Welch Edwd. Welch Jno. Gordon Danll. Butter, Thos. Lamb, Henry Lamb, Richd. Marshall Na. Tucker, Matthew Dyer, Henry Clark and Wm. Pratt.

reverse of p. 335
Tomozena Wykan Proves Rights for the Importation of himself and wife into this Government.

Laurence Martin Proves Rights for the Importation of Laurence Patience and Ann Martin into this Government.

Matt. Capps proves Rights for the Importation of Matthew, Eliz. Senior Elizabeth Junior Mary and Ann Capps, and Mary and Elizabeth Powell.

p. 340
(Oct. 1715) Thos. Crank proves Rights for the Importation of Thos. Crank Senior Thos. Crank Junior Ann Crank Senior Ann Cran [*sic*] Junior Eliz. Crank and Danll. Storey.

Lewis Bryan proves Rights for the Importation of Symon, Wm. Edwd., Jannett, Lewis, Elizabeth, Mary, Joanah, Sarah and Ann Bryan, Lewis Bryan Junior and Eliz. Bryan Junior.

reverse of p. 344
(July 1716) Epaphraditus Benton Proves Rights for the Importation of Elizabeth Lazarus, Elizabeth Junior Lemuell, Job Sarah Epa. Benton and Wm. Hardy

p. 351
(July 1717) Benjn. Foreman prov'd Rights for the Importation of Benjn. Foreman Senior Verrily, Wm. Mary and Benjn. Foreman Junior.

Thos. Roundtree prov'd Rights for the Importation of Thos. Roundtree Junior Eliz. Roundtree Senior Eliz. Roundtree Junior Charles and Judeth Roundtree.

Thos. Roundtree prov'd Rights for the Importation of Francis Anne, Wm., Joan, Susannah, Moses, John, Sarah, Elizabeth, Jethro and Christian Roundtree.

Jams. Griffin prov'd Rights for the Importation of Jams. Griffin Senior Jams. Griffin Junior Sarah Griffin Senior Sarah Griffin Junior, John, Joseph, Susanah and Moses Griffin.

Moses Hill prov'd Rights for the Importation of Moses Hill Senior Moses Hill Junior Dorothy, Elizabeth, Guy Susanah Hill and Thos. Fullerton.

Chowan County Minute Docket, County Court, Apr. 1730-Oct. 1734, Jan. 1740-Jul. 1748, State Archives, Division of Archives and History, Raleigh. [CR.24.301.2].

reverse of p. 51

(Apr. 1742) Edward Arnal appeared and made proof that his family onely Consisted of himself and prayed a Certificate of the Same to take up a hundred Acres of land

p. 59
(Apr. 1742) Edward Arnell appeared and proved his family consised only of himself and prayed a Certificate of the Same to take up a hundred Acres of Land

p. 81
(Oct. 1743) Johnathan Parker proved Seven white persons in his family (to wit) himself Charity, his wife, William, Rachel, Jess, Elizabeth Prisilia

reverse of p. 85
James Parker Came into Court and made Oath that his family Consis[ted] of four White Persons (Videlicet) himself and his wife William and James

p. 96
(July 1744) Mr. Peter Adams appeared in Open Court and Made Oath that his familey Consisted of twelve Persons one White and 11 Blacks, Videlicet, Peter Adams Stepney Joe Marrea Betty toney Jack Pat Lucey Dena Mol James

p. 104
(Oct. 1744) Personally appeared Mr. Luke Gregory and Made Oath that he has Seven Persons in his family Videlicet, Luke Gregory Samuel Mary and Sarah Gregorys Blacks Joe Venus Jenne. issued.

reverse of p. 104
Personally appeared Mr. Isaac Hunter and Made Oath that his familey Consisted of Two Persons Videlicet, Isaac Hunter and one Negro Called London. issued.

Personally appeared Mr. Joshua Haughton and Made Oath that his familey Consisted of Seven Persons Videlicet Joshua Sarah Thomas Joshua Deborah Haughtons Blacks Jamey and Janey. Issued.

Personally appeared John Halsey Esqr. and Made Oath that his familey Consisted of Eleven Persons Videlicet, John Halsey Mary Halsey James Halsey Willm. Halsey Jeremiah Halsey Joseph Halsey Samuel Halsey Blacks Sam Kent Venus Jenny. issued.

p. 105

Personally appeared Mr. Francis Penrice and Made Oath that his familey Consisted of three Persons Videlicet, Francis Penrice Sarah Penrice and Samuel Hall. issued.

p. 111

(Jan. 1744) Personally appeared Mr. Robert Powell and Made Oath that his familey Consisted of Six White Persons and one Negro Videlicet Robert Powell Mary filisha Jacob Shadrick Daniel Powels and one Negro Named Mark. issued. fees pd.

Edgecombe County Court Minutes, 1744-1746, (Partial), State Archives, Division of Archives and History, Raleigh. [CR.37.301.1].

p. [4]

(Feb. 1744) Nathan Rowland proves 3 Rts. White Viz. himself Mary Ux. and Sarah his Child.

p. [19]

(Nov. 1744) Wm. Parker Proves three Right (Videlicet) Wm. Parker, Mary Parker, Anne Parker

p. [21]

Alexr. Avery Proves 6 Rights Alexr., OLive his wife Alexr., jr. Wm., Jacob, Sarah Fees not pd.

[Jn]o. Knight Proves 6 Rights (to wit) Jno., Isabell, [torn]s., Moses, Eliza., [torn]

New Hanover County Court Minutes, 1738-1769, State Archives, Division of Archives and History, Raleigh. [CR.70.301.1].

p. 66 [lower left corner]

(Mar. 1741) Edward Porter Came into Court and Claimed to prove his Right to Lands which is only himself.

Onslow County Records, Vol. I, Precinct Court Minutes, 1734-1737 Jan.-April; County Court Minutes 1741-1749 May-April [CR.72.301.3].

reverse of p. 28 [stamped in lower left corner]
(Apr. 1742) John Burly Comes into Court and proves his right being
only himselfe

p. 36
(Jan. 1742) Jno. Gourley Comes into Court and proves his right being
only himselfe. Certificate Issued. fees pd.

reverse of p. 39
(July 1743) Wm. Barbor Comes into Court and proves his right being
only himself. Jas. Foyle pays fees

reverse of p. 42
(Oct. 1743) Jacob Hugens proves his rights for 1 White person

Mr. Andrew Murray Proves one Right

p. 44
John Stenson Comes into Court and proves Rights for himself onley.

**Onslow County Court Minutes, October Term, 1741-October
Term, 1743, State Archives, Division of Archives and
History, Raleigh. [CR.72.301.4].**

p. 3b [lower left corner]
(Jan. 1741) Lazarus Kenny proves his right being only himselfe

p. [10b]
(Apr. 1742) John Burley Comes into Court and proves his right being
only himselfe

p. [24b]
(Jan. 1742) John Gouerley Comes into Court and proves his right
being only himselfe

p. 35b
(July 1743) Wm. Barbour Comes into Court and proves his right
being only himself

p. 39b
(Oct. 1743) Jacob Huggin[s prov]es his righ for 1 white person in his
family

p. [40b]
Mr. Andrew Murray proves one Right.

p. 41b
John Stinson comes into Court and proves right for himselfe only

Pasquotank County Court Minutes, Apr. 1737-Jul. 1753 (Partial), State Archives, Division of Archives and History, Raleigh. [CR. 75.301.1].

p. 1 [second enumeration]
[1741] On Motion of Israel Lambert praying he might Prove his right for takeing up land Granted

p. 18
(Apr. 1743) Daniel Dan made Proof that his family Consisted of one White Person for takeing up of Vacant Lands. pd.

p. 45
(July 1744) Randell Kelly Came into Court and made Oath that his familly Consisted of five white persons for takeing up Vacant Land Videlicet Randell Kelly Elizt. Kelly Bridget Madrom James Kelly Sarah Kelly

Timothy Meads Came into open Court and prov'd his rights as follows (to witt) John Meads Ann Meads Penelope Meads Mary Meads Millisett Meads for takeing up Vacant Land.

Perquimans Precinct Court Minutes, 1697-1706, State Archives, Division of Archives and History, Raleigh. [CR.77.301.2].

p. 2
(July 1698) Samuell Hearst proved Rits for fower persons transported Into this County Whos Names are under Wretten vis. him Selfe Jane Chaddock John Doughatre Jane Jane Doughatr

p. 3
Hennery Norman proved Rites for eigh persons transported Into this County Whoes Names are under Wreten vis. him Selfe Mary his Wife Andrew Ross Mary Ross Thomas Ross John Simmon, Georg Waide James Ross

p. 12

(Apr. 1699) John Watts Proved Writs for three persons tra[n]sported Into this County Whoeses Name ar under Wretten John Watts Senior John Watts Junior Catterin Watts

p. 21
(Apr. 1700) William More Proved two Writs for two persons Transported Into this County Whoes Names Are under Written vis. Him Selfe Elisabeth His Wife

p. 22
Thomas Hancock Proved five Writs for five persons transported Into this County Whoes Names Are under Written vis. Him Selfe Mary His Wife Mary His daughter Elisabeth His daughter John His Sonn

John Hare proved three Writs for three persons transported Into this County Whoes Names Are under Wretten vis. Him Selfe Sarah His Wife Sarah Shadock

William Fryle proved on Rite for His transportation and Asigned It to Robart Murre

Robart Murre Proved on Rite for His transportation

p. 26
(July 1700) John Benet Proved Rits for Six persons transported Into this County Whoes Names Are under Written vis. Him Selfe Rose His Wife John Benet Junior Elener Benet Jean Benet Thomas Benet

p. 52
(Nov. 1702) Timothy Clare Proved too Rites for too persons transported into this County Whoes Names Are under Wretten John Dixson Elisabeth Jackson

Thomas Winslo Proved on Write for His Freedom An Asignd It to Timethy Clar

p. 54
(Jan. 1696/7) Francis Segrave proved five Rits for five persons transported into this County Whoes Names are under Wretten vis. him Selfe Lucrecia his Wif[e] Thomas his Sonn Francis his Soon William Powel

John Dunston proved three Rits Whoes Names ar under Wreten vis. him Selfe Francis his Wife Sarah Moore

p. 55

Thomas Speight proved tenn Rits Whoes Names ar under Wretten vis. him Selfe Richard Mallone Nich. Perru John Morres Elisabeth Morres John Morres Junior William Morres Mare Morres Nathanel Rave Fone a Negro

Charles Scot Proved fower Writs for fower persons transported into this County Whoes Names are Under Wretten vis. him Selfe Mary Scoot Elisabeth Scot Charles Scot on for his Servetue

Denis Meclenden proved aleven Rits Whoes Names are under Wretten vis. Him Selfe Charles Cafen Mary his Wife Margret Dun Dennes Dun Rebecka Carpender Elisabeth Mackclenden Brient Mackclenden Dennes Mackclenden Francis Mackclenden Thomas Mackclenden

John Oden proved Six Rits for Six persons Whose Names are under Wretten vis. Him Selfe Ann his Wife Ann his Daughter Jan his Daughter Mary his daughter Rachel his daughter

Abraham Williams proved fower Rits Whoes Names are under Wretten vis. him Selfe Ame his Wife Edward Williams John Williams

p. 56

Francis Foster Proved Six Rits Whoes Names are Under Wretten William Foster John Foster Elisabeth Foster Francis Foster Jeane Swetman A Negro Hanna

p. 66

(July 1697) Edward Homes proved Writs for fifteen persons transported Into this County Whoese Name[s] are Under Wretten vis. him Selfe Elisabeth his Wife Tho. Homes Edward Homes Junior Edward Homes Senior Elisebeth his Wife Tho. Homes Edward Homes Junior Sarah Homes Elisabeth Homes Edward Homes Senior Elisabeth his Wife Thomas Homes Edward Homes Junior, John Homes

p. 70

(Oct. 1697) John Spence proved three Rits for three persons transported Into this County Whoes Names ar under Wretten vis. him Selfe Cattern his Wife Robart Spence

Alexander Spence proved Rits for five persons transported Into this County hoes Names are under Wretten vis. him Selfe Dorety Spence John Spence Daved Spence James Spence

p. 71
John Shaw proved on Rite for his transportation

p. 76
(Apr. 1698) Daniel Hall proved two Rits one for his transportation And one for his freedum

Robart Smith proved on Rite for his transportation Into this County And Asigne It to John Dawson

p. 77
John Dawson proved on Rite for his transportation Into this County

Rose Ingan proved one Rite for hir transportation Into this County And Asigned It to John Dawson

p. 85
(Feb. 1702/3) upon a Petition of Mary Coffen Widdow The said Mary proves three rights being for the transportation of Francis and Mary Coffen and Jno. Thursten and assignes them to her Sonne in Law Richd. Rose

p. 86
Richd. Rose proves one right to 50 acres of Land by transportation of him selfe

p. 93
(July 1703) James Forster by a Petition requests leave to prove five rights (videlicet) two for himselfe Hannah Forster Samll. Wright and Mary White and is granted

p. 97
(Oct. 1703) Thomas Speight proves Rights for 350 acres of Land by the Importation of Mary Speight Senior Ditto Junior John

Hetterter Mary Fitt Garratt Elizabeth Do. Negro Hannah and himselfe.

Thomas Dorton proves his Rights to 150 acres of Land by the Importation of himselfe Thomas Davis and Anne Davis.

p. 122
(July 1704) Wm. Williams proves his Right to 50 acres of Land by the Importation of him selfe.

p. 127
(Oct. 1704) Upon Petition of Captain James Coles praying to prove Rights to Two Hundred and Fifty acres of Land by the Importation of himselfe John Brock John Falconar Edward Daniel Pison and Charles an Indyan and is admitted.

p. 135
(Jan. 1704/5) Upon Petition of Danl. Snooke praying to prove Rights for Four Hundred and Fifty acres of Land by and Importation of John Williford and Jane Williford Wm. Williford Sarah Williford Mary Watts Mary Avengton Phillis Love Saml. Boasman and 1 Child and is admitted.

p. 136
Upon Petition of Dennis Macclendon praying to prove Rights to a Hundred Acres of Land by the Importation of two persons videlicet Michael Dorming and Habella A Negro and is Admitted.

Upon Petition of Henry Spring praying to prove Rights to A Hundred acres of Land by the Importation of two persons videlicet himselfe twice and is Admitted.

p. 138
Upon Petition of Thomas Parker praying to be admitted to prove Rights to A Hundred Acres of Land by the Importation of Elizabeth Parker and Lucy Parker and is Admitted and Assignes them to Henry Spring.

Upon Petition of Timothy Clare Esqr. praying to prove A Right to A Fifty acres of Land by the Importation of Jenny A Negro is Admitted and Assignes the Same to Dennis Macclendon.

p. 168

(Jan. 1705/6) Isaac Wilson by his Subscription proves Rights to Twelve Hundred acres of Land by the Importation of Mary Boasman Eliz. Boasman John Morris Richd. Ruckman Negroe Phebe Indian Mall Negroe Patt Negro Maria James White 2 Anne Barker George Baits 2 my Wife Rebekah Ratcliffe George Rice Richd. Gove Simon Alderson Joseph Carnerle Richd. Turner Wm. Barstable John Hooks Isaac Ricks and Abraham Ricks.

Upon Petition of Ralph Boasman praying to prove Eight Rights is admitted and proves Rights to Four Hundred acres of Land by the Importation of himselfe 3 times for his wife for Eliz. Boasman and 3 times for Saml. Boasman.

p. 169

Upon Petition of Saml. Bond praying to be admitted to prove Eight Rights is Admitted and proves Rights to Four Hundred acres of Land by the Importation of Saml. Bond Eliz. Bond Mercy Bond Susannah Bond Eliz. Bond Mathew Potter Sarah Johnson and Luke Grace

p. 170

Upon Petition of James Nuby praying to prove Six Rights is Admitted and proves Rights to Three Hundred acres of Land by the Importation of John Nuby Magdalen Nuby John Nuby Eliz. Nuby and James Nuby 2 and assignes the Same in Open Court to Isaac Wilson.

Upon Petition of Saml. Bond praying to prove Three Rights is admitted and proves Rights to One Hundred and Fifty acres of Land by the Importation of Henry Grace James Hurt and William Bruing and assignes the Same in open Court to Isaac Wilson.

p. 178

(Oct. 1706) Upon Petition of Mr. James Minge praying to be admitted to prove Rights is admitted and proves Rights to One thousand Acres of Land by Importation of James Minge Six times Ruth Minge Thrice Robin A Negro Four times, Beb Sam Sue Jone Doll Sam and Voll.

Richd. Turner by his Subscription proves Rights to Four Hundred and Fifty acres of Land by the Importation of Richd. Turner Thrice his wife Bridgett Turner William Barnstable 2 Elizabeth Turner John Turner and John Hooks.

Saml. Charles by his Subscription proves Rts. to Two Hundred acres of Land by the Importation of Charles Scott Mary Scott Eliz. Scott and Mary Scott

Robert J. Cain, ed., *Records of the Executive Council, 1664-1734*, vol. VII of *The Colonial Records of North Carolina* [*Second Series*], (Raleigh: Division of Archives and History, 1984).

p. 33 Madam Catha. Hyde Came before this Board and was admited to prove upon Oath the Importation of Eight persons into this Government (Videlicet) Edwd. Hyde Esqr. Mrs. Penelope Hyde Wm. Clayton Jno. Lovick Mary Tudo James Gregory Andrew Stephenson and her Selfe. Jan. 12, 1712/13.

Major Christo. Gale was admitted to prove upon Oath the Importation of Four rights for which he has not as Yett taken up any Land (Videlicet) himselfe twice his Daughter Eliza and Arthur Harris And Assigned the Same over to Colonell Wm. Reed. Jan. 12, 1712/13.

Index

INDEX

As mentioned in the Introduction, all variants of personal and place names have been made a main entry, even when they are known to refer to the same individual or place. Similarly, no attempt has been made to differentiate between and among people bearing the same name. A limited number of subjects have been included.

Brown, Temsela, 38
Brown, Tenisell, 213
Brown, Tho., 177
Brown, Thomas, 177
Brown, Thomasell, 73
Brown, William, 210
Brown, Wm., 7, 21-22, 40, 203
Browne, [*torn*], 88
Browne, Fra., 62
Browne, Jacob, 5
Browne, Jno., 107, 139, 160, 163, 190
Browne, John, 59, 139
Browne, Tho., 141
Browne, Willm., 114
Browne, Wm., 143
Bruck, John, 6
Bruing, William, 16, 223
Bryan, Ann, 39, 214
Bryan, Edward, 39
Bryan, Edwd., 214
Bryan, Eliz., Junior, 214
Bryan, Elizabeth, 39, 214
Bryan, Elizabeth, Jr., 39
Bryan, Janette, 39
Bryan, Jannett, 214
Bryan, Jno., 35, 50, 78
Bryan, Joanah, 39, 214
Bryan, Lewis, 39, 214
Bryan, Lewis, Jr., 39
Bryan, Lewis, Junior, 214
Bryan, Mary, 39, 214
Bryan, Mathew, 32
Bryan, Needham, 206
Bryan, Sarah, 39, 214
Bryan, Susanna, 206
Bryan, Symon, 39, 214
Bryan, William, 39
Bryan, Wm., 206, 214
Bryant, Needham, 206
Buck, Jno., 189
Buckley, Ellinor, 106, 174-175
Buckley, Henry, 174
Buckley, Mary, 106, 174-175

Buckley, Rowland, 106, 174-175
Buckley, Rowland, Junior, 106, 174-175
Buffkin, Ralph, 32
Buftin, Christopher, 40
Bugles, Rob., 181
Buller, Richard, 6
Bullock, Rich., 2
Bundy, Caleb, 73, 102, 111-112, 141, 144-145
Bundy, Eliza., 102
Bundy, Mary, 102
Bundy, Saml., 76, 111-112, 141
Bundy, Willm., 102, 144
Bundy, Wm., 102, 106, 111-112
Bung, Humphrey, 111, 145
Buntin, _____, 102
Buntin, Alice, 102
Buntin, Jno., 102
Buntin, John, 44
Burd, An, 129
Burd, John, 129
Burd, Mary, 129
Burkhead, John, 30
Burley, John, 217
Burley, Margrett, 157
Burley, Margrt., 106
Burly, John, 217
Burnsby, Jno., Junior, 158, 164
Burnsby, Tho., 173
Burtenshall, Dorcas, 76
Burtenshall, Eliz., 76
Burtenshall, Prcilla, Junior, 76
Burtenshall, Prcilla., 76
Burtenshall, Pricilla, 196
Burtenshall, Priscilla, 197
Burtenshall, Rich., 196, 197
Burtenshall, Richd., 76
Burtenshall, Susan, 196
Burtenshell, Henry (?), 76
Burton, John, 79
Burton, Leonard, 87
Burton, Mary, 192

Homes, John, 12, 207, 220
Homes, Lydia, 207
Homes, Mary, 207
Homes, Moses, 207
Homes, Sarah, 207, 220
Homes, Simon, 207
Homes, Simon, Junior, 207
Homes, Tho., 12, 220
Homes, Thomas, 12, 220
Homes, Timothy, 207
Honora (Irishwoman), 102, 117, 147
Hoodson, William, 201
Hooker, Wm., 51
Hooks, John, 16-17, 223-224
Hoolbeach, Jno., 162, 167
Hooper, Elizabeth, 85
Hooper, Rob[t]., 85
Hooper, Robt., 85
Hopkins, Haniball, 74
Hopkins, Jno., 179
Hopkins, John, 32, 85-86, 141, 179, 201
Hopkins, Sam'l, 43
Hopkins, Samuel, 76
Hopkins, Sarah, 85, 179
Hoplin, Charles, 40
Hopton, Cha., 73
Horn, Joel, 47
Horn, Mary, 47
Horn, Moses, 47
Horn, Wm., 49
Horne, Thomas, 6
Horning, Eliz., 201
Horton, _____, 126-127
Horton, Eliz., 205
Horton, Hugh, 205
Horton, Sarah, 205
Horton, Tho., 126-127
Hosea, Jno., 64
Hosea, Wm., 200
Hoskins, Tho., 135
Hossold, Mary, 9, 24, 91
Hossold, Tho., 91
Hossold, Tho., Junior, 91

Hossold, Thomas, 9, 24
Hossold, Thomas, Junior, 9, 24
Hotkins, Tho., 98
Hotkins, Thomas, 156
Houghton, Thomas, 58
House, Abraham, 43
House, Daniel, 43
House, Elizabeth, 43
House, John, 43
House, Sarah, 43
House, Thomas, 43
How, Lidia, 1
Howard, Charles, 80
Howard, Wm., 5
Howards, Phillip, 80
Howcott, John, 40
Howden, Mary, 44, 75, 77
Howel, [*faded*], 76
Howel, Daniel, 76
Howel, Eliz., 76
Howel, John, 76
Howel, Thomas, 76
Howell, Alse, 207
Howell, Arthur, 207
Howell, Danl., 138, 140, 153
Howell, Eliz., 140, 153
Howell, Elizabeth, 138
Howell, J., 187
Howell, Jean, 210
Howell, Jno., 31, 187
Howell, Johanah, 140
Howell, John, 207, 210
Howell, Mathew, 207
Howell, Robt., 48
Howell, Sarah, 48, 207
Howes, Thomas, 202
Howson, Eliz., 6
Howson, Wm., 80
Hubbard, Anna, 46
Huchison, Wm., 202
Hudson, [*torn*], 83
Hudson, Henry, 83, 186
Hudson, Jno., 102, 134, 155

Nuby, James, 16, 223
Nuby, John, 16, 223
Nuby, Joseph, 198
Nuby, Magdalen, 16, 223
Nuby, Mary, 198
Nuby, Wm., 32, 198
Nueman, Elis., 201
Nueman, Jane, 201
Nueman, Tho., 201
Nuton, Will, 60
Nyer, Charles, 32

O'Neale, Margaret, 41
O'Neill, Ann, 43
O'Neill, Deborah, 43
O'Neill, Michael, Jr., 43
O'Neill, Michael, Sr., 43
Oadam, John, 31
Oakely, Geo., 3
Oats, James, 70
ODains (?), Roger, 184
Odam, Jacob, 47
Odam, John, 187
Odam, Sarah, 47
Odam, Susannah, 47
Odam, Thos., 47
ODaniel Pat, Junior, 72
ODaniel, Eliz., 72
Oden, Ann, 12, 75, 220
Oden, Jan, 12, 75, 220
Oden, John, 12, 75, 220
Oden, Mary, 12, 75, 220
Oden, Rachel, 12, 75, 220
Odom, An, 187
Odom, Jane, 187
Odom, John, 187
Odom, Mary, 187
Odom, Rachell, 187
Odum, An, 187
Odum, Jane, 187
Odum, John, 187
Odum, Mary, 187
Odum, Rachell, 187

Offee, Olive, 26
Okeham, George, 31
Old Mary (negro), 191
Old Will (negro), 58, 94
Olford, Jabez, 48
Olford, Jno., Junior, 48
Olford, Jno., Senior, 48
Olford, Wm., 48
Oliver (negro), 201
Oliver, Alex, 181
Oliver, Alexander, 59
Oliver, Alexandr., 126
Oliver, Alice, 120, 148, 194
Oliver, An, 120, 148
Oliver, Ann, 194
Oliver, Eliz., 126
Oliver, Feelix, 120, 148
Oliver, Felix, 194
Oliver, Jno., 14, 33-34, 41, 53, 81
Oliver, Margarett, 194
Oliver, Margeret, 120, 148
Oliver, Mary, 120, 148, 194
Oliver, Rich., 120
Oliver, Richard, 120, 148, 194
Oliver, Sarah, 120, 148, 194
Oliver, Thos., 4
Olliver, Allice, 194
Olliver, Felix, 194
Olliver, Margarett, 194
Olliver, Mary, 194
Olliver, Rich., 194
Olliver, Sarah, 194
Olton, Jno., 5
Oneal, Charles, 183
Oneal, Danl., 183
Oneal, Frances, 183
Oneal, Hugh, 183
Oneal, Joice, 183
Oneal, Margarett, 201
Oneal, Mary, 183
Oneal, Robert, 201
Oneal, Winifred, 183
[O'neale], Bobert, 41